Christ at the Center:

What Christians Should Know

Essays on Christian Apologetics

By Janet E. Rea

Christ at the Center

"Jesus Christ is the end of all, and the center to which all tends. Whoever knows Him knows the reason of everything." – Blaise Pascal, *Pensees* #556

Jesus said: "Now this is eternal life: that they may know you, the only true God, and Jesus Christ, whom you have sent." (John 17:3)

This work is copyright © 2011, 2014 by the author, Janet E. Rea. ISBN: 978-0615879727

Unless otherwise noted all Bible quotations are taken from the New International Version of the Bible, copyright 1984 by International Bible Society, Published by Holman Bible Publishers, 1986.

Scripture quotations marked (ESV) are from The Holy Bible, English Standard Version, copyright 2001 by Crossway Bibles, a publishing ministry of Good News Publishers.

Other Books by Janet E. Rea

All Things in Christ- What Christians Should Understand

Other Books by Workshop for Writers

The Raven Stone (A Novel) by Michael L. Rea

Justice (A Novel) by Michael L. Rea

This Side of Reality (A Novel) by Michael L. Rea

Old Bones (A Novel) by Greg Picard and Wendy Gorham Picard

Connected: Remaining Human in a Networked World by Michael L. Rea

www.workshopforwriters.com

Table of Contents

Essays on Christian Apologetics 1
INTRODUCTION 6
Part 1 – God Revealed 9
Chapter 1 -- TRUTH, GRACE AND BEAUTY: The Heart of Christianity 9
Chapter 2-CREATION 18
   Part 1: Knowing How It All Began 18
   WHAT THE BIBLE AND NATURE SAY ABOUT CREATION 20
   HOW GOD CREATED 24
   Creation and Time 25
   Israel and the Creation Story 28
   Hearing God's Voice in Science 30
Chapter 3-CREATION 33
   Part 2: Finding the truth about Creation 33
   CREATION AND EVOLUTION 33
   Evolution 34
   Theistic Evolution 37
   When God Doesn't Create 38
   Life Comes From God 40
   Creationism -- Young Earth Creationism 42
Progressive Creationism – Old Earth Creationism 45
   Intelligent Design 48
   THE CONTROVERSY BETWEEN SCIENCE AND FAITH ... 51
   A CHRISTIAN APPROACH TO THE DEBATE 55
Chapter 4-THE BIBLE: Read the Word 61
Chapter 5-JESUS: All or Nothing 75
   Preexistence 78
   Incarnation 79
   The Hypostatic Union 80
   The Proclamation of the Word 80
   The Substitutionary Death 81
   The Glorious Resurrection 82
Knowing the God-Man 84

Part 2 – The Problem We Face	88
Chapter 6- MAN: Who We Are	88
The Image of God	92
MIND	97
BODY	101
SOUL	106
Chapter 7- SIN: The Heart of What We Do	111
Salvation For All?	125
Chapter 8-FALL . . . AND REDEMPTION: What's Wrong and How It Gets Right	130
Part 3 – Who We Become	146
Chapter 9-THE CHRISTIAN: In Christ and Christ In Us	146
Chapter 10-CHRISTIAN VIRTUE: Christianity from the Inside Out	158
Chapter 11-PRAYER: Communication Between Heaven and Earth	168
Part 4 – Life in the Body of Christ	177
Chapter 12-THE CHURCH: Christianity Together	177
Chapter 13-WORSHIP: The Connection Between Heaven and Earth	194
Chapter 14-HEAVEN OR HELL: The Journey's End	209
Choice at the Crossroads	211
Walking in Virtue	214
Prudence (Wisdom)	216
Fortitude	217
Temperance	217
Justice	218
The Other Road	219
Suffering on Both Roads	223
A Glimpse of Heaven	225

Christ at the Center

INTRODUCTION

When I started writing this book, I did so because, at the age of 50, I realized that I had something to say and I might as well try to say it. I felt I could write, but I had no idea whether or not I could write *a book*, so this project came together somewhat like Jonah's vine on a hot day. I just started writing until I realized that I was writing a book.

The principle inspiration for this book came from the many people who sat under my husband's tutelage in an adult Sunday School class he taught for many years. I noticed that some of these people were quick to *ask* him questions, just to see how he would answer them. Then they listened to him with a kind of awe that he "knew so much," but were oblivious to the fact that what he knew were the very things they also could know.

These people seemed to be content to try to ride to heaven on someone else's coat tails, so to speak. Although they trusted in Christ for their salvation, they seemed to lack depth in their knowledge of the truths of the Christian faith.

On the other hand, others of his students grew greatly through what they were taught, and were enabled and inspired to go on to actively pursue their own ministries in the body of Christ. So, I decided to focus in on the importance of **knowing** the truths of Christianity and how that makes us stronger in the faith upon which our lives must be built.

From my years of observation as a Sunday School teacher of elementary age students, the wife of a Christian School educator, and as a Christian School librarian and Bible teacher, I have become intimately aware of the crisis in "knowing" faced by today's evangelical church. A wave of ignorant disaster, coming on the heels of modern false teaching, threatens now to further weaken the church. Christians, like many of my high school students, just want the answers; they don't want to think about things. Some even believe that some things are unknowable; that there are realms where the truth need not be applied.

In a post-modern world, many hold that no absolute truth can be found, and no center for the soul is needed. One need not pursue truth beyond what one feels to be true. Consequently, if one were to ask some evangelical Christians of today what it is that they know to be *true*, a whole mish-mash of ideas would surface, usually based on feelings, not on facts.

Even though truths exist which will not be fully known until we enter heaven, it is still possible to know much of what now is so often neglected. In Col.1, Paul explains the importance knowing what one believes. He tells the believers that they will "live a life worthy of the Lord and please him in every way (v. 10), and, as they continue to grow in knowledge, they will be "strengthened with all power (v. 11).

The people who know the truth are the ones who really live and truly serve. They have found Christ to be the quiet center of their lives. Each day brings them closer to God on their journey of faith into the glory that will be revealed – that is, it will be *made known*, both now and in eternity.

While writing this book, I went on a journey of my own as I gained insights into things I had previously taken for granted or thought little about. I actually grew to know things that I had not realized before. I hope that this little study in Christian apologetics will be of practical value to the reader. I did not intend to philosophize; in fact, I only began to study philosophy while writing this book; but I do intend to provoke thought. I also realized that I could have gone into much deeper theological detail on the topics I chose to address in this book. I did not do so, because it was not my intent to write a systematic theology.

I hope, however, as a librarian, that the readers of this book will be encouraged to look further into the writings of the great Christian authors that I have quoted. In addition, I hope that my readers will not be dismayed by the quotations from the Catholic Catechism. I used it because it does such a great job of explaining orthodox Christian truth and offers insights that I have not found in evangelical sources, especially on the topics of creation and the virtues.

It is my wish that, through the pages of this book, the life of the evangelical church will be strengthened. I hope the Christians will be reminded that the only basis for what we

Christ at the Center

believe must be Biblical; therefore, I make no apology for the many passages of Scripture that I quoted. May we all learn (as I hope I will continue to learn) that Christ can, and ultimately will be, the center of all things.

Christ at the Center

Part 1 – God Revealed

Chapter 1 -- TRUTH, GRACE AND BEAUTY: The Heart of Christianity

"My purpose is that they may be encouraged in heart and united in love, so that they may have the full riches of complete understanding, in order that they may know the mystery of God, namely, **Christ, in whom** are hidden all the treasures of wisdom and knowledge." – Col.2:2,3

I have been a Christian for over 45 years – almost all my life – and my journey has taken me far, but it was only recently that I realized I was on a journey at all. I did not see that salvation goes beyond a mere point in time to a whole lifetime of walking with God. Like many evangelical Christians, I thought one was saved and then began to walk. I did not understand that salvation is not only the beginning of that walk, but also the walk itself.

During my life and through my experience in the church, I have been acquainted with many Christians who are quite unclear about walking with God and living the Christian life. So many are just walking down ordinary paths on ordinary days with nothing more than a "Christian charm" in their pockets and a tiny, dulled glimmer of hope for Heaven in their hearts. Do contemporary Christians really know truth? Do they really want it to set them free to "know God, whom to know is life eternal?"

The truth is that we can live a life that is true, beautiful and good where Christ is at the center. We can emulate Enoch and walk with God. But in order to do this, we must first know the truth and then give up everything else to "know him and the power of his resurrection." I offer this apology to help others on this journey and to clarify what it is that Christians should know if they are to know the truth. But it all begins with being able to discern what is true and what is beautiful and how, in turn, those things bring goodness into our lives.

I always thought that people have a built-in sense of beauty, that is, we can perceive it even though we may perceive it differently; until the day my husband and I took our youngest daughter to Yosemite National Park. She had been adopted from Russia a couple of years earlier and had lived through some very difficult times. We thought she would express some sort of awe and appreciation for the wonders seen throughout the park, but she only declared that it was boring and dull and suggested a trip to a famous California fun park instead. My husband and I were shocked, because we have always loved natural beauty and, furthermore, our two older children do as well. What was wrong? How could anyone not see and appreciate the splendor of that beautiful place?

And then it hit me (so hard that I felt a little sick,) *she could not see beauty*. Because of the hardships she had endured, (in a land where truth is also at a premium), she had no sense of what is beautiful, she had no aesthetic center. But the amusement park was pretty to her, full of fun and glitter. In contrast, we who know true beauty see the amusement park as fun but folly.

But she is not the only one trapped in this mindset. Beauty is fading fast in this world, both in and out of the church. It is as if beauty, once exiting the stage, was never invited back. She stands waiting in the wings, forgotten, while her sister truth is parodied about on stage. Like righteousness and peace, which once kissed each other (Ps. 85:10), they are partners now estranged. Many will never see or hear their moving performance of grace.

Truth and beauty were once firmly united in Christian thought and permeated all of scholarship. The medieval cathedrals bear witness to this relationship. The truth of the gospel was held in such high esteem that the only proper place for the proclamation of truth was one that was glorious. Therefore, we see in the cathedral the soaring arches leading our eyes upward toward God, the colored glass breaking the infinite light into a thousand hues, and the gilt paintings telling the precious story. Everything in a cathedral illustrates the marriage of truth and beauty, because the building was constructed as a representation of the dwelling place of God, where truth and beauty abide. It pictures Christ, who is truth and is beautiful.

Christ at the Center

Psalm 29:2 states that God is to be worshiped in the "splendor of holiness" as is fitting for one so great, and the cathedrals certainly echoed this sentiment. The medieval church builders were possessed by the idea that any manifestation of truth should be beautiful. From the priest's robes to the patterns of the marble pavement, symmetry, form and elegance were fully evident. It was heaven, if you will, in the best earthly imitation.

Today we live in a pluralistic society where many things are accepted to be true; for if one *feels* an idea is true, it then becomes possible to use it to get as close as one can to the truth. This mindset resulted from the propagation and proliferation of Enlightenment and Modernist humanistic philosophies, which served to replace God's revelation with man's opinions as the source of truth. The result was a world guided by individual interpretations of truth rather than by dependable, absolute truth itself.

In the melee, truth was divorced from beauty. We see a picture of this in the ancient Babylonian king, Nebuchadnezzar, who boasted of creating a glorious empire – "is this not great Babylon, which I have built," he boasts. (Dan. 4: 30) But soon after saying this, he was reduced by God's judgment to an ugly creature living like an animal in the woods. When truth switches from God to us, beauty vanishes. As Samuel's daughter-in-law lamented, "The glory has departed from Israel, for the ark of God has been captured." (1Sam. 4:22)

It used to be that the difference between truth and falsehood was as clear as the difference between black and white, but all that has changed. We live in a world where the light of truth has been fractured into a thousand shades of gray. A twilight has settled over our minds. We "wander about in darkness, not knowing the truth." (1Jn. 1:6) Isaiah describes this very idea when he says, "we hope for light and behold darkness, for brightness, but we walk in gloom." (Isa. 59:9)

In this postmodern world, people are merely hoping to get the right idea, hoping to find a truth to give them direction, yet they are dead men walking all the while. When we lost truth we lost our foundation, when we lost beauty, we lost desire, resulting in the emptiness and darkness so many people experience today.

A wonderful picture of what happens when "the glory departs" is found in Charles Dickens' *A Christmas Carol*. The Spirit of Christmas Present had taken Scrooge on a merry romp through England, showing him scene after scene of happy Christmas celebrations, but as his earthly time comes to a close, he reveals a dark and deadly secret. Pulling aside his beautiful robe, he reveals two dreadfully poor and despicable children whom he identifies as "Ignorance" and "Want." They are indeed the antithesis of truth and beauty.

The Spirit warns Scrooge to fear the boy Ignorance the most. "Beware them both...but most of all this boy, for on his brow, I see that written which is Doom..." (Dickens, p. 86) When truth departs, when glory leaves, we are left with a world stripped of all that is good, all that is beautiful, and we live in fear. Ignorance, resulting from this departure from truth, surely spells the doom of our age.

When the horror-struck Scrooge observes these two woebegone children, he asks, "Have they no refuge or resource?" This is the very question we must ask today. In a world where truth has met its doom, and want has devoured like a flood, where can we find a refuge? Where can we go to find the place where glory dwells?

The answer is stated so simply by the Apostle John; "From the fullness of his grace we all received one blessing after another...grace and truth came through Jesus Christ." (John 1:16,17) Jesus came to rekindle right relationships, to bring restoration to a fallen system, to set everything back on a journey to righteousness. He accomplishes this task through grace, for we are unable to know the truth on our own and are unworthy to gaze upon his beauty.

The Apostle Paul bears testimony to the transformation of grace in his life by saying, "But by the grace of God, I am what I am, and his grace to me was not without effect." (2Cor. 15:10) Creatures that rebel against their Creator do not really deserve to be rescued, yet God never once failed in his thoughts of loving grace toward us. So he put a plan in motion to realign the world with truth and to right the wrongs that separate us, in order to restore all that is good and beautiful.

It is, no doubt, perfectly obvious to us that we live in a world defaced by sin, and this fact limits us. But it also should be equally clear that we are, at the same time, living in a world where God is at work, and this fact liberates us. The kingdom of God, in which the earth is restored to God's total rule and jurisdiction, **comes**. It is not that it is coming, entirely, on some future date, and it is not that it appears only in some kind of spiritual dimension.

God reigns and his truth is always at the heart of justice. 1Corinthians15:25 says, For he must reign until he has put all enemies under his feet." This is happening *now*, for many enemies possess our world, but a culmination will come – "then the end will come." (v. 24) The coming of the kingdom will be at once terrible and glorious. The incredible power of grace will be completely known; all that is ugly and ignorant will be swept away and beauty will finally be made permanent.

To approach the topic of truth is overwhelming, for in doing so, we face something of an infinite nature because we are talking about the fundamental nature of God himself. Passages in the Old Testament such as Psalm 31:5 declare that God is a "God of truth," and in John 14:6, Jesus says he is "the way, the truth and the life." Citing this passage in his great *Summa Theologica*, St. Thomas Aquinas concludes, "Whence it follows not only that truth is in Him, but that he is truth itself and the sovereign and first truth." Truth is as "big" as God is, and the only way we can know truth is by knowing God.

Perhaps the most well known Biblical passage about truth is John 8:32: "you will know the truth and the truth will set you free." If we know God, we live forgiven of our sins, and we thrive in the glorious light of freedom, far away from the dark jailhouse of sin and fear. In order for us to see this light, for us to know this truth, God had to reveal it to us. Wandering around in a state of blindness, we are only freed from our dependence on this world when God, and no other, purposefully shines "the light of the gospel of the glory of Christ" on our faces. The truth of God is the pure light by which beauty is revealed. We discover it, first, by knowing Christ, and secondly, by studying God's Word.

This life of knowing and studying is described in the Bible as a walk, or a journey with God. It leads us to Heaven, our beautiful home; the eternal abode of truth, grace and beauty. The Apostle John said that his greatest joy was to hear that his children (in other words, the believers he had trained) were "walking in truth." (3Jn. 4)

In Psalm 25, David describes our journey in terms of an educational process, asking, "Make me to know your ways O Lord, teach me your paths. Lead me in your truth and teach me." Knowing the truth is a long and arduous journey, directing us not only to higher and higher plains of insight here on earth, but also continuing on into Heaven. We will never stop learning truth, for it is infinite, just as God, who is truth, is also infinite.

At the door of death, we turn the corner from a knowledge of God that gives us strength and insight for our lonely earthly walk, to a glorious never-ending voyage of infinite education where we shall "know, even as we are known." The Apostle Paul expresses this desire for the eternal knowledge of truth when he says, "That I may know him . . . becoming like him in his death...that I may attain the resurrection of the dead." (Phil. 3:10,11) In eternity, God's glory will shine out from his eternal truth -- the light that shines on beauty and finally makes it real.

When the Bible describes our Heaven-bound journey towards knowing truth and being free, it teams up Mercy (in the O.T.) or Grace (in the N.T.) with truth, and beauty with goodness. As blind sinners, we cannot see truth without the light of grace. But grace and truth have come through Jesus Christ. Once they are received into our hearts by faith, the Holy Spirit then "guides us into all truth" as he helps us to understand the gospel so that we may live good and holy lives. As Christians, we perceive truth through the twin lights of Jesus and the Word. If anyone should be able to see beauty, if anyone should be able to glimpse pure good, it should be us – God's very own.

The life we now live as we journey down this path of insight is a genuine version of what is rightly called "the good life." When our sense of goodness comes from God, and not from ourselves, we live at peace, echoing David's familiar words: "Surely goodness and mercy shall follow me all the days of my life." In Psalm 145, David also writes, "The Lord is good to all; he has compassion on all he has made."

He points out that this inner realization of God's goodness (and the peace and joy that comes with it) is dependant on knowing and understanding the works of God. "They will tell of the power of your awesome works...They will celebrate your abundant goodness." When we realize that the power evident in God's mighty deeds is the same power we have at our disposal every day, we will face life with confidence, discerning and reflecting truth and beauty – "the light of the knowledge of the glory of God in the face of Christ." (2Cor. 4:6)

In his renowned sermon, "The Weight of Glory," C.S. Lewis discusses our desire for true beauty, our longing deep inside for something greater, for a type of beauty that is not an illusion as it is now, but intrinsic in all that is good. He says we perceive a "...secret we cannot hide and cannot tell, though we desire to do both. We cannot tell it because it is a desire for something that has never actually appeared in our experience. We cannot hide it because our experience is constantly suggesting it..." (Lewis, p. 3) He is saying that when we see something beautiful in this life, it is so fleeting that we are left with only a momentary illusion of something far greater; something that will reveal the eternal glory of God.

Last summer, while I was taking a flight from St. Louis to San Diego, I saw a sunset from *within the clouds*. It looked as if a clear and distinct line of brilliant light had been drawn between the earthy clouds and Heaven itself. I was then struck by this truth: a distinct line exists between heaven and earth; it is *redemption*, and we the redeemed alone may walk upon that line and genuinely experience truth, grace and beauty.

In "The Weight of Glory," C.S. Lewis also saw this line, a line that he describes as falling between being "left utterly and absolutely outside" of God's presence or being "called in, welcomed, received, acknowledged." He concludes, "We walk everyday on the razor edge between these two incredible possibilities." (Lewis, p.7)

Christ at the Center

The Christian life is walked upon this line, where we "trip with light fantastic toe" (as Milton said). Through God's redeeming grace and indwelling Spirit, we are the only mortal beings who can see that line or path between the light of truth and the beauty of light. Zechariah, the father of John the Baptist, describes it so well in his song – "the rising sun will come to us from heaven…to guide our feet into the path of peace." (Luke 1:78, 79) As we follow our Beautiful Savior on this heavenly path, may we marvel at all beauty, treasure all truth and share all that is good with grateful hearts.

Bibliography – Truth and Beauty

Ball, Phillip. *Universe of Stone: A Biography of Chartres Cathedral.* New York: HarperCollinsPublishers, 2008. Print.

Dickens, Charles. *A Christmas Carol.* New York: Scholastic Publishing Services, 1962. 86-87. Print.

St. Thomas Aquinas, *The Summa Theologica of St. Thomas Aquinas.* 2nd and revised ed. 1920. Web edition 2008. New Advent. Web. 11 May 2010.

Lewis, C. S. "The Weight of Glory." Preached originally as a sermon in the Church of St. Mary the Virgin, Oxford. 8 June 1942, published in Theology, November 1941, and by the S.P.C.K, 1942. Retrieved online at http://www.verber.com/mark/xian/weight-of-glory.pdft.

Chapter 2-CREATION
Part 1: Knowing How It All Began

"[Christ] is the image of the invisible God, the firstborn over all creation. **For by him all things were created:** things in heaven and earth, visible and invisible…He is before all things, and in him all things hold together." Col.1:15-17

GOD'S PLAN

When discussing the Biblical teaching on Creation, it is easy to jump to the controversial issues first, like diving into the deep end of a frigid swimming pool. But I have learned that it is best to start with a discussion of God's plan for the universe. Why did God create? What was his purpose or goal? How does this go beyond the mere creation of a physical world into all of God's purposes for mankind? Creation, you see, is all encompassing; it goes far beyond the events of the beginning and is really all about the revelation of God's Plan – his plan for the past, for today and for an eternal reality.

One of the best doctrinal statements I've ever found concerning the topic of Creation as it relates to God's plan is found in the Catholic Catechism, so I'm going to begin this look at the issues surrounding this very controversial topic by referring to it and commenting on it. (Admittedly, my comments on this passage may be tilted towards an evangelical slant, but I am trying to be as objective as possible.) Furthermore, this is probably uncharted territory for Evangelicals, but sometimes it helps to look at things from a different vantage point. We can think about truth in a new way, and as a result, see our way a little clearer.

The Catechism begins with Creation finding its culmination in the New Creation: the restoration of all things in God's eternal kingdom. To this end, the Spirit strives to present the Church holy and blameless on that future day. We are all progressing toward the goal of eternal glory. Colossians 1:19 says that one day, through Christ, all things will be reconciled.

Our beliefs about Creation do not only concern the creation at the beginning of the world. They also come to bear on our perception of a new creation at the end of the world. Further, they influence our understanding of how fallen souls are liberated by Christ's sacrifice to become new creations in Christ. In other words, the Creation story and its theological implications do not begin and end in Gen.1 and 2, and it cannot be said that Gen.1 and 2 say everything there is to say about God's creative acts.

The catechism goes on to make the point that "God the Creator can be known with certainty through His works, by the light of human reason." (Catechism, p. 84) This is an important point, because what is meant here is that through study and critical thinking about nature, God can be known or revealed. The study of nature (which in our day is adsorbed in scientific thought) can show us the truth.

The Catholic Catechism goes on to explain that this reason is confirmed by faith and faith leads us to the truth. In other words, you can learn facts about nature, which are in turn facts about Creation, and faith, including belief in the Scriptures, will confirm those facts as being true.

The catechism further states that God created out of his wisdom and goodness. He created out of nothing (*ex nihilo*). Hebrews 11:3 says, "By faith we understand that the universe was formed at God's command so that what is seen was not made out of what was visible." God did not use any preexisting material to create or *begin* anything. It all came from his divine Word, which constructed physical realities. He declared things to exist. What he made was orderly and good; that is to say, it works correctly and God sustains that working as He guides and upholds it.

We often mistakenly say that God created things "perfect." Initially, before sin, the world was *very good*, but not absolutely perfect, because perfection is a characteristic of God and not of the physical world and universe. Change was built into the physical universe, and whenever something changes, it is progressing toward a goal; something beyond or better than what it is now.

The catechism relates this orientation to God's providence. I like the phrase that says that the universe is in "a state of journeying." It moves by God's direction toward its divinely appointed purposes. In his providence, God may use secondary causes; meaning that, to carry out his will, creatures may freely act and carry out their own cause and effect relationships.

So, if we were to summarize the Catholic stance on the theology of Creation we could say: God created out of nothing a universe, which is proceeding by his guidance to his ultimate perfect ends. We can learn about this universe in two ways; by the testimony of God's word and the truth revealed by the universe itself. As we can see, the Catechism gives us a captivating framework upon which we can build a realistic thesis concerning the truth about Creation.

WHAT THE BIBLE AND NATURE SAY ABOUT CREATION

In order to learn the truth about creation, we will first study what the Bible has to say about it (chapt. 2) and then go on to look at some of the controversies surrounding the debate between Creation and Evolution (chapt. 3). In order to gain a comprehensive understanding, we must look at all of the Bible passages, not just Gen.1 and 2. What concepts comprise the truth about creation as revealed in the Bible? How can we construct a complete Biblical framework?

One of the most interesting foundational verses about Creation is found tucked away in Job 38:33. God is speaking, and he says, "Do you know the ordinances of the heavens? Can you establish their rule on the earth?" (ESV) Also, in Jer. 33:25, God declares that he will not break his covenant with Israel because it would be the same as breaking "the fixed laws of heaven and earth." These verses tell us (as scientific research has born out) that the universe is indeed governed by certain fundamental rules (or **laws**) that God built into it from the very beginning. God wanted the universe to work in a certain way, and he laid the ground rules for this operation at the start.

Everything developed from these laws, and everything operates under their jurisdiction. And, as we know, scientists who study nature have discovered these laws, for nature is a revelation of God, and in it, the details of God's plan are made known. (Some scientists have acknowledged God in their discoveries while others have not.) When we look at scientific laws, we see a marvelous consistency and intricacy that belies the Creator's hand and his timing as well.

It is also interesting to note that the study of nature and its laws (science) has only come into its own in modern times. We know more about science and can do more with science than at any other point in history. It is almost as if we have been waiting and wondering until the right time came for us to see the things God put in nature for us to see.

At a time when God's revelation in his Word and through Jesus Christ has been diminished in many circles, God's revelation in nature has exploded out with the message of who God is and what he has done, if we only have eyes to see it. As Christians, we must be careful that we do not trivialize the truths which science discovers.

In addition to this foundational principle of laws, we also see a clear distinction drawn between the creation of the heavens and the creation of the earth. An **order** is established; the heavens are created first, the earth second, growing out of the creation of the heavens, with the waters as an intermediary step. Genesis 1 follows a poetic framework of heavens, waters, and earth.

This framework is also found in Psalm 33. Verse 6 says, "By the word of the Lord were the heavens made." A statement about the division of the waters follows – "he gathers the waters," and then by a verse describing the creation of the earth – "Let all the earth fear the Lord . . . for he spoke and it came to be." This psalm also refers back to God's overall plan – "the plans of the Lord stand firm forever." (v. 11) Psalm 104 also confirms this order – "he stretches out the heavens" (v. 2), "he lays the beams of his upper chambers on the waters" (v.3), and "he set the earth on its foundations" (v. 5).

Creation appears to come together in accordance with God's plan for the heavens to antedate the earth and then for the earth to be established as a home for humanity. Conversely, at the end of time each will consecutively be destroyed as a part of God's plan. 2Peter 3:10 says, "The *heavens* will disappear with a roar; the *elements* will be destroyed by fire, and the *earth* and everything in it will be laid bare."

It was not until I started to look at Biblical Creation passages other than Gen.1 and 2 that I even became aware of this distinction. The heavens were set up for the earth, so what went on in the heavens impacted the earth, and the earth, in turn, impacted people. At the same time, the waters were taking from the heavens and giving to the earth.

A thorough understanding of creation, therefore, begins with **cosmology** – the science behind what was going on in the heavens – rather than biology/evolution, what was going on here on the earth. The Big Bang has to do with cosmology, the revelation of the heavens, whereas evolution has to do with biology, the study of living, earthly organisms. (The waters, perhaps, have to do with chemistry, the basis for life.)

Dr. Hugh Ross, in his book *Creator and the Cosmos*, contends that the Big Bang event and star formation were some of the causes behind our earth being the way it is so that we could live here and be an integral part of God's plan. In fact, the universe tells us that the events occurring during and after the Big Bang, had to happen in order for our planet to be suitable for us to live on it.

Studying the cosmos also reveals that these events happened over a time period of about 14 billion years. We know this because God used light (specifically, the speed of light) as a built in clock with which we can count backwards to the creation event. Psalm 19:1 states that, "The heavens declare the glory of God; the skies proclaim the work of his hands. Day after day they pour forth speech; night after night they display knowledge." The revelation of God in nature is first seen in the skies above.

The stars contain and demonstrate a record of what God did. He placed within them clues for us to trace, in order to find an explanation for our existence. It is interesting to note that God says this record can be discovered and understood by mankind – "there is no speech or language (human elements) where their voice is not heard." (v. 3) If we want to interpret this revelation of God, we must read his nature-book.

Christ at the Center

Both the Bible and cosmology also seems to qualify the heavens as being quite ancient and old. Psalm 68:33 describes the Lord riding in a heavenly chariot in "the ancient skies above," and Psalm 102:25 says, "of old you laid the foundations of the earth and the heavens are the work of your hands." The words used seem to indicate times before us, times beyond human comprehension when God engaged in ancient goings-on. This agrees with what we observe in the night skies.

One of the most common arguments I've heard against an ancient universe is that God could have created the world in six twenty-four hour days if that was what he wished to do, because God can do whatever he wants. In response, I would say, first of all, God cannot lie. (Titus 1:2) If God's revelation of the truth in nature points to something other than a literal week, a much greater amount of time, then that is exactly what God is trying to tell us. Some say that God constructed the universe and the earth so that it only looked old, but I think that would be deceptive, and God does not deceive or trick us.

The verse I just mentioned is related within the context of God's plan – "…a faith and knowledge resting on the hope of eternal life, which God, who does not lie, promised before the beginning of time, and at his appointed season brought his word to light…" (Titus 1:2,3) Notice how salvation is a part of God's creative plan, and how he does things at exactly the right time in his sequence of events and does not deviate from his eternal purpose. God's plan operates in his way under the jurisdiction of his laws. It is incredible that God even allows us an insight into his operations, so we must take care to interpret the truth he gives us in as accurate a manner as possible.

Another truth that the Bible makes clear to us is that **God creates**, and he **always** creates. In John 5:17 Jesus says, "My Father is always at his work to this very day, and I, too, am working" -- right now and always. Interestingly, this verse is in the context in of a discussion about the Sabbath, the one day in which God is said to *not* have worked.

Of course, neither the Sabbath nor any other day was made for God's benefit; they are for people. Mark 2:27, 28 says, "…the Sabbath was made for man, not man for the Sabbath. So the Son

Christ at the Center

of Man is Lord even of the Sabbath." The Sabbath was given to mankind to provide rest amid his continuing life of labor.

God's completion of creation and rest on the seventh day means that he delivered a finished product, meaning that he had completed things in the way they were going to be, nothing new and different was going to be added or "tweaked." God rested only because he wanted us to rest. But He is always working, especially to create and sustain life both physically and spiritually, a task that only God can do and one that he eternally does.

HOW GOD CREATED

One of the things we don't think about very often is the dynamic of God actually doing that work. What would that look like? When we work, we go through individual steps to achieve a completed product. For example, imagine making chocolate chip cookies. We perform several small consecutive steps (measuring, mixing, eating a few extra chocolate chips! etc.) in order to get the job done and doing the steps takes time. But what if you didn't have to use time to do the steps? What if "what-you-said," became?

That's the way it is for God; no time passes for Him when He creates, not even 24 hours or 6 days or 14 billion years. He speaks and it is done. Frances Schaeffer refers to this as "divine fiat;" a statement delivered by God by which things are made. (Schaeffer, p. 28, 29) Psalm 33:6 &9 teaches this by saying, "by the word of the Lord were the heavens made," and "For he spoke, and it came to be."

C. S. Lewis created an interesting spin on this when he described the creation of Narnia in *The Magician's Nephew*. Aslan stands in a dark void and begins to sing – one note at first, and then, adding other notes, a song begins, and the song becomes an amazing symphony. As the song progresses, more and more things appear and exist and "be." Narnia is created with a song.

If we carefully read Scripture, we can see that this is probably not too far off from what actually happened during the creation of our earth, speaking in a symbolic sense – and even then, it may be more literal than we think. In Job 38:6, 7, God asks this question, "...who laid its (the earth's) foundation – while the morning stars sang together...?" Music seems to be "playing" at the very beginning of time.

Fundamentally, music is based on math. (In fact, good musicians are usually good at math.) Music is comprised of rhythms to count and sounds that are vibrations, which proceed according to mathematical frequencies. Could it be that the "word" God used to create was math expressed in music? Math regulates everything in our universe. Every object has dimension. Each chemical reaction has a formula. All movements in physics can be quantified. All scientific concepts have a mathematical basis. (One could almost say that, by creating, God 'did the math!")

In addition, the Bible speaks repeatedly about God creating with words. It's very interesting to note that the words *are* actions. Psalm 148:5 says, "He commanded and they were created." We can use words to describe things that happen, or regulate the way in which things happen, (give directions), or to try and persuade people to do things. Words and actions are separate. But this is not so with God. Why is this? It may be because when God performs an action it takes no time to do it; it doesn't take God any time at all to do things. "Saying it" and "doing it" is the same thing.

Creation and Time

It is interesting to note that the primary controversy surrounding creation revolves around the amount of *time* it took – be it 6 days or 14 billion years. But remember, for God, the one doing the actual creating, no time passed whatsoever. Time only passed in the physical universe as each creative endeavor was "added" to the whole. God spoke many things into existence, but as soon as they began, they existed in a physical world. As such, they fell under the jurisdiction of time.

The Bible teaches that God did certain specific things when he created. Psalm 104 mentions several of these precise things – stretching out the heavens, laying beams for water chambers, and setting the earth on foundations. He raises mountains and lowers valleys, makes springs of water gush out, and grows grass. He plants trees and forms Leviathian to play in the sea.

When we think of someone doing these types of things, we think of time passing by as they are done. I can make chocolate chip cookies, but it takes time. God does these things (and many, many other things at the same time) in literally no time at all, and he actually accomplishes something. He makes real things that exist in real time. Think of how it would look if you saw a sped-up video of me baking the chocolate chip cookies. It would look like it took a lot less time, yet, because I am human, time still passes.

In spite of the illusion of time behaving much differently than it normally does, the cookies can only come together in real time. God works, you might say, incredibly "fast", but he takes no time. However, the actual process of creation was performed within the confines of time. This is one of the great paradoxes we encounter when we explore the great mystery of creation; therefore, it becomes one of the most important components of creation that we must accept by faith.

St. Augustine points out that a process of change indicates a process of creation; "We look upon the heavens and earth, and they cry aloud that they were made. For they change and vary." (St. Augustine, p.213) Then he dives into a detailed discussion of time and concludes that God, being completely outside of time, and not necessitated by it, created time, and as a result, time passed when he created but the time was inconsequential to God.

Think about how much time it took Jesus to perform a miracle. If you really think about it, it took no time at all. He may have put mud on a blind man's eyes and told him to go wash it off in a pool (John 9), but the placing of the mud and the washing (actions that take time) weren't the miracle. The giving of sight was the miracle. It happened instantaneously; or maybe we can say "super-instantaneously." That's because miracles are not physical actions, but spiritual ones and do not involve time. When God performed the miracle of creation, it all happened in a "timeless" way from his vantage point. But, from our vantage point (earth-based), time is the first dynamic we observe.

Christ at the Center

The words "in the beginning" are time-indicators. The first act/word of creation was "Let there be light" (Gen. 1:1), and this set time into motion. When we look at the message of the stars, time is one of the principle things we see. We measure time by the speed of light – about 186,000 miles per second – something that the heavens have revealed to us. Accordingly, at the initial point of God's creative activity, time starts to pass and God keeps creating. We might say, in our human way, that God got so wrapped up in his work that He lost track of time!

Between the command to create light and man's appearance, God is preparing the earth so that it works in a certain way, a way suitable for man to live in. Finally, when people are created, time becomes important because people are going to live in the context of time. We call it history; God's plan for the lives of people, carrying out his purpose for the redemption of people.

We need to be careful, then, about putting God into a kind of "24/7 box." God wasn't in that box when he created. Remember, he still creates life and that week is long gone. Think for a minute – if God spent 6 days creating and the 7th resting, what did he do on the 8th day? Creation was done – did he suddenly need to find something else to do? And on the 14th day, did he rest again? And when Christianity got up and going, did he switch His rest day from the 7th to the 1st?

And what about the problems introduced by time zones? Because of the earth's rotation on its axis, 2 days are always going on at the same time on our planet. So on the 6th day, was God creating and resting at the same time? It just doesn't work to put God in a 24/7 box. He is outside of time and it has no influence over what he does. God is not bound by time in anyway or, so to speak, at "anytime."

But, some may protest, "what about those pesky days mentioned in Gen.1 and Gen. 2:1?" First of all, remember that the Bible uses the word "day" in many different ways and so do we. "Day" can mean a period of 24 hours, daytime when it's light outside, or a long period of time like an age. Or it can refer to an event that only takes place during a small portion of a day, a birthday (the actual moment of the day when you were born) or one's wedding day (the ceremony lasts for a small portion of the day).

Take, for example, the 3 days during which Jesus was in the tomb. Jesus predicted that he would be buried for "three days and three nights" in the same way that Jonah was in the whale for three days and nights. (Mt.12:40) However, if we look at the accounts of the crucifixion, it is very clear that Jesus was not in the tomb for 72 hours. He was there *on three days*, that is, from Friday at about 6:00pm and all day Saturday until about 6:00am on Sunday. Just as those 3 days were somewhat imprecise, the days of Creation are used to express the idea of the passage of time as God creates, not the exact time.

The use of the concept of a "day" is telling us that God created time and that he created certain things so that they appeared at certain times, and as time passes, his plan comes into fruition. It is significant, I think, that the days of creation are only mentioned once outside of Gen.1 and 2:1. Jesus himself never speaks of them. Exodus 20:11 says that the Jewish people were supposed to rest on the 7th day because God created the world in 6 and rested on the 7th. It's a part of the Law, and the Law says a lot about the Sabbath. In fact, the whole Creation story is more about the 7th day than the other 6. And, in its redemptive sense, God's plan of creation culminates in a sort of Sabbath; a permanent day of rest to which we strive, as Hebrews 4 describes.

Israel and the Creation Story

In order to understand the significance of God's emphasis on the Sabbath, it's helpful to look at who wrote the Genesis creation account and why it was written. Gen.1 is part of the Pentateuch, the first 5 books of the Bible or the Jewish Law. Charles Hummel gave an interesting view of this in his book, *The Galileo Connection*. The Hebrews had just come out of Egypt, where they had lived for 400 years -- a long period of time. At the beginning, they were a large family, and at the end, they were a nation within a nation. But now they would be a nation all their own, and they would need certain laws and concepts to guide them. After all, it was happening rather quickly. So, God took Moses aside and began revealing a series of truths (the Law), which were to guide and give continuity to this new nation.

One of the concepts God wanted them to understand was the week. We have very little trouble understanding weeks, because they are an integral part of our culture. But ancient Hebrews didn't have weeks. They had days – it's light and then gets dark at regular intervals – the sun told them that; and months – the moon told them that – but that's all they had. They knew plenty about work, but very little about rest.

Moses starts off his book with a bang – a real attention-getter – a poem about a week, a grand epic poem to glorify God for his glorious act of Creation. In his book, *Searching for God Knows What*, Donald Miller talks about his experience of learning that Moses often chose to write in poetic style because he was more concerned with communicating *meaning* than *facts*. Miller talks about the incredibly moving experience of hearing passages read in Hebrew; moving, even though he couldn't understand the words.

The ancient Hebrews understood this. Creation is about relationship with and emotional attachment to the Creator. The whole point of the poem is the 7th day, the day that God wanted the Jewish people to set aside to honor Him and to build relationship with Him.

We know that the passage in Gen.1 is a poem or, at least, poem-like, because it has poetic qualities like a repetitive refrain and a 3-within-3 structure. (The first three days are related to the last three.) Some scholars think that the poem was composed before the time of Moses and handed down from generation to generation. Maybe it was sung around the campfire, as it were; surely, it was greatly revered and honored because it was the story of how everything came into existence by the word of a powerful and loving Creator.

If this was so, the Israelites probably sat up and took notice right away when they first heard it. "Hey, it's that creation poem," they might have said, "so it means we should put 6 days together to work as God worked, and devote the 7th to worship

God, the Creator – wow, what a concept!" And so, the idea of a week of work and rest took off.

Even though we can keep track of time a bit better than the ancient Hebrews, we're still rather loosey-goosey about how we reference it, and so were they. We use a lot of figurative phrases when referencing time: someday, whenever, that'll be the day, any day now, back in the day and once upon a time. But we don't often fuss about the exact dimensions of the "day" itself.

Perhaps this is what is going on in Gen.1, especially since it is a poetic passage. Figurative language can convey truth – as we know from the truths we learn from Psalms and Proverbs, for example. The fact is that God created; it was great, good, and a work of art. In light of this glory, we are to rest in worship.

Hearing God's Voice in Science
We need to remember that God has revealed himself to us through creation. He has given us insight into His character, will, love and plan through nature; through what has been created. Romans 1: 20 says, "For His invisible attributes...have been clearly perceived...in the things that have been made." The study of Nature (created things) is called science. When we study science, we are studying God.

Today, at the edge of what scientists do, we find spiritual tension because God is revealed in nature. The study of science has become increasingly complex as the years have gone by, and at the same time, by the influence of the Evil One, it has become increasingly removed from the study of God. Nowadays, many scientists will have nothing to do with God. But God is still there in nature/science. His math still speaks. He is still revealing Himself like a candle shining in a dark room.

When unbelieving modern scientists catch a glimpse of that candle, they are forced by the blindness of their own hearts to turn and run, protesting as they go. I Corinthians 2:14 states, "The man without the Spirit does not accept the things that come from the Spirit of God..." This explains why there is so much tension between the world of science and Christianity; it is part of a deep underlying conflict between God and evil, particularly, the evil of denying God's revelation of truth.

At the same time, Christians have undermined the glory of Creation in various ways. As mentioned earlier, some have tried to stuff God in a "24/7 box", justifying this by concocting "scientific" explanations for everything that happened. Their focus is limited to a very literal interpretation of Scripture. Others have tried to link up with the secular side by embracing various premises of evolution, calling it theistic evolution.

But God reveals the truth, and He wants us to know the truth about Creation, not our best guess or what feels like a plausible explanation. Our viewpoints (as discussed in the next chapter) should not dictate what God did or didn't do when he created. Who God is should determine what we believe about creation, and sometimes in this debate we have forgotten just who God is – he is almighty, his "thoughts are not our thoughts" and he works in a supernatural way in all that he does.

What it all comes down to is that Creation is an all-consuming miracle. How do we experience miracles? It is by faith. Hebrews 11:3 explains, "By faith we understand that the universe was formed at God's command, so that what is seen was not made out of what is visible." What "is not seen" is God's Word; and yet at the same time, the Word is Christ, Who was "made flesh and dwelt among us." (John 1) You see, faith is not of this physical world; it is spiritual; and yet, it is the very thing that makes reality understandable!

Not only were words the vehicle of Creation, they are the essence of the Creator himself. John 1:1,2 says, "In the beginning was the word, and the word was with God and the word was God. He was with God in the beginning. Through him all things were made." God's revelation becomes as real as he is. Creation is the speaking of the divine word, a voice that goes out to the whole world. Everything is touched by it; everything sings it, mathematically and otherwise.

The word of creation speaks to point us to God, to Jesus who creates our life and our new life in him. God's purpose in creation was to reveal himself to his creatures by displaying his glory through his speaking as the eternal Word. His plan was that they would, in turn, live in that glory and reflect it back upon him.

Hebrews 4:9 says, "So then there remains a Sabbath rest for the people of God." As I said before, the whole point of the Gen.1 Creation hymn was the Sabbath. The Bible teaches that something greater than the physical Creation, a new Creation, lies ahead for believers. When we become new creations in Christ, we start on our way to this new universe. Our souls are the first things to be re-created as we enter, through salvation, the Kingdom of God. Later our bodies will be transformed when they rise from the dead so that they will be able to function in a brand-new, heavenly system.

The Gen.1 creation will not last forever; it will be replaced by something altogether different. 2 Peter 3 describes this amazing event in which the old universe will be literary torn apart by fire and God will create, again, by His Word, a new universe, ruled by the dynamic of timeless righteousness. Because we are creatures of time, we cannot imagine this unbounded universe. By faith, however, we can live as citizens of it. And so – we were made for so much more – a heavenly reality will someday be made real to us. By faith our journey began, by faith it will be fulfilled.

Chapter 3-CREATION
Part 2: Finding the truth about Creation

"For his invisible attributes, namely, **his eternal power and divine nature**, have been clearly perceived, ever since the creation of the world, in the things that have been made. So they are without excuse." Rom. 1:20, ESV

CREATION AND EVOLUTION

Now, if we take a step back, and revisit the teachings of the Catholic catechism on creation, we remember that it explains that Creation proceeds from God, by his miraculous word, and is a part of God's redemptive plan for the world. The Bible and nature reveal the truth about creation to us. It is all about the unfolding of God's beautiful, intricate plan directed to bring us home to him.

This being said, however, I found it surprising that the Catholic Church (and for that matter, the Episcopal Church and others as well) espouses **evolution** as the means by which God created. Why do they subscribe to what is such a radical view in the (typical) Christian world? How can they hold this view and maintain their orthodox position on the divine person and unlimited power of God?

In order to understand how this could come about, one has to understand the Catholic Church's position on authority, that is, how they determine the basis for truth. Just like Protestants and Evangelicals, the Catholics believe the final say on truth comes from the Bible. But in addition to this, or perhaps, superimposed on this, it is the Catholic belief that the church can make various types of statements on certain issues and these statements are to be taken as authoritative.

Therefore, if the Catholic Church says that if man, using his God-given powers of reason, has found evidence for a process of evolution leading to the development of life on this planet, then, if the church condones this as being in keeping with divine revelation, evolution can be endorsed as a valid scientific theory. Remember, the Catholic Church puts a lot of emphasis on the use of human reason, so that it is believed that man, divinely endowed with reason, can arrive at the truth.

The Catholic Church condemns a view of evolution devoid of God. They say that one must not account for the existence of life in a purely materialistic sense – nature is all there is, and nature evolved on its own, independent of any divine intervention. Divine providence is said to guide the evolutionary process. Evolution has to fall into a pattern of divinely ordered procedures and outcomes. (*Catechism*, p. 82-84)

The question is, can this happen? Can evolution, as a scientific theory, be viewed as a mechanism used by God to create? Before this question is answered, it would do us well to look at the various theories and ideas often discussed in the creation/evolution debate.

Evolution

First, we will take a brief, simplified look at what the theory of evolution states. Most of the information I will relate here comes from a typical high school biology textbook called *Biology the Dynamics of Life*. Since many of us were not paying attention in high school, or like myself, were severely biased against what we were hearing, this basic information bears repeating.

Charles Darwin's book, *The Origin of the Species*, was published in 1859, and his second book, *The Decent of Man*, in 1871. During this time, people were beginning to move away from thinking about things from the standpoint of faith in God to reasoning about things from a purely human viewpoint. Darwin wanted to develop a view of the origin of life that was the opposite of the traditional view based on faith; he saw it as a completely natural process. Nature, by means of random mutations based on coincidence, was, so to speak, in charge of its own processes, not God.

A very basic summary of the theory of evolution states that it is the process by which changes occur in populations of organisms over time. The vehicle for this change is *natural selection*, sometimes called "survival of the fittest." Changes that benefit species are retained when they are passed on to offspring, thus insuring their survival. These changes and adaptations occur over vast amounts of time.

Another important factor in evolutionary theory is *speciation*, in which genetic changes occur in isolated groups as that group adapts to its environment. New species are formed when they can no longer interbreed with their original group. Evolution also takes into account *common decent*, that is, dissimilar species display genetic traits in common which can be traced back to a common ancestor.

Scientists have been fleshing out Darwin's theory and refining it over the years. They have studied fossils and genetics and biochemistry and so on, in an effort to discover the hows and whys of evolution. This has given rise to neo-Darwinism, the idea that evolution occurs purely through natural selection acting in a completely random (or aimless and unpredictable) way.

In fact, the randomness is seen to be the very "structure" of evolution. Natural selection acts on inherited genetic variations within populations and mutations can cause these variations. Positive mutations are very, very rare, so a lot of time is needed for changes to occur – a lot of time!

The idea that genetic changes can occur in organisms, which enable them to adapt to changes in environment while not changing the organism into a different species, is called microevolution. The fact that this phenomenon occurs has been widely observed and is not called into question by either creationists or evolutionists. Creatures can change and adapt to environmental pressures, provided that the changes are in the range of their particular genome.

In evolutionary thought, however, microevolution takes the leap into macroevolution, as, over a long period of time, the changes accumulate and a new life form emerges having a completely different genetic code. Scientists extrapolate macroevolution (changes resulting in a new species) from microevolution (changes within a species) because they place so much stock in the role of time. In other words, they believe if a change in an organism can be observed to occur over a short period of time, it is viable that vast amounts of time can precipitate changes that result in new and better organisms.

For example, they have observed that disease-causing bacteria will change and become resistant to drugs. Bacteria go through many, many generations in just a short period of time; therefore, they say, if you give the bacteria enough time, it will change into something else entirely. But the lifetime of a person might not be long enough, so one could not observe this change taking place.

However, they feel that the observable small changes will ultimately result in the big changes. When these changes do occur, they feel it will happen very quickly in relationship to the vast amounts of time leading up to the change. This is called *punctuated equilibrium*, an idea purposed by the famous evolutionist, Stephen J. Gould.

The most important feature of evolutionary theory is **natural selection**, which is viewed as the basic, primary "force" behind the process of evolution. It is, practically speaking, the natural process by which an organism uses changes in its genetic traits (causing useful developments in the organism) to help it survive and reproduce. When reproducing, the organism will pass on these traits to its offspring, thus helping them to be stronger and better able to survive. Natural selection is believed to be positively influenced by a favorable environment, and it is more successful if a large degree of succeeding generations inherit the positive genetic traits.

This all-important feature of evolution is held in such high esteem by evolutionists that it has taken on a kind of god-like quality, in that it makes organisms what they are; it gives them their existence. It is, in essence, a powerful natural process that creates nature.

In his book, *The Blind Watchmaker*, evolutionary biologist and atheist Richard Dawkins says, "Natural selection, the blind, unconscious, automatic process which Darwin discovered, and which we now know is the explanation for the existence and apparently purposeful form of all life, has no purpose in mind." Natural selection, in god-like fashion, produces life and gives it a sort of meaning, but unlike the true God, having no plan, it never had, nor was able to have, any good reason for why life came about and no idea of what life is good for anyway.

Theistic Evolution
What I have been describing is secular evolution as opposed to theistic evolution, the viewpoint of the Catholic Church and other Christian groups. Secular evolution is completely naturalistic and materialistic; nature is all there is and nature intrinsically possesses the power to change itself. Theistic evolution recognizes the mechanisms of evolution, but purposes that God initiated the overall process. The first moment of the cosmos coming into being is seen as God's great creative act.

Many scientists who are Christians, not just Catholics, hold the idea of theistic evolution. In the Feb. '08 issue of Christianity Today, Dorothy Boorse, associate professor of biology at Gordon College, says, "I'm to teach the best available biology and the best evidence is that God used extensive evolution. I think most scientists in biology would agree with that, including Christians." Furthermore, many Christian colleges teach theistic evolution in their science classes, or maybe they would just say "evolution."

So, if scientists, who are Christians, look at the evolutionary process and see God's hand in it, and recognize God as the Creator, they may endorse the validity of evolution, but, as we shall see, this may not be the wisest course of action. It is important to note here that modern Christian scientists are not so much in agreement with "classical" theistic evolution (God intervened at certain times to make changes occur – the "God of the gaps" theory), as they are seeing the entire scope of evolutionary processes within God's work.

It is also important to understand that most of the proponents of theistic evolution show a lot of respect for God and his work. They are not trying to be antagonistic to the historical Christian faith, but they are trying to see creation in a modern scientific light. Therefore, they hold evolution and Christianity as parallel, not congruent, truths. Also, some theistic evolutionists see God's guidance in the evolutionary process to a greater degree than others.

Christ at the Center

One questionable aspect of theistic evolution is its overall insistence on the idea that God's influence over creation was only primary – he got the ball rolling, so to speak. Since God is said to be using evolution as his method of creating, he is allowing evolutionary processes to do the entire work of creation. Even the switch from non-life to life is seen purely as an evolution-time event. Life arose because it got to the point where it could arise. (Biologos)

Theistic evolutionists also embrace evolution as an aimless, undefined, non-designed process. Other than that initial all-encompassing first act of creation, evolution is the vehicle for the development of all physical life. They feel that discovering evidence of evolution in nature is revelatory that it is God's method of creation.

The trouble with theistic evolution, I feel, is that it simply does not allow God to be God. Despite what theistic evolutionists say about the centrality of God's creative act, they seem to relegate him, in some kind of deistic context, to the backseat of creation. The great, unregulated mechanism of evolution upstages anything that God is needed to stick around and do. Theistic evolution scientists will, at times, carry on for page after page of biological, evolutionary preponderance, seeming to give only a slight nod in passing to God, the all-powerful Creator, who, as the Bible declares, created "all things."

When God Doesn't Create

In Romans 1, Paul talks about those who are able to clearly see God in his creation, but who turn aside from this revelation instead of embracing it. He writes, "For although they knew God, they neither glorified him as God, nor gave thanks to him, but their thinking became futile...[they] exchanged the glory of the immortal God for images made to look like mortal man and birds and animals and reptiles."

Although this verse is commonly sited as a reference to man's decent into idol-worship, I feel it is very applicable here. Evolutionists know God, but they are not allowing God (Jesus, the Creator) to be the "firstborn over all creation." He is not given the "supremacy" that he deserves as the one who has created all things. (Col. 1) Instead, they have turned to "futile" explanations for creation. Secular evolutionists in particular embrace this type of thinking, and some theistic evolutions seem to lean in this direction also.

It is interesting to note that this Greek word translated "futile" carries with it the connotation of aimlessness – the very bedrock of evolution itself. The glory of God, as manifested all created things -- because he made and formed them in every detail, and he personally, continuously and perpetually gives life to all mortal creatures -- is transferred to glorifying an idolatrous construct. Evolution is the modern idol of man, birds, animals and reptiles. God will have no other gods alongside and next to him, as the first commandment states. As Jesus said, we cannot serve two masters; we cannot serve God and mammon (something served other than God) simultaneously.

Consider this statement made by Dennis Venema, writing on the BioLogos website: "Biologists are well aware of a natural mechanism that does add functional, specified information to DNA sequences (and in some cases, creates new genes *de novo*): natural selection acting on genetic variation produced through random mutation. Not only are biologists aware of some examples of natural selection adding functional information to DNA, this effect has been observed time and again, and in some cases it has documented in exquisite detail." Notice how he gives natural selection the credit for creating the changes in the DNA and how he uses microevolution as proof for macroevolution.

Although theistic evolutionists may say that God made evolution to act in these ways, they are not saying that God alone actively and supernaturally creates. Instead evolution creates, because God triggered it. The proof of macroevolution arising from microevolution is only theoritical; no one really knows if small changes add up to big changes in the end. Their faith seems to be placed in the forces of evolution and not the power of God who has given us proof of his creative powers and deeds wherever we look in nature.

A variant of theistic evolution is **evolutionary creationism**, which also contends that God created through the forces of evolution, but it gives more credence to God's overall guidance in the process. In other words, God actively created with the mechanism of evolution. They hold to the basic principles of evolutionary theory, such as common ancestry and natural selection, but feel that God superintended these processes more closely than theistic evolution would allow. Evolutionary creationists take a high view of God and Scripture, but they combine it with the idea that scientific research has produced ample proof that evolution is the force behind biological life. However, they hold to the foundational core of creationism – God created all things and he alone gives life.

Evolutionary creationists have benefited from recent studies in evolutionary biology that indicate that the processes of evolutionary development are more directed than previously thought. For example, it is becoming much clearer that evolution changes only occur in certain ways, not every which way, as it were. It is also now believed that evolution is self-organized around certain laws of development that take it down particular pathways. (Moritz)

I believe this viewpoint is worthy of continued scrutiny, because it involves the study of God's revelation in nature as well as respect for Scripture. The scientists who are Christians involved in this study are open to seeing God's hand in the processes of creation that also incorporate evolutionary paradigms, and this is to be commended.

Life Comes From God

When looking at this issue from a Biblical standpoint, I believe that the most telling fallacy of any evolutionary viewpoint (theistic or secular) is their disregard for the origin of life (and all succeeding life in its fundamental structures as well) coming directly and exclusively from God. To dismiss life as a happy cosmic accident or a broad genetic generality is to go directly against all that the Bible teaches us about the living God and his powerful relationship to life.

In John chapter 1, the Apostle John tells us that Jesus, the eternal Word, who was one with the Father, both made all things and gives life – "In him was life." In 1Sam.2:6, Hannah, who miraculously received a child from God, said, "The Lord brings death and makes alive."

In Job 12:7-10, Job calls upon the creatures of the earth as witnesses to the life-giving power of God: "Which of all these does not know that the hand of the Lord has done this? In his hand is the life of every creature and the breath of mankind." As God points out to Job later in the book, the gift of life comes to all living creatures directly and miraculously from him.

God repeatedly questions Job (a person, a natural entity) about whether or not he has creative powers greater than his – "Do you know?" "Do you give?" "Do you make?" God inquires. No, these things go beyond the limits of human comprehension, and to question God's authority in this area is to discredit God as the supreme and all-powerful Creator. (Job 40:8,9)

It seems, too, that God gives life to all animate things at all times. Nothing could live without his special gift of life. Life itself is not simply a biological construct. We are all a miracle. Referring to creatures such as birds, trees, lions and sea creatures, as well as to man, the Psalmist writes, "when you take away their breath, they die and return to the dust. When you send your Spirit, they are created, and you renew the face of the earth." (Ps. 104:29, 30)

Life is not a part of something merely because it is physical and contains genetic material. God says that he put the breath of life in all the animals, and caused the green (living) plants to grow for their food. He formed man and "breathed into his nostrils the breath of life, and the man became a living being." (Gen 2:7)

I am reminded of the segment from a well-known children's program that my children used to watch: "Is it alive or is it dead?" Various images of things would appear on the screen, followed by a shout of "alive!" or "dead!" It always made me think of that razor's edge between the living and the dead, an edge as thin and infinite as the breath of God. Our physical life trembles on this fault line at each and every moment, and our eternal life, once we receive it as a gift from God, explodes outward from it into fuller and broader dimensions of unlimited possibilities in God's eternal kingdom. But it always comes and keeps coming from God our Creator.

Creationism -- Young Earth Creationism
In opposition to the whole spectrum of evolutionary thought, stand the creationists, who believe that God created the cosmos, the world and all that is therein. (Theistic evolutionists view themselves as a particular type of creationist, because they believe that God did, in fact, create. But as I previously mentioned, they appear to give far more credence to the role played by evolution than to the supernatural aspect of creation.)

Old Earth creationists believe that God created the universe beginning with the Big Bang event and continuing over billions of years with the formation of Earth until, finally, man was made. I feel, as you may have noticed, that this position is most consistent with the twin revelations of Scripture and nature. Most evangelical Christians, however, have only been exposed to the young earth position. So, the questions remain, "How?" and "When?" and this leads to the disagreements so commonly seen among *Christians*, not scientists.

The most vocal of the creationist groups are those in the "Creation Science" movement, who can hold to a young earth or old earth position, but most of them are young earth. I'm going to call those in the young earth camp "literalists." On a website called "creationism.org," I discovered links to 28 creation science websites, only one of which portrays an old earth/intelligent design point of view. I felt that these 27 websites revealed a lot about the literalist position, but I'll only look at their two most common constructs here.

First, they believe in a **literal interpretation** of Genesis and other Biblical passages, and that through these interpretations, actual scientific facts are revealed in the Bible. They state that around 10,000 years ago, God created the universe and the earth in 6 literal 24-hour days and rested on the 7th day. He made things with an appearance of being older than they actually are.

Other geologic phenomena can be explained through the effects of a literal, planet-covering flood in Noah's day. (Gen.6)

The Creation Research Society's webpage says, "All its (the Bible's) ascertations (sic) are historically and scientifically true...Genesis is a factual presentation." They are using divine inspiration to give credence to their scientific findings, but they are working backwards from the Bible to the science.

Secondly, they place a lot of emphasis on finding **answers**. They will pose a scientific question, go at it from a predetermined viewpoint (literalist creation), and attempt to answer the question in a scientifically valid way. They also spend a lot of time "debunking" other people's answers, as if to give increased validity to their point of view. (This, of course, is not using the scientific method correctly; but perhaps the evolutionists do this also. It seems as if many of the parties in this debate are determined to see the facts the way they see them!)

In addition, it seems like there are a great many questions to be answered. Here are a few from Answers in Genesis (Ken Hamm's site). Did dinosaurs turn into birds? Are elephants developing smaller tusks? A fused chromosome – proof of evolution? Was there really an ice age? And on and on. My answer to these questions is, quite frankly, who cares? Must these issues be resolved from a literalist point of view?

No – remember, God will reveal Himself in Creation whether we like it or not, whether we believe or not. There's no reason to go around fussing about connecting every little scientific dot to Gen.1 and 6. If one studies nature, God will be seen sooner or later, but we need to be careful that we are not predisposed against what we are observing!

It is very easy for the literalists to get lost in their own sea of "answers." The explanation of the "answers" is often a convoluted maze of circular reasoning that wanders around and around and eventually arrives back at their preconceived notions. One needs to look at the literalist position in its most basic form to see if it makes sense. One must objectively ask the question, "Can what the heavens teach us and what we observe here on earth explain a Creation which took 144 hours and not approximately 14 billion years?"

Also, in response to their argument about there being no validity to salvation without a literal interpretation of Genesis, remember that salvation is a purely spiritual concept; we are speaking about the salvation of **souls**. God can and does save people who have never heard of young earth creationism. He delivers them from sin and makes them new creations in Christ; they are spiritually born again. Agreeing to a time framework for creation is not a prerequisite for salvation.

Remember, the whole of Creation, physical as well as spiritual, is on a journey toward the New Creation and it will arrive at its predetermined end. All things, spiritual and physical, will be united in a new dynamic. "But according to His promise we are looking for new heavens and a new earth, in which righteousness dwells." (2 Pet.3:13) Salvation is a part of this new creation, not the "old" one.

But the young earth creationists are very firm on taking Gen.1-6 literally because they believe that the doctrine of Biblical inspiration rests on it. Writing on the Answers in Genesis website, Ken Ham states, "When we consider the possibility that God used evolutionary processes to create over millions of years, we are faced with serious consequences: the Word of God is no longer authoritative and the character of our loving God is questioned."

They feel that if we do not take the numbers 1-7 and the word "day" literally, and the words "all the high mountains under the entire heavens" in Gen. 6 to be literal, we are denying the absolute truth of Scripture. If we do that, then everything else, including salvation can be questioned also. They believe that no death could have occurred before the fall of man into sin. All of these things have to be **literal** to make their theory work.

To arrive at these conclusions the literalists do 2 things: 1.) They do not harken to the validity of a poetic framework for Gen.1, and 2.) They fail to distinguish between physical realities and spiritual ones. Physical realities are true, and spiritual realities are true, but they are not exactly the same. Spiritual things can't be physical; therefore, a miracle cannot have a purely physical explanation, which is what the literalists are doing when they try to scientifically explain each and every element of Creation.

Making everything literal makes everything physical (real things in real time), thus shutting out the timeless implication of miracle. However, physical phenomena can be brought about by miracles, which can never be explained by science. For example, Jesus turned real water into real wine, a miracle showing that Jesus was the Creator, but, try as we might, we cannot measure the moment in time when the water became the wine, nor can we explain exactly what transpired.

Therefore, when we read the Bible, we need to realize the spiritual truths God is teaching us about Creation, things that we accept by faith. As Christians we should not discount the use of inspired poetic language as a vehicle God used to express truth. The words of Scripture are more than just words – "they are spirit and they are life." (Jn. 6:63) In these spiritual words, we are introduced to physical realities, themselves created by those very spiritual words.

When we study nature, we need to recognize God's truth revealed in it. The ability to reveal truth is built into Creation by God; at the same time, we are programmed by God to receive it. When we do this with pure hearts, we should see the same thing in 2 different ways – Biblical revelation and natural revelation. This viewpoint is known as the "Concordist" position; that is to say that the truth about creation is revealed through the twin sources of the Bible and Nature, which must be taken together.

God created physical things in a spiritual way, so as Christians, we see the glory of God with both our spiritual eyes and our physical ones. Unbelievers are blind in spiritual sight, so they only see the physical; that is to say (as it pertains to this discussion) they only see the naturalistic, evolutionary processes. Literalists are misdirected in their spiritual sight, so trying to fit the physical into a literal, temporal framework takes precedence over everything else.

Progressive Creationism – Old Earth Creationism

The old earth perspective on creation differs from the young earth view not only on the obvious question of the amount of time that passed as God created, but also in the way the scientific method is used to study the creation event. Progressive creationists believe that God supernaturally created all things, and when we look back on that event through the lens of nature, we can see that this process took billions of years and not a week.

They also see in the fossil record the rise and fall of many organisms. As time passes, God is actively creating and getting the planet ready for us. It is as if a great deal of time passed like "water under the bridge" as God used many now extinct species of plants and animals as well as astronomical and geological phenomena to arrive at his moment of completeness when he saw that "it was good," and decided to crown his creation with man made in his image.

At first glance, this view does seem to contain a very strong "God-of-the-gaps" component, for it appears that God is creating various organisms at specific times. But, like I said earlier, time does not figure in to God's work. He is timeless, and his creation-work is done (continuously) outside of time. Yet, in ways known only to him, his works enter into time. A true progressive creationist would not classify this "process" as "God-of-the-gaps."

(When taken as an old earth view, as it often is, (or is not, as the case may be!) evolutionary creationism looks at this a little differently. It reasons that evolution means change, and because this change is evident in nature, it would say that God orchestrated those changes by means of evolution. Remember, in this viewpoint, God is more actively involved in the evolutionary processes than as perceived by theistic evolution.)

Progressive creationism rests firmly on the Concordist (or, "two books") position, drawing scientific study of God's revelation in nature together with revealed truth from the Bible. On one hand, God wants us to use our powers of reason to pick up on what nature teaches us about the creation event because it teaches us about his great power and plan. Studying nature will lead us to discover how God made natural processes work, and how, in turn, this can benefit us.

On the other hand, the Bible is not a source of scientific knowledge (as the young earth view would contend,) but, as far as scientific things are concerned, it always proves to be accurate or fitting. If Scripture is truly inerrant, it does not contain a false construct of natural phenomena.

The writers of the Bible may have seen things from an ancient near-eastern point of view, but that does not mean that they were not careful observers of nature. In fact, based on shear observation, they were probably far more knowledgeable about nature than the average person is today, simply because they interacted with it much more than we do. When Scripture was written, the Holy Spirit intended that it declared truth in every area.

Therefore, we may look at nature and Scripture interchangeably in a sense; they work together to reveal God's truth to us. However, because of the period of time when it was written, the Bible sometimes merely hints at a scientific truth or points us in a direction that bears further exploration.

Progressive creationism rests on the idea that God has made each species of plant or animal life as a special creation. Evolution, as commonly defined, was not a factor in the formation of life forms. Once created, organisms did not change into different kinds of organisms. (Answers in Creation)

Psalm 146:6 supports this idea: "[God is] the Maker of heaven and earth, the sea, and everything in them, the Lord, who remains faithful forever." God is responsible for the existence of the physical universe as well as for all the organisms living in it. According to Genesis 2:19, God formed animals and birds from the soil, and he made man in the same way.

The word "form" means to fashion, mold or shape, and denotes a sense of purpose or plan for the product. It is used in the passage in Psalm 139 that refers to how we were formed in our mother's womb. We were "knit together," "woven together," and "made in the secret place." Today we know that this is how the DNA code works. Every organism finds its identity and code for life in the DNA from which we are formed.

When God created each organism, he essentially wrote the DNA; he did not allow it to assemble itself on its own. The word "faithful" from Psalm146 quoted above teaches this. It means to guard, to care for, to preserve. As God so dramatically impressed upon Job -- he created, knows and gives life to every living thing in a way that is beyond our understanding, yet filled with his love.

In addition, God intended each organism to pass its DNA along to its offspring. In the Gen.1 creation account, the phrase "according to their kinds" is used several times, meaning that God intended that genetic material to be passed on unchanged.

However, because God was actively working during the period of Creation and because different climate conditions on the planet Earth supported different life forms, organisms would eventually die out and newly created ones would replace them. Progressive Creationists believe that the days of Creation mentioned in Gen.1 are indicative of this process, because combined with the scientific data we observe, they point to long stretches of time. The "days" can overlap or be somewhat distinct from each other, but, taken together, they indicate that certain things happened at particular points in space-time.

The early and medieval church idea of the "hexameron" conveys this idea by taking the 6 days and combining them into one unit. Creation was a sweeping long-term event that may be loosely divided into 6 significant parts. The days show us the grand design of the Creator who worked very hard to make things according to his plan – a plan that somehow involved the use of time. The grand goal of creation was to develop a world uniquely suited to mankind, who would use the gifts of creation to enrich their lives as well as to glorify and honor the Creator.

Intelligent Design

In recent years a new concept (or maybe an old concept in new terms) has been introduced into the creation/evolution debate, the concept of Intelligent Design, or "ID." The idea behind intelligent design is that since we can directly observe structure, organization, and overall design in nature, this leads us to believe that a designer who knew what he/it was doing put it there. Some proponents of ID are reluctant to say that this designer is God -- it could be an intelligent being from another galaxy, or the intelligence of nature itself -- however, ID is pretty much a creationist idea.

Most of the different schools of thought within creationism embrace ID to a greater or lesser degree. Secular evolutionists, on the other hand, abhor ID, because it upsets the apple cart of their belief that randomness is the driving force behind the evolutionary process. Theistic evolutionists also dislike ID because they see life and biological change in a strictly scientific sense; therefore, they feel organisms are only capable of arising from evolutionary processes, even though God may have set the whole thing in motion.

Two of the champions of this debate are Michael Behe, a Catholic, who has written a book called *Darwin's Black Box*, and Richard Dawkins, an atheist, who wrote *The Blind Watchmaker*. Behe introduced the idea of *irreducible complexity,* which means that organisms cannot even begin to live or work correctly without certain complex traits. The organisms couldn't have waited around to evolve these traits, because they could never have lived in the first place. Dawkins, however, contends that natural selection put the complex traits together (randomly), sometimes taking traits originally used for one thing and later using it for something else.

The problem is that both the theistic evolutionists and the secular evolutionists don't see any reason to put design into the equation. The atheists don't want design, because they don't want God. The theistic evolutionists want God, but not design. (And even the literalists want design to work *their way!*)

Yet, if they would really stop and think about it, there just can't be a world without design. We see it everywhere, and are governed by it everyday. For example, when I bake chocolate chip cookies I use a recipe, a "cookie-design." When the atheist writes a book criticizing ID, he uses a language, combining specific words in a certain order. Design is built into the system; it's the designer who's up for grabs.

Intelligent design is a sort of qualifier for creation models. It is qualifying how Creation happened – an "intelligence" was at work that guided the whole process. Modern day scientists are correct in making the quick assumption that this "intelligence" was God. The Bible supports the idea of intelligent design in great detail; in fact, God himself gives a splendid description of it in Job 38-41. He seems to say, "If you want design, I'll give you design!"

The word "made" in Gen.1 denotes doing something with a purpose in mind, making something to assist in achieving a certain function, and doing something to achieve a particular goal. God did not make things mindlessly, nor did he allow a natural "force" to aimlessly put his plan together. As the Almighty God, he acts with power and purpose.

In John 1:3, the acts of Creation are attributed to Jesus Christ: "Through him all things were made; without him nothing was made that has been made." Once again, the word "made" is defined as something having its origin brought about by an agency that has as definite purpose in mind. The making and the purposefulness also apply to each individual thing – every organism is designed, constructed and animated by God.

Another difficult aspect of this debate is that while ID scientists work very hard to do legitimate research in their field, as do the literalists, not to mention the progressive creationists, the evolutionists categorically dismiss their research. (The literalists, however, exhibit a sort of quasi-science, working from their own biased premises, which are in turn, pretty much the only thing they have been taught. Both ID scientists and evolutionists pretty much hold degrees from similar evolution-teaching institutions, so they are more "main-stream" in their science that some of the creation science proponents.) In the end, parties involved only seem to respect the results of research that comes from their "side."

But, there again, from both sides of the issue, one is talking about a spiritual reality when discussing Creation, and faith is not accepted as a basis for knowing truth in the modern scientific world. William Dembski and Sean McDowell, the authors of the book, *Understanding Intelligent Design*, summarize the debate by saying, "Intelligent design is so important because the evidence for it is compelling, but Darwinists suppress that evidence to promote a naturalistic worldview." (Dembski, p. 29)

They go on to point out that most people will naturally view the universe as designed, but the prevailing naturalistic worldview diverts their attention from the truth and demands that they embrace a self-conflicting way of seeing things. As the Apostle Paul stated so long ago, "[wicked men] suppress the truth by their wickedness." Their wicked act, remember, was to deny the Creator God. (Rom.1)

THE CONTROVERSY BETWEEN SCIENCE AND FAITH

Now I want to go back to the curious question of how the Catholic Church could condone biological evolution and, at the same time, present in the catechism such an accurate picture of God's Plan, purpose, and active participation in Creation. To figure this out, we must go back to the 17th century when the Catholic Church condemned the astronomer Galileo for propounding the idea of the heliocentric solar system; that is, the earth revolves around the sun. From his study of nature (the heavens), Galileo was persuaded to take a scientific stand against the Church's teaching that Scripture says that the sun revolved around the earth.

Galileo was reading God's nature-book; the Church was reading the Bible, specifically, the passage in Joshua 10 which tells the story of the sun standing still as Joshua and the Israelites fought a battle against the five kings of the Amorites; a battle that God miraculously gave them extra time to win. If the *earth* was moving, the Church reasoned, why was it the *sun* that stood still? Surely, the sun was moving, as we observe daily as it makes its transit across the sky.

The conflict over the heliocentric solar system had a huge impact on the way the Catholic Church dealt with scientific discoveries, because, when the smoke cleared and it was demonstrated that indeed the earth orbited the sun, the Catholic Church was put into an embarrassing position, one which they desired not to have repeated.

I found a recent response to the Galileo situation in an article featured on the website americancatholic.org., in which Bishop Pagano, a Vatican archivist, says, "The Galileo case teaches science not to presume to teach the church on matters of faith and Sacred Scripture and, at the same time, teaches the church to approach scientific problems...with much humility and circumspection."

150 years ago, when Darwin's evolutionary theory appeared on the scene, the church was compelled to take a rather ambivalent stand, sort of "we'll see how this goes." Because Catholics believe that reason enables us to learn about God, they say that the study of evolution can purpose some answers to the question of how creation unfolded itself. The church gradually came to the position that it is not outside of the realm of possibility for God to have used evolution to create.

In another article from the website cited earlier, Catholic biologist Kenneth Miller explains, "Look at what evolution tells us; we live on a planet and in a universe where the very laws of nature remarkably hospitable to the emergence of new life...Evolution is a way to understand the wisdom and creative power of God."

The negative response of the Catholic Church to Galileo's science followed by the positive response to Darwin's science has much to teach us about the conflict between faith and science, between creation and evolution. Can they truly relate? How should Christians look at their relationship?

Evolution is a branch of biology that seeks to answer questions concerning how life began, how it developed, and how it changed. It is fundamentally a study of nature, which is, as I said before, a study of God's revelation to us concerning himself and his works. I have come to the conclusion that *something like evolution* can be seen in this study, for apparently, change happened over long periods of time and life changed over time as we see by the evidence for the rise and fall of various organisms in the fossil record. But we must bear in mind that evolution was one of the first scientific ideas to be purposed outside of a belief in a Creator God. Galileo saw God in the heavens, but Darwin did not see him on the earth.

I believe that this makes all the difference in the world about how Christians should look at evolution. Evolution has come to mean a materialistic and purely naturalistic phenomena

– self-guided (though unguided), self-determined (though lacking direction.) This is precisely where the separation between Creation and evolution takes place and must indeed occur, for we cannot have a God with a plan who allows unplanned events to rule the day.

When we take the scientific studies of biology and cosmology all the way back to their point of origin, we must cross the line between the physical to the spiritual. There's no getting around it. At the moment of creation, at the moment life began, God was there with a miracle to set his laws and plan in motion. We owe our existence to that timeless miracle which made physical realities appear. As a result, because of our God-given intellect and reason, these physical realities become apparent to us and as we study them, we learn spiritual realities about God.

Science and faith, I feel, are not to be perceived as parallel lines pursuing the same end, but as a circle or even as a Mobius strip that constantly moves from Creation to revelation to redemption and back again, infinitely, as we continually grow in our knowledge of the truth. This circle, connecting the physical to the spiritual, was designed to cast glory upon our loving Creator, Jesus Christ, who upholds creation by his eternal word, and who is eternally the one who is over all and in all and creates life in all.

Both creation and secular evolution express a philosophy about why we're here and where we're going. This is consistent with our internal desire for meaning and purpose. Creation says that we are here because of the will of a loving God who made us and everything else, and who causes us to come to the place where he will perfect us forever. Rom.8:19-25 categorizes this as our journey of hope, stating, "the creation itself will be liberated from its bondage of decay and brought into the glorious freedom of the children of God."

Conversely, secular evolution places us here by chance and takes us on a self-determined (yet unguided) course toward improving ourselves. This goes against our longing for order and purpose, and places the burden of redemption on society's shoulders. Evolution teaches that we can and will progress, but this is a hollow promise due to the fact that science also teaches that all physical things are on a negative course of regression (entropy) – which is, in fact, one of God's foundational laws. Having lost the true spiritual center for life, mankind abandoned God and abandoned hope. Evolution is turning out to be an empty promise.

We must also believe that this Creator God operated according to a plan. Remember God is all-knowing; he knows the end from the beginning (Isa.46:10). He does not make things up as he goes along. Cardinal Schonborn, who has written extensively on the creation/evolution/ID debate, says that if science did end up finding out (proving) that everything came about as a result of random chance, then Christians would be stuck with no answer to why life is here, because God would have never planned it, and therefore, performed no actions to carry out His plan. We would lose meaning, and in turn, faith.

Science can only go so far in being able to explain how and why life came to be. Once we start talking about what caused life and what exactly life is (its essence) we stop dealing with scientific questions and start dealing with philosophical ones. Then, if we start looking for answers outside of ourselves, we start dealing with spiritual, theological questions. All roads, it seems, lead us back to God.

Just studying biology requires intelligence and freedom – two spiritual qualities. So, when we look at life in the context of the whole of reality, it takes on a spiritual dimension because God created each of us with a soul and in the image of God. Our response to (or rejection of) God whenever we search for truth is "built in." This is why discussions of creation/evolution are never purely scientific discussions. The minute we start thinking about life, we enter the realm of the spiritual, and the minute nature starts acting on the life principle, it proceeds from a spiritual impetus.

Clearly, Christians cannot identify themselves with the purposeless outcomes of evolutionary theory. Whether or not they can identify with evolution solely as a biological theory is nebulous, for, if we believe that God actively and intricately creates, we cannot abandon creation to any kind of a hands-off process. And yet, it is not wrong for Christians to acknowledge a process of change in the creative development of life.

The question of whether or not we should call this evolution naturally arises here because of the implications of the historical precedent set by the strictly secular, godless study of the subject. Theistic evolutionists seem to be either creationists to secular society or just plain compromised in the eyes of many Christians. Christians missed the boat, I think, when, early on in the debate, they turned the sharp corner from evolutionary theory to literalist Creationism. Maybe the Catholic Church had a point when they said, as it were, "we'll study this and see where faith and reason line up." Galileo's theories were not confirmed until 100 years after his death, likewise, I think we can say, 150 years after Darwin, the jury is still out on a complete biological picture of what happened.

A CHRISTIAN APPROACH TO THE DEBATE

As Christians, however, we are obligated to study not only the Bible to find out the truth about Creation, but also we need to study nature as well. This is where many Christians drop the ball; they eagerly sharpen their pencils waiting to write down a list of pat answers to the evolution/creation controversy. "Tell me what to believe," they seem to say, "and I'll believe it." Having done a lot of thinking, research and Bible study on this topic for a while now, I think that Christians struggle with what they can know about Creation because they want somebody to spoon-feed them the answers because they are too lazy to realize or think about what God has clearly revealed to each one of us.

How easy it is to absorb the literalist answers and feel that we have God squared away in the "24/7 box!" I did this for many years myself, until my scientist husband encouraged me to think from a different perspective. (At first, I thought I had married a heretic!) But then I became aware that I had to study both the Bible and nature to get a picture of what was really going on as God created. It is important to note that we must study **both** when we study creation because God used both to reveal the truth to us.

On the other hand, some Christians embrace evolutionist theory and just slap God's name on it, thinking that God just used evolution as his means to create. Here we must stop to realize that natural processes did not control God when he created, because he was performing one miracle after another, and miracles are spiritual, supernatural processes. We must also possess a robust knowledge of evolution in order to evaluate it properly.

This is why I have come to appreciate the old-earth creationist viewpoint as primarily expressed by Dr. Hugh Ross of reasons.org. My lifelong acquaintance with science helped me to see that his creation model appears to make the most sense from both the Biblical and natural perspectives.

I hope that, taken along with Charles Hummel's social context interpretation of Gen.1and 2, I have spelled out in these chapters a valid, logical creation paradigm. I am not saying that I am a special person with special knowledge, nor am I saying that Christians should believe exactly what I believe, but I feel that the time has come for each and every Christian to carefully and personally examine the truth about creation. Its time to stop being spoon-fed the answers.

The way I see it, when 21st century Christians now engage in the argument of creation vs. evolution, it is as if they are trying to put a jigsaw puzzle together *without* looking at the picture on the box. The literalists are looking for the pieces that will answer their many questions, the theistic evolutionists are looking for the puzzle pieces that will work well together, and the intelligent designers are trying to find overall structure in the puzzle. But I think God is calling us to look at the **picture on the box** – His revelation in nature itself – and become "totally Creationist."

Unfortunately, Christians struggle with figuring out the picture on the box because, on one hand, their knowledge of the Bible is limited, and one the other, to put it bluntly, many Christians are "science wimps." Many Christians blithely accept "scientific" explanations for the hows and whys of Creation simply because they don't know any better. We must be able to draw from our own knowledge base when evaluating the validity of any scientific theory.

Instead of paying attention in science class, and being serious life-long learners, many Christians bury their heads in the sand and whine, "it's too hard, I hate science and aren't all scientists atheists anyway?" As a daughter, wife, and mother of 3 scientists, Christians who have influenced me greatly, I am personally quite sick of this. We *can* figure out the picture on the box – God gave us minds to use – and we are obligated to compare scientific study to what the Bible says as we personally read and study God's word.

Finally and fundamentally, Creation is a matter of faith; it is basic to the life lived by faith. We may see "parts" of evolution, a creation week, and overall design, but that is not really what we should be seeing. We should see God, who "has given us eternal life and this life in His Son." (1Jn.5:11) Once again, Creation is about God's great, all-encompassing plan of redemption that will culminate when everything will be made subject to Christ and "God may be all in all." (1Cor.15:28)

Today's creation (all of it, including us) longs to be set free from decay and enter into a glorious eternal freedom. (Rom.8:19-21) There we shall be forever beholding Him. If we live our lives in hope of that glory, we will be living out the daily purpose for which we were created. We partake in His Glory and express that glory to a fallen world. This is, in the end, more important than having a complete scientific knowledge of how we were created.

However, the more understanding we gain, the more glory we can express toward God. One day that glory will be **all there is**, as Creation comes full circle. Only then we will understand, only then we will see the answers -- yet today and everyday we live within the context of the perfect plan of our gracious Creator who "loved us and gave himself for us," and who calls us, in this physical world, to "come, learn of me."

Christ at the Center

Bibliography – Creation (chapters 2 and 3)

Catechism of the Catholic Church. New York: Doubleday, 1995. Print.

Ross, Ph.D., Hugh. *The Creator and the Cosmos*. 3rd. Colorado Springs, CO: Navpress, 2001. Print.

Schaeffer, Francis A.. *Genesis in Space and Time*. Downers Grove, IL: InterVarsity Press, 1972. Print.

Lewis, C.S.. *The Magician's Nephew*. New York: HarperCollinsPublishers, 1994. Print.

St. Augustine, *Confessions*. Indianapolis: Hackett Publishing Co., Inc., 1993. Print.

Hummel, Charles E.. *The Galileo Connection*. Downers Grove, IL: IVP Books, 1986. Print.

Miller, Donald. *Searching for God Knows What*. Nashville, TN: Thomas Nelson, Inc., 2004. Print.

Biggs, Alton. "Biology: the Dynamics of Life." Glenco McGraw Hill, 2000. Print.

Green, Jocelyn. "ID Tagged." *Christianity Today* Vol.52. No.2Feb. 2008 1-2. Web.17 Aug 2009. <http://www.christianitytoday.com/ct/2008/february/4.15.html?start=1>.

"home page." *www.creationism.org*. creationism.org. 17 Aug 2009 <http://www.creationism.org/>.

Rusch, W.H.. "History and Aims of Creation Research Society." *The Creation Research Society*. 2001-2009. Creation Research Society. 17 Aug 2009 <http://www.creationresearch.org/hisaims.htm>.

"home page." *Answers in Genesis*. 2009. Answers in Genesis. 17 Aug 2009

Behe, Michael J.. *Darwin's Black Box*. New York: Free Press, 1996. Print.

Dawkins, Richard. *The Blind Watchmaker*. New York: W.W. Norton and Company, Inc., 1985. Print.

Strong, James. *Strong's complete word study concordance*. expanded ed. Chattanooga, TN: AMG Publishers, 2004. Print.

Giberson, Carl. "The Modern Creation Story." *The Biologos Forum*. The BioLogos Foundation, 28 Feb 2011. Web. 29 Apr 2011. http://biologos.org/blog/the-modern-creation-story/.

Venema, Dennis. "Evolution and the origin of biological information Part 1: Intelligent Design ." *The Biologos Forum*. The BioLogos Foundation, 10 Mar 2011. Web. 29 Apr 2011. <http://biologos.org/blog/evolution-and-origin-of-biological-information-part-1-intelligent-design/>.

Lecture 10 -- The Creation and Evolution of Life. Perf. Joshua Moritz. Vimeo, 2013. Film.

Neyman, Greg. "Old Earth Creationism: Progressive Creationism." *Answers in Creation*. Answers in Creation, 2011. Web. 29 Apr 2011.
<http://www.answersincreation.org/progressive.htm>.

Neyman, Greg. "Old Earth Belief." *Answers in Creation*. Answers in Creation, 2011. Web. 29 Apr 2011.
<http://www.answersincreation.org/old.htm>.

Ross, Hugh. "Designed to live, designed to die." *Reasons to Believe*. Reasons to Believe, 01 Jan 2008. Web. 29 Apr 2011.
<http://www.reasons.org/designed-live-designed-die>.

Dembski, William A., and Sean McDowell. *Understanding Intelligent Design*. Eugene, OR: Harvest House Publishers, 2008. 29. eBook.

"Evolution and the Roman Catholic Church." *Wikipedia*. 2008. Web.15 Jan 2008. <http://en.wikipedia.org/wiki/Evolution_and_the_Roman_Catholic_Church>.

Wooden, Cindy. "Vatican Secret Archives Prefect: Church can still learn from Galileo case." *Catholic News Service* 03 Jul 2009 1. Web.30 Jul 2009. <http://www.americancatholic.org/news/report.aspx?id=1327>.

Sadowski, Dennis. "After 150 years, evolution debate continues among people of faith." *Catholic News Service* 26 Feb 2009 1. Web.30 Jul 2009. <http://www.americancatholic.org/news/report.aspx?id=745>.

Schonborn. Christoph. "Finding Design in Nature," *The New York Times* 07 Jul 2005. millerandlevine.com. Web.23 Jan 2008.

Schonborn, Christoph. "Reasonable Science, Reasonable Faith." *First Things* Apr 2007 Web.23 Jan 2008.

Ross, Hugh. "Summary of Reason's to Believe Testable Creation Model." *Reasons to Believe*. 2009. Reasons to Believe. 18 May 2009 <http://www.reasons.org/summary-reasons-believes-testable-creation-model>.

Chapter 4-THE BIBLE: Read the Word

"**Let the word of Christ dwell in you** richly as you teach and admonish one another with all wisdom . . ." Col. 3:16

Ecclesiastes 12:12 makes an interesting statement: "of the making of many books there is no end." As a librarian, I call this "the librarian's Bible verse;" for it gives, so to speak, a divine endorsement for what keeps us in business. As opposed to it, however, there is the librarian's mantra, "people don't read," which explains why our business is suffering!

An article in the Washington Post called, "One in four read no books last year," (Aug. 21, 2007) describes this decline. It seems that television, movies and the Internet are stealing people's attention away from the printed word. Another 2007 study called, "To read or not to read: a question of national consequence," done by the National Endowment for the Arts, reports a sharp decline in reading by young people. Young people aged 15-24 read less than 10 min. per day; free time that could be spent in voluntary reading is spent instead interacting with visual media such as TV and the internet. They are less focused on what they do read because of their habit of multitasking – listening to music or surfing the internet while reading. Annual spending on books dropped sharply between 1997 and 2002.

And, the most interesting statistic of all, I think, as a children's and school librarian, is the huge divide between reading scores of 9 year olds and 17 year olds. From 1999 on, the 9 year olds' scores have risen sharply, while the 17 year olds' have fallen dramatically. Beyond a certain age, reading is no longer "cool." I once asked my 5th grade students (10-11yrs old) about this, because it is the year in which I have always observed a sharp drop off in reading. They said that other things suddenly become more important in their lives -- sports, music, shopping, talking on the phone, homework -- and reading is no longer enjoyable. What a terrible thing it is for society, young and old, to lose such an essential foundational pillar of civilization.

Christ at the Center

As a Christian and a librarian, I have often thought about the importance of reading as it relates to the Word of God. After all, **God wrote a book**, and He expects us to read it. It is the most important book of all, the work on which all knowledge is ultimately based. It contains the knowledge of Him who gives us all we need for life and godliness. (2Pet. 1:3) We ignore it and diminish it at our own peril.

I recently heard a student make a very revealing statement about the Bible. He said something like, "I know it's bad, but I don't look at the Bible very much. I ask my (Christian) friends for advice. I think they can guide me better than stories about people who lived 2,000 years ago." This statement certainly reveals a lack of understanding about the universal, timeless nature of the Word and a failure to realize that people are people no matter when they lived. But add to this the fact that the student attended a Christian school, where he had taken Bible classes for 6 years. Certainly something fundamental had not been communicated to him; the fundamental truth that the Bible is no ordinary book; it is contains the spiritual truths which are the foundation of learning and life itself.

I see several points of failure in this student's story. The first is the failure to recognize the true significance of the Bible itself, how important it really is. Many people, Christians included, see the Bible as an old, dry and dusty book enjoyed by preachers who have to use it to write a sermon, and by people who are older, drier and dustier than the book itself. Even though there are many excellent modern translations of the Bible available today, many people still think that the Bible is and always will be written in the King's English, and therefore impossible to understand.

When we think of the story of how we got the Bible, it is amazing that it ever came together in the first place, and that it still exists today. Approximately 40 people wrote the Bible over a period of about 1,600 years. It was originally written in three languages, Hebrew, Aramaic and Greek, but has been subsequently translated into hundreds of languages. Although written over a long period, the Bible displays a single, overarching theme – Creation, Fall, and Redemption. This theme is expressed in many literary forms; narrative, poetry, drama, storytelling and logical discourse, to name a few.

For those who take the time to read it, the Bible seems to have a personal message. People are touched and moved by the messages communicated to them on its pages. It doesn't matter when they lived or what their cultural experiences are, those who read and study the Bible are better because of it, their lives are changed and their perceptions of reality refocused so as to understand the truth behind all of life.

The timeless, spiritual nature of the Word is the reason for this amazing personal application of truth. Hebrews 4:12 says, "For the word of God is living and active. Sharper than any double-edged sword, it penetrates even to dividing soul and spirit...it judges the thoughts and attitudes of the heart." Psalm 119:89 says, "Your Word, O Lord is eternal; it stands forever in the heavens." Timeless, alive, penetrating; God's word is a spiritual reality manifested in ink on paper. For this spiritual reality to become a personal reality, however, the Bible must be read, the mind engaged.

My purpose is not to reiterate the many, many unique properties of the Bible that are proofs of its supernatural origin. Almost any book on Christian apologetics has done a thorough job of that. But I want to look first at the one that is the most central; the Bible is accurate and true and is a conduit of truth.

The failure that we are dealing with here is the failure to realize what the Bible means. Some think that the Bible has something to do with ancient history because it contains the traditional Jewish law and references to ancient Egypt, Babylon and Rome. Others think that the Bible is a collection of moral precepts outlined in stories, poems and rules. They fail to realize that while the Bible does speak about history and morals, it speaks ultimately about truth.

John 1:1 and 2 says, "In the beginning was the Word, and the Word was with God, and the Word was God. He was with God in the beginning." These verses link three fundamental Christian truths, which are also the three revelations of God to mankind: the Bible, Jesus Christ and nature. 1.) The Word as truth comes from God, 2.) Jesus and the Word are the same, and

3.) Jesus is the Creator God, who creates by means of the Word. The Word is always portrayed as truth itself. It is reliable, trustworthy, and foundational, for the answers to the heart's deepest questions are found in the Word of truth.

Luke 4 tells an interesting story about Jesus, the Word, reading the Scriptures and teaching about them using words. Jesus began his teaching ministry by reading from the Isaiah scroll in his hometown synagogue. The passage (Isa. 61:1,2) was a prophesy concerning himself, which stated that he would teach the poor, set prisoners free, and perform healing miracles. After reading the passage, Jesus said that on that Saturday, beginning at the Nazareth synagogue, the prophecy had found fulfillment.

The audience was amazed at his "gracious words." The Greek word "charisma" used here denotes a gift freely given that comes from God Himself. So the words that Jesus read and the word he spoke were both immediately recognized as divine. But as Jesus continued to talk about his mission, the people grew angry with Jesus, because his words pointed out their unbelief, their failure to see the truth.

Jesus then goes to the synagogue in Capernaum and once again begins to teach on the Sabbath day. The people instantly realized that Jesus spoke with authority – they knew that Jesus was speaking the truth and that he was singularly the source of truth. (v.31, 32) In fact, the power of the truth caused evil spirits to publicly proclaim the deity of Christ.

Jesus retreats to a solitary place, but when found by the curious crowds, says, "I must preach the good news of the kingdom of God to other towns also." The words that Jesus was going to speak during his earthly ministry were to be taken as words of revelation, words from God spoken directly to men.

Because Jesus is the Word, every word He spoke while teaching was important. One must know the words of Jesus to know the truth. The New Testament writers knew how critical their job of recording his words would be to the education of future generations of Christians. The Bible had to be written, so the truth could be known. At the end of his book, the apostle John says, "This is the disciple who testifies to these things and who wrote them down. We know that his testimony is true." He further says that if he had written everything that could have been told about Jesus, "even the whole world would not have room for the books that could be written." The words and stories we have about Jesus are exactly what God wants us to have. They are the truth we need.

Jesus Himself says of his words, "The words I have spoken to you are spirit and they are life." When praying to God His Father, Jesus says, "I gave them the words you gave me and they accepted them." In the gospels, Jesus uses the word "truth" over and over again when referring to his words. We can see that more than good moral principles or solid advice is at stake here. The Bible contains words of truth to live by – forever. The Word of God/Truth is the pivotal point of the New Creation, linking the old universe with the new – "heaven and earth will pass away, but my words will not pass away." (Mark 13:31)

When a person comes to faith in Christ and becomes a new creation in Christ, hearing and believing God's words are of primary importance. In Romans chapter 10, we learn that in order for one to receive God's righteousness, the acceptance of the words of Scripture is the starting point of one's spiritual journey. One does not find God by "searching high and low," but reading, believing and acting on the words "right in front of you," the Word of God. Paul says this word which he proclaims verbally and in writing is "near you; it is in your mouth and in your heart." In order to come to faith, one must believe the gospel words in the heart so that a confession of faith in the form of spoken words can be made.

He goes on to explain the dilemma faced by those who desire to believe but possess no information about the gospel. Before they can believe, someone must travel to their location and speak the words of the gospel. Jesus Himself commands us to spread the words of truth around the world – "Therefore go and make disciples of all nations..." (Matt. 28:19)

The truth of God's word is not something that is perceived purely through the mind or the imagination. It is validated and brought to life through the ministry of the Holy Spirit's work in the believer's heart. John 14:26 explains that the Holy Spirit will "teach you all things and will remind you of everything I (Jesus) have said to you." Once again, we see that Christ's words are important, but one does not have to struggle on one's own to figure out what the words mean. The Holy Spirit brings clarity to the mind and security to the soul as the Word is read.

Another failure I see among modern Christians is the failure to realize that the Bible is a living book and that in order to maintain a healthy spiritual life, we must partake in the life of the Word. So many times we see the Bible as long spiritual advice column, a Godly how-to book, or a sugary sweet inspirational poem. And not only that, we get this feeling that if we're not reading it in order to benefit from the advice and the inspiration, the hammer of God's wrath will fall upon us.

Many people struggle with what part to read and what it really means. If we see the Bible just as an ancient book, (or even as an ancient *holy* book), we will wonder if reading it is worth the time and effort. We will not understand its true power.

As far back as the time of the apostles, when the Bible itself was being written, we see evidence of believers neglecting the word. Paul scolds the believers for being "worldly and not "spiritual" and therefore only able to receive "milk" (basic, elementary truths) from him. Peter told the Christians to whom he wrote to set aside evil practices and "crave pure spiritual milk, that by it you may grow up in your salvation." (1Pet. 2:1,2)

From our day of birth into God's family, we need to receive God's word in order to grow and develop. As we continue in the Word, we can digest harder and more complex truths and teachings. The writer of Hebrews says that this "solid food is for the mature, who by constant use have trained themselves to distinguish good from evil." Those who look at the Bible as if it were old stale bread, and express no desire to make progress in God's ways, become stagnant and stunted in their spiritual growth and well-being.

However, if we see the Bible as a living document, and partake of it as if it were food for the soul, we can begin to live transformational lives, changing not only our thought processes, but the world around us as well. Jesus compares the Bible to bread when, in Matt. 4:4, He quotes Deut. 8:3 – "man does not live on bread alone, but on every word that comes from the mouth of God." In the Old Testament passage, Moses is telling the Hebrews that God sent them manna to eat to teach them a lesson about the Word of God. It is just as important to our spiritual life as bread is to our physical life.

Jeremiah says, "When your words came, I ate them; they were my joy and my heart's delight." In the same way that our bodies store food to be converted into energy, we need to store God's Word in our hearts and minds in order to combat sin and negativity. Psalm 119:11 says, "I have hidden your word in my heart, that I might not sin against you."

Language, in and of itself, is a commodity; we use many ways to sustain our life. Marilyn McEntyre writes, "Words are entrusted to us as equipment for our life together, to help us survive, guide and nourish one another. We need to take the metaphor of nourishment seriously in choosing what we 'feed on' in our hearts, and how to make our conversation life-giving." Biblical words aside, words and language enrich our lives, help us to interact in meaningful ways and help us to express ideas, thoughts and feelings.

But if the words take on a spiritual significance, as the words of the Bible do, then we are talking about enriching the life of the soul. The Word of God is the source of soul nourishment as read God's word and perceive the meaning of its life-giving words. Our thoughts and feelings about God and His will for us are maintained by the food of Scripture.

This interaction with scriptural food is important individually, but it is also important to the life in the Christian community. The words of Scripture should flow between us, as if we were passing food around a table. Whenever we give comfort, advice or information to a fellow Christian, biblical passages need to be a part of it. Paul tells the members of the church in Thessalonica to "stand firm and hold to the teachings we passed on to you, whether by word of mouth or by letter."

In Colossians 1, Paul says the Christians have love, faith and hope "that you have already heard about in the word of truth, the gospel that has come to you. All over the world this gospel is bearing fruit and growing..." The good news communicated to us in the Bible is good news for all of us, and as

Christ at the Center

we share it, and discuss it, and pour over it, the entire church grows into a deeper relationship with Christ – everyone benefits.

One of the first churches to experience the powerful effect of studying the Bible together was the church in the city of Berea, mentioned in Acts 17. When the Berean Jews first heard the gospel message from Paul, they eagerly began to study the scrolls in their synagogue to see if Paul's references to the Old Testament were valid. The Bible says that they did this with open hearts and regularity, earnestly looking for truth every day. By contrast, today, many Christians fail to **read** and therefore fail to **know** – the greatest failure of all.

When persecution against the apostles spread from Thessalonica to Berea, Paul left and went to Athens, but Silas and Timothy stayed in Berea. Later, in his letters to Timothy, Paul seems to point Timothy back to lessons he may have learned while working with Berea's scripture-searching church. Twice in 1Timothy Paul warns Timothy to stay away from the likes of "false doctrines," "myths," "endless genealogies," and "old wives' tales." These false sources of knowledge stand in sharp contrast to the Scriptures poured over in Berea.

In 2 Timothy, Paul advises Timothy to stay away from "godless chatter" and "stupid arguments" which produce "quarrels." He then reminds Timothy of his lifetime exposure to Scripture and how this has made him wise and discerning, one who can handle the Word of God with confidence. (2 Tim. 3:14, 15)

In this passage, Paul comments that Timothy has known the Scriptures "from infancy." The first step on the road to reading the Bible begins before we can read; the Bible must be read to us. In Deut. 6:7-9, parents are instructed to constantly remind their children of God's commands. They are supposed to talk about them throughout the day, carry portions of Scripture with them, and write and display passages in prominent places in their dwellings. Familiarity with the Word of God should begin at an early age and it begins at home.

Education in the Jewish and early Christian traditions was related to one primary goal – one must learn to read in order to read the Bible. The individual's personal encounter with the Word of God is beautifully described in Psalm 119. Although each verse is packed with meaning, and a great deal could be written about this Psalm, several key principles relating to the profits to be gained by Bible reading stand out.

- Reading the Word enables one to live a pure and blameless life.
- Reading the Word fills the heart with joy.
- Reading the Word gives one confidence to face the trials of life.
- Decisions are better made in the light of God's words.
- In order to be effective in one's daily life, Bible passages must be memorized as well as read.
- The true message about eternal salvation is only contained in God's word.
- The words of God live on forever.

One of the biggest mistakes people make about Bible reading is thinking that the Bible is hard to understand. They never get far enough into it to experience the delight expressed in Psalm 119. This feeling leads people to look to Christian teachers, preachers and authors to explain the Bible to them. Instead of engaging in personal Bible study, they cling to the explanations others give to Biblical topics and stories. Almost everything they go on is second hand.

The effectiveness of this procedure is only as effective as the teacher himself. If the teacher is "thoroughly equipped for every good work" (2 Tim. 3:16), Christians should be able to correctly understand the Bible message when they receive instruction from teachers who carefully study the Word: But I see dangers in exclusively following the practice of learning the Word through teaching alone.

First, those who don't read and study the Bible personally never really learn anything. They are like teenagers who only want the answers to the test questions and could care less about reading the book they are being tested on. They are content in

Christ at the Center

repeating what so-and-so says, rather than knowing what the Bible says. They are never able to spiritually stand on their own two feet.

In the Spiritual battle described in Eph. 6, the Bible is called the "sword of the Spirit." Both physically and spiritually, it is the key piece of armor when it comes down to the actual fighting. A soldier is helpless without his sword. But many Christians want others to do the fighting for them when they do not desire to carry God's words in there minds and hearts.

Secondly, non-readers are open to lots of crazy ideas about what the Bible says and means. They can't distinguish between the viewpoints of reliable and unreliable teachers. Jesus rebuked a group to religious leaders by saying, "Are you not in error because you do not know the Scriptures or the power of God?" (Mark 12:24) The Berean Christians wouldn't even recognize the authority of **Paul** to teach without first checking his message against the scrolls of Scripture! Today, the failure to read has caused all kinds of misconceptions to creep into the church.

When we read the Bible, the Holy Spirit leads us along the path of truth, but those who do not read it will never receive this wonderful gift. Before his death and resurrection, Jesus' great concern centered on how his followers would always be convinced of the truth of his words. He petitioned his Father to give us the gift of the Counselor (or, the Holy Spirit) so that the church would forever be certain of the meaning of the word of truth. (John 14:16, 17)

No one needs to be reluctant to read the Bible out of fear of not understanding it. With prayer, the Holy Spirit will make the meaning clear. John 15:26 says quite simply, "He shall testify;" (KJV) that is, His words, His insights, His knowledge can be accepted as reliable evidence for truth in the courts of Heaven where God is the righteous judge of all, and we can know this truth with certainty in our hearts.

Therefore, in today's church we are facing situations where children do not have the Bible read to them nearly enough and individuals do not faithfully read the Bible on their own. But a third problem is also evident, though not talked about very much, the failure to read God's Word corporately, together, when it is read aloud in church. The Bible has a lot to say about the value of reading the Word aloud to groups of people. I'd like to look at a few examples from the Old and New Testaments.

The book of Deuteronomy tells the story of how Moses received the words of the Law on Mt. Sinai, wrote them down, and read them to the people. At the conclusion of the book (Deut. 31), Moses explains how he wrote the Law, gave the scroll to the priests for safekeeping, and commanded that the Law be read out loud to the people every 7 years during the Feast of Tabernacles. He says that they were to "listen and learn" and adds that children especially were to hear the Law and learn to fear God.

It was at this point that Israel switched from being a nation with oral traditions (having stories about God handed down to them from the Patriarchs) to being a nation with a written tradition (the Law). The words of the written Law were to be carefully guarded and copied in order to pass them down verbatim from generation to generation. They were not a series of stories that were to be told verbally, although discussion and education are still important. Telling the stories repeatedly could cause them to become legends; writing them down and being able to read them brought permanence and authority. If a question arose over what to do or how to act, the written Law could be referred to.

Twice in the Old Testament, we read how the Law became neglected and lost when the Israelites turned away from God. In 2Kings 22 and 23, King Josiah, a good king who followed a succession of evil ones, gives orders to repair the temple. During the reconstruction, the book of the Law was found somewhere in the dusty old building. When the king heard the words of the Law read to him (probably for the first time in his life), he realized that God's judgment was about to fall because Israel had neglected God's Word and worshiped idols. Josiah then has all the people gather in the temple court to hear the Law read out loud.

A similar scene takes place when Nehemiah returns to Jerusalem after the Babylonian captivity and supervises the rebuilding of the temple. Ezra the priest called an assembly of the people together in the Water Gate square where he the Law out loud – for six hours! Out of respect for God's words, the people stood the entire time. When he read the part mentioned earlier concerning Moses' command to read the Law during the Feast of Tabernacles, they realized that they had not observed that feast in a long, long time. They built "booths" to live in during the seven-day long feast and Ezra read the Law out loud each day.

In both of these cases, the reading of God's Word brought the people to the point of repentance and opened their eyes to God's expectations for a righteous life. As a group, they confessed their sins and learned how to walk in God's ways. Now they could move together to the goals God had for them, because everyone had heard the same thing. The word of the Law unified them in a common purpose.

I've already mentioned how Jesus was familiar with the Jewish custom of reading the Scriptures out loud on the Sabbath day. Paul mentions this practice in a speech he gives in the city of Pisidian Antioch. In fact, he is giving the speech because he was asked to expound on the reading for the day. He said that Jesus' trial and death were a fulfillment of "the words of the prophets that are read every Sabbath." (Acts 13:27)

Having heard the Scriptures read every Saturday; the Jewish people should have recognized whom Jesus was. They should have known the truth because they had heard the Scriptures read. On a couple of occasions, Jesus asks religious leaders a rhetorical and incredulous question – "have you not read?" Within the framework of hearing the Bible read each week, no one should have had an excuse for not knowing what it said.

I think that if Jesus came into many evangelical churches he would ask the same question – "have you not read?" The reading of Scripture aloud by a reader or reading together as a group has all but vanished; eclipsed by the showiness of the typical service. It is not enough to flash verses up on the screen and read them during the sermon. Timothy was told to give attention to the **public reading** of Scripture (1Tim. 4:13).

Christ at the Center

The church must continue the ancient tradition of reading aloud from the Bible. It is meant to be a process by which we become familiar with what the Bible says and by which we honor the Holy Word as we stand out of respect when it is read. Knowing the words of Scripture, the church then has the power to act as a body to stand for truth and oppose evil.

The failure to read God's Word, which is so prevalent among individuals, families and churches today, is an extension of the failure to read. As I said before, *people don't read*. God has given us his Word to guide us into truth, but if we do not read it, we cannot go there. I think that behind the failure to read lies an evil plot – if people don't read in general, they will be less likely to read the Bible specifically.

People will go back to trusting what they hear (oral tradition), instead of trusting the Holy Spirit to reveal meaning and truth to them as they read. In fact, 2 Timothy 4:3,4 says the time will come when people will gather around teachers "who say what their itching ears want to hear." The less people read the precious eternal words of the Bible, the closer we come to that evil day.

Those of us who know the great value of the written word overall and the Word of God specifically must daily take up the Sword of the Spirit to wage war against the Enemy. We are engaged in a battle between truth and lies, all bound up in the conflict between truthful words and false ones. In fact, today people can scarcely tell the difference between lies and truth. A post-modern society wonders if truth actually exists and lives accordingly.

In Luke 18:8, Jesus asks an amazing rhetorical question: "when the Son of Man comes, will He find faith on the earth?" This statement indicates that in the end those who know the truth will be few and far between. We could say, "When the Son of Man comes, will he find readers – readers of the Word?" It's up to all of us who read it to take up "the sword of the Spirit, which is the Word of God" and fight for the preservation of truth with a precious, ancient-yet-eternal book which lights our way to God. We must not fail.

Bibliography – Bible

Manso, Kathleen Kennedy. "Young People Seen Losing Love of Reading." *Education Week* 19 November 2007: n. pag. Web. 27 November 2007. <http://www.edweek.org/ew/articles/2007/11/19/13read_web.h27.html?print=1>.

Fram, Alan. "One in Four Read No Books Last Year." *Washington Post* 21 August 2007: n. pag. Web. 29 Feb. 2008. <http://www.washingtonpost.com/wp-dyn/content/article/2007/08/21/AR2007082101045_p...>.

Lightfoot, Neil R. *How We Got the Bible.* 3rd, revised and expanded edition (2005). Grand Rapids, MI: Baker Publishing Group, 2003. Print.

"Why Read the Bible?." *Bible Reading Plans*. BiblePlan.org, n.d. Web. 14 Feb. 2008. <http://www.bibleplan.org/whyread,htm>.

McEntyre, Marilyn. "Care of the Word." *Westmont College Magazine* Fall 2007: 12-15. Print.

Chapter 5-JESUS: All or Nothing

"God made him who had no sin to be sin for us, so that **in him** we might become the righteousness of God." 2Cor.5:21

When I started to think about writing this chapter, I realized fairly quickly that a chapter would not really do. In order to write about Jesus, it would be necessary to write a book, and a very long book at that. Of course, many people have already written books of this sort; therefore, many excellent books about Jesus (his life, ministry, teachings, death and resurrection) are readily available. (On the other hand, many books have been written which try to refute the idea of Jesus ever having existed at all!) But even the Bible says that it would be impossible to write all the books that could be written about Jesus.

The Apostle John, who made this statement, also said that what has been written serves an important purpose. John 20:31 says, "But these are written that you may believe that Jesus is the Christ, the Son of God, and that by believing you may have life in his name." The Word of God, which tells us about Jesus, the Word, requires us to make a commitment to what has been written, for belief is the key not to just knowing about Jesus, but knowing him as well.

Our primary source of information about Jesus comes from the first four books of the New Testament, the Gospels, Matthew, Mark, Luke and John, who are sometimes known as the four Evangelists. Historically, the Church has considered the contents of these four books to be accurate and reliable, delivered by the Holy Spirit to the authors. Very few, within or without the Church, raised questions about them or doubted their authority. It has only been recently that controversy has been swirling around the Gospels, who their authors really are, when they were written, and the truthful or mythological essence of their contents.

For almost 2,000 years, the Church and indeed the world associated with it, whether under its auspices or apart from them, admitted that, if nothing else, Jesus was sent from God. In

Christ at the Center

the very least, the world and the Church concurred that he was very, very important. His death was seen to be (especially as testified to by numerous works of art) a very momentous event; a turning point in history, the tipping point between heaven and hell itself. Even the way time was measured, the calendar, was altered to fit this inarguable view. Christ was at the center of time and history.

In 1985, a group of religious scholars began meeting together with the intended goal of diminishing 2,000 years of historical precedent. Instead of trying to prove the historical existence of Jesus Christ, they set about to prove his non-existence. The Jesus Seminar, composed of about 200 liberal theologians and operating under the flagship of the ubiquitous Westar Institute, met annually for several years to discuss (or perhaps, just to bandy about) their ideas on whether or not Jesus actually existed, whether or not he said the things he supposedly said, and whether or not the Bible, as an historical record, has any validity at all.

After first translating the Scriptures to their own satisfaction, and adding in the Gospel of Thomas (no doubt just because it was *there*), they proceeded to vote on the historical factuality of the life, words, actions and surroundings of Jesus Christ. They were trying to reach a consensus on the following types of questions: did Jesus really live as a citizen of 1st century Israel, did he and would he have said the things the Bible says he said, did he accomplish anything significant at all (much less supernatural), and, is it necessary for us, all these years later, to believe that his life had any impact whatsoever on our lives, our world, or even the world to come?

In order to reach a consensus on these obscure events of the dim past, never mind the substance of the enduring legacy of the Church herself, nor the permanence of the resilient honor of those who died for her sake and for her Divine Founder, the Seminar very democratically decided to cast their votes with colored beads. Voting a red bead meant, 'it's quite likely this is authentic,' a pink bead, 'maybe it happened,' gray, 'maybe, maybe not equally,' and black – 'forget it.' The upshot of their efforts was a color-coded edition of the five Gospels (Matthew,

Christ at the Center

Mark, Luke, John and the trendy Thomas) printed almost entirely in "forget-it" black ink. Jesus, along with any significance he may have ever had, was essentially washed down the drain.

As yet, the Jesus Seminar folks have not gone around putting signs on the Christian martyr's graves, saying, "Here lies so-and-so, who died for **nothing**." (But maybe that's next: a red sign, 'really died for nothing,' pink, 'maybe died for nothing,' gray, 'maybe, maybe not,' and black, 'just died anyway.') Seriously, who would die for Jesus if he was a nobody from nowhere who never said or did anything important?! Abraham Lincoln is more exciting and worthy of devotion. (Of course, in 2,000 years maybe the Lincoln Seminar will come along and declare him nonexistent also.) As it is, the Westar Institute has gone on to debunk the book of Acts and is hard at work at voting the early church into oblivion.

Now, just doing what they were doing, in a completely human sense, the Seminar was right. Without the presence of the Divine and the foundation of spirituality expressed by faith, Jesus is nothing. The big factor missing from their deliberations was **belief** – they simply did not believe in Jesus. If I do not believe that someone existed and doubt the truthfulness of the records written about him, of course it will be very difficult to prove that that person existed. But if I believe and something within me assures that belief, in fact provides the belief, (the Holy Spirit) I will be unmovable in my confidence towards the person or concepts believed. The Bible says, "And without faith it is impossible to please God, because anyone who comes to him must believe that he exists." (Heb. 11:6)

In a world devoid of faith, a world brought about by purely natural accidents, Jesus naturally looks like a legendary figure, a poor, traveling minstrel who uttered a few pithy sayings (maybe). But in the world of belief – the world touched by Heaven – Jesus is everything. When I look at the life and ministry of Jesus, I see six key concepts about Jesus that must be entirely accepted as truth or not accepted at all.

Preexistence

Jesus, as God, exists for all time, eternally, beyond the confines of time. Jesus forcefully proclaimed this truth in John 8:58, when he said, "Before Abraham was, I am." Centuries before, God had told Moses that his Holy Name was "I AM." (Ex. 3:14) The Hebrew word used here means "I am" – first person, present tense. However, the Jewish people were never allowed to say that specific name out loud. To do so was to admit to being God, as in, "I am God."

Instead, they were to call him Yahweh, which literally means, "He is" – third person, present tense. By speaking this name, they were affirming that that their God was the one who lives, who exists, the One who is the one true God. The only one to ever come along and verbally proclaim the name "I AM" was Jesus, the one who was and is forever God.

The eternal can enter time, but time can't enter eternity. Our souls, for example, were created eternal (spiritual), but our bodies are bound by time (physical). Jesus, as perfect Man and eternal God, could enter time and return to timelessness, and when he did so, no time passed in heaven. Jesus' life did not begin in a stable in Bethlehem. He always *was*, but it was essential to the process of redemption that a blameless sacrifice be made a sinful world. Jesus, while in the glory of Heaven, stepped forward, if you will, to be the one, the only one, to be this sacrifice.

Our sinful souls have no other way of getting to heaven than through the eternal Christ's eternal sacrifice. Revelation 13: 8 says the Christ was "the Lamb slain from the creation of the world." The sacrifice of Christ would be just another ritual Jewish sacrifice if he were not eternal. Philippians 2:5-8 says that Jesus was "in very nature God" who was "made in human likeness" and ultimately "became obedient to death – even death on a cross!"

He who created this physical world became physical in order to redeem his creation. Colossians 1:21 and 22 explain that Heaven and earth suffered a great separation due to sin, but the death of Jesus "reconciled" the two, reunited them, because the creator's death and resurrection is able to bring new life to our souls, to re-create us, as it were.

Incarnation
John 1:34-36 tells the story of one of the first encounters several of the disciples had with Jesus. They had already been stirred by John the Baptist's message about a mighty deliverer who was on his way, coming to interact with our world. One memorable afternoon, they came face-to-face with Jesus as they were walking down the road. It must have seemed to them that time skipped a beat when John the Baptist shouted, "Look, the Lamb of God!" Suddenly they were looking into the face of God, who had a human face. (Every Christmas our hearts, too, skip a beat as we celebrate the incarnation – God showing up on Earth as a baby.)

The mission of John the Baptist was to point people to the person of Jesus Christ; a real person, the only one worthy to set us free from sin. Hebrews 2:14-17 explains that Jesus took on flesh and blood because that's what we are; being an angel, for example, would not do. Jesus wasn't going to shed real blood for angels. He took on the flesh and blood so that he, like a perfect High Priest, could present (and as the same time *be*) the atonement-sacrifice.

In his great work, *The Incarnation of the Word of God*, St. Athanasius writes, "...it was our sorry case that caused the Word to come down, our transgression that called out His love for us, so that he made haste to help us and to appear among us. It is we who were the cause of his taking human form, and for our salvation that in his great love he was both born and manifested in a human body." (*Christian Apologetics*, vol.1, p. 177)

The humanity of Jesus was essential to the accomplishment of his mission. Jesus existed as a man-in-time; sent here to be the bridge to God for us who are trapped between time and eternity. Upon those of us whose hearts the blood of his sacrifice is poured, we are set free to live forever unbounded. "If the Son sets you free, you will be free indeed." (John 8:36)

The Hypostatic Union

When I was in Bible college, one of my professors gave us a rather simplistic description of the hypostatic union – the concept of the God-Man. He said something like, "Jesus is 100% God and he is at the same time 100% man – but it doesn't add up to 200%, it adds up to 100%." Of course, whenever I start trying to get a handle on this, it never seems so simple. You could twist your brain into a pretzel trying to get a grip on this idea and never quite get it. By faith we accept this fact about Jesus; in fact it's why he's called Jesus Christ – Jesus, representing his humanity, Christ, referring to his heavenly mission.

He is completely God, he is really human, and in so being, he is a unique individual in all of time, earth, heaven and eternity, not to mention whatever else may be out there. You can't make Jesus only one or the other; he just wouldn't be Jesus Christ anymore. The apostle John calls him "God, the one and only." (John 1:18) Paul says that the fullness of God dwelt in him." (Col. 1:19) In Philippians 2, Paul describes Jesus as "being in very nature God" and that he was "made in human likeness."

Throughout the history of the church, it has been considered heresy to prefer one to the other. A few of these historical controversies include: the Arians who taught that he was not God, but a created being (a perfect god-like man), the Gnostics who said he only appeared to be human and had the special divine knowledge or "*gnosis*", the Nestorians, who felt that he had a split human/divine personality, and the Monophysites, who deduced that his human side was absorbed by his divine side. These heresies appear and reappear in various forms in their unrelenting bombardment of the truth. Yet, the truth is that if Jesus is not completely God and completely perfect man in one person, he disappears into nothingness.

The Proclamation of the Word

Most people, even if they have not made up their minds about the divine veracity of Christ's teachings, would agree that Jesus was a great teacher. Very few would argue that he had nothing or very little to say. Jesus got into debates, logical arguments, and explosive verbal confrontations with all sorts of people (loving them all the while.) As children, we are taught his righteous sayings and his fascinating stories.

Yet taking a step of faith reveals that there is so much more to what Jesus said than a mere expressions of his opinions, powerful as they were. No, the words Jesus spoke were not trivial earthly sayings; they were profound heavenly truths. Jesus, as the Word, spoke the words of God.

Of all the evangelists, the apostle John was, I think, the most diligent about revealing Jesus as the Word. The deceptively simple language of John chapter 1 belies the profound meaning behind this spiritual "equation" – *The Word = life = light*. The equation is the key to why Jesus came, who he was, and why it matters to us.

Just as this world came into existence through the words of Christ, so now, Jesus, the living Word of God, a revelation of God, brings the light of truth and the life of salvation to dead, sin-darkened souls. He not only gave life to all created life forms, he gives life to spiritually dead souls. John 1:12 says, "Yet to all who received him, to those who believed in his name, he gave the right to become the children of God."

Everything Jesus said or did on this earth was an expression, a verbalization of God's Word. He spoke truth into the void of sinfulness engulfing our planet so that everlasting life could blaze up in the souls of the redeemed. The Greek word for "word" is "*logos*" – from which we get the English word "logic." You might say that Jesus did not come just to say things that made sense, instead, he made sense of it all, and nothing makes sense without him.

The Substitutionary Death

Whether or not people agree that Jesus was God, most people agree that he died by crucifixion on a Roman cross. **Why** he died is the big question. If Jesus was just a man, the reasons for his death could range anywhere from "died the death of a glorious martyr" to "in the wrong place at the wrong time." However, if one believes that Jesus is God, his death has just one distinct meaning – "he died to be my Savior."

Looking at it from a strictly human viewpoint, if **God** came to earth, one would think that he would want to be worshiped and adored as he assumed supreme power -- but not Jesus. He (in his own words) "did not come to be served, but to serve, and to give his life as a ransom for many."(Matt. 20:28) Jesus came to live a humble life, destined to end in sacrifice. In 2Corinthians 5, Paul says that "we once regarded Christ in a [worldly point of view.]"

In other words, as unbelievers we only saw Christ as a good person who died an unfortunate death. But now, since the light of God through Christ has shone through the cross, we realize that, "God made him who had no sin to be sin for us, so that in him we might become the righteousness of God." (v. 21) The perfect man, Jesus, paid the price for our sins and if we apply this truth to our hearts by faith, we are forgiven.

Leviticus 16 describes the Day of Atonement, which the Jews still celebrate once a year. During the Old Testament ceremony, the high priest sprinkled blood from a bull and a goat in the Most Holy Place in the tabernacle or temple. At the same time, a scapegoat who had symbolically received all the people's sins was set free in the desert. The Jews believed that by observing these rituals as an expression of their faith in God, their sins would be forgiven for one year, but the next year the ceremony had to be repeated.

Yet, as the author of Hebrews points out, Jesus was a once-and-for-all priest *and* sacrifice – "he has appeared once for all at the end of the ages to do away with sin by the sacrifice of himself" (Heb. 9:26), and "when this priest (Jesus) had offered for all time one sacrifice for sins, he sat down at the right hand of God." (Heb. 10:12) The death of Jesus was the ultimate sacrifice leading to the forgiveness of sins; through him our sins are lost in a wilderness, as it were – if it had meant anything else, it would be meaningless.

The Glorious Resurrection

Controversy arose over the resurrection of Christ on the very day it happened and has been swirling ever since. Satan did not take his defeat lightly. Matthew 28 tells the story of how the

Roman soldiers who were guarding the tomb went to the chief priests and gave an (no doubt) animated account of the spectacular events they had just witnessed. The upshot of this meeting was that the guards were paid off to start a rumor that the disciples stole the body of Jesus. Matthew remarks in Mt. 28:15 that "this story has been circulated among the Jews to this very day." (I know this is true because I had a Jewish friend tell it to me once, unsolicited.)

Certainly, a lot of people, Jewish or not, have bought into the falsehood that Jesus never really, bodily, rose from the dead. When you think about it, an event of this sort could not take place without supernatural underpinnings. It just doesn't happen in "real life." The resurrection is a miracle, one that only God, who creates life and is life, can perform. The Apostle Peter, writing about Jesus Christ stated, "Through him, you believe in God, who raised him from the dead and glorified him so that your faith and hope are in God." (1Pet. 1:21)

Notice how the ideas of faith (belief) and miracle (an act of God) are combined to give validity to the resurrection; without them, the resurrection has no meaning (hope) in our lives. If we look at the resurrection in a natural light, we will get nowhere, because, of course, such an event would be impossible. The resurrection only becomes a real event when it is supernatural – God raising Jesus to life because Jesus, as God, was Life itself.

So, in summary -- if you don't have preexistence, you don't have *God*. If you don't have the Incarnation, you don't have his humanity. If you don't have the hypostatic union, you have either God or Man, but not both. Without the 'speaking of the Word,' you have no life, and without the substitutionary death, you have no gateway to Heaven and no forgiveness of sins. Without the resurrection, there is no eternal life and no hope of it. Who would want to deal with a Jesus who possessed none of these qualities? Certainly, he would not do anyone any good. He would be a useless being, an empty life, and not worthy (at the very least) of having a religion named after him.

Knowing the God-Man

If we look at the life of Christ, we clearly see that the dynamic between the perceived dichotomy of Jesus-as-man and Jesus-as-God is constantly being played out. When he is born, the angels praise God, but Herod hunts down a baby boy. The disciples are convinced that they are hearing Jesus speak the words of God, but the Pharisees are only interested in trapping him in human arguments. While hanging on the cross, the Roman soldiers gamble for the right to take his garments, but the believing thief receives the gift of eternal life.

The debate has raged throughout the history of the church. Was he just a man? Is he God? These questions are not universal questions, in the sense that all mankind must come to a consensus, but they are very personal; each person must come to the crossroads where he deals with the question Pilate posed, "What shall I do then, with Jesus who is called Christ?" (Mt. 27:22)

The determining factor which answers this question is wrapped up in what one believes about the resurrection, because the resurrection is all about our new life in Christ (salvation) bringing the power of God into our lives. The resurrection is the catalyst of radical change in our lives, and through us, in the world. Paul says that he wants "to know Christ and the power of his resurrection." (Phil. 3:10) Nothing will change a person quite like knowing that the living God lives through you.

Those who think that Jesus is a mere man may be "inspired" but they will never be **empowered** to live lives in which God actually does his work through them. If the resurrection had never happened, the disciples would have dispersed and gone back to their everyday lives and never bothered to change the world. But it did happen, and they spread change across the world, establishing God's kingdom built on love.

As I mentioned earlier, I realized that so much could be written about Jesus that a chapter would not do, and even many books could not cover the material. But I went on to realize another thing, almost the opposite of what I saw at first. For a

Christ at the Center

long, long time I have taken Jesus for granted. Growing up in a Christian home, going to a conservative, fundamentalist church every Sunday, I saw Jesus as a "given." Even after learning about Jesus in Bible college, I *knew* more, but experienced the same well-worn familiarity.

Now, it's not a bad thing to assume that Jesus is a reality in one's life, or to feel that he is always present. It is, however, a fatal flaw not to live in the power of Christ; the power through which his life is being lived out through us -- in every circumstance. In an interview with the publication *Preaching Today*, Anglican bishop N.T. Wright says, "To preach the resurrection is to announce the fact that the world is a different place, and that we have to live in that 'different-ness.'" The difference lies between merely telling the world about Christ and powerfully loving the world to Christ.

In Ephesians 3:14-20, the apostle Paul offers a prayer for the Ephesian church in which he refers to the resurrection power of Christ as the key to a life lived in love. He asks that God would "strengthen us with power through his spirit" which will cause the **life** of Christ to be a real, motivating force within us. This will enable us to live a life of love toward others and empower us to know Christ, not just to know about him.

Love is the foundation of this kind of life; we are "to grasp how wide and long and high and deep is the love of Christ" (v. 17) and feel that his power is at work in us (v. 20). Philippians 2:12 & 13 says, "Continue to work out your own salvation with fear and trembling, for it is God who works in you to will and to act according to his purpose." As we reverently attempt to produce the fruit of our salvation (good works), God steps in and helps us to do the right thing as we perform tasks in loving service to God.

As I looked at the life of Jesus, after a while of struggling with what to write about in this chapter, I realized that all we know about Jesus, all that the Evangelists endeavored to communicate to us was **love**. If you take away the *drama*, it comes down to one thing – a life of love, nothing else.

The apostle John drives this point home in chapters 3 and 4 of 1John by saying that the great love we see in Jesus began in the heart of the Father, was "lavished" on us by the Son, enabling us to become the beloved children of God. Now we are to take that love and in the same way pour it out on the people around us as we express this love in actions and truth.

The essence of being a Christian, being *like Christ*, is the surrender of our selfishness in exchange for a love that conquers everything. Just like Jesus himself, the life lived in love is all or nothing. Either we reach out to our brothers and neighbors in love, or we care nothing for them and only for ourselves. Phil. 2:3-5 teaches us that we should "consider others better than [ourselves]," "look to the interests of others," and possess the same attitude as Jesus had. What was this attitude? Simply that he gave himself (all that he was) away. We turn around and give ourselves (nothing without him) back to him.

Bibliography – Jesus

"Jesus Seminar." TheFreeDictionary.com. 2010. Farlex, Inc. 11 May. 2010, http://encyclopedia.thefreedictionary.com/jesus+seminar

"Historical Jesus." TheFreeDictionary.com. 2010. Farlex, Inc. 11 May. 2010, http://encyclopedia.thefreedictionary.com/historical+jesus
– Jesus

"Excerpt on voting and color-coding from the introduction to The Five Gospels." *Westar Institute*. Westar Institute, n.d. Web. 11 May 2010. <http://www.westarinstitute.org/Polebridge/Excerpts/voting5g.html>.

Gonzalez, Justio L. *The Story of Christianity*. One volume ed. Prince Press, 1994. Print.

Lowery, Brian. "N. T. Wright on Resurrection." *Preaching Today*. Christianity Today International, 19 Mar. 2008. Web. 11 May 2010. <http://www.preachingtoday.com/2008/03/interview with n t wright.html>.

Christ at the Center

Part 2 – The Problem We Face

Chapter 6- MAN: Who We Are

"... you have taken off the old self with its practices and have put on the new self, which is being renewed in knowledge **in the image of its Creator**." (Col. 3:9,10)

One frosty day during the winter of 1619, the French philosopher Rene Descartes sat in a cozy room heated by a stove – or he sat in a room next to a stove, or he actually sat in a stove; there are several theories – and pondered what a later philosophically inclined writer would call "life, the universe and everything." (Of course, now that I think of it, Douglas Adams would have had quite a bit of fun with that stove!) Descartes, on his part, wanted to know what in life was real and how he could know it was real. Were his body, mind, and all the things around him real? And what told him about this reality so that he could know it in certainty?

On the wintery day when Descartes set about to write down his thoughts about life, the universe and so on, he was beginning to verbalize a series of thoughts that had been bouncing around in his brain for quite some time. He decided that he would get to the heart of reality by breaking everything down to its most basic level, tearing away all the ideas about each thing that he could doubt. (Lawhead, p. 64) He was determined to get down to the lowest common dominator of existence.

Thinking in this manner, he concluded that thinking or reason was the key – he was certain of his existence because he was thinking and he did not doubt that he was thinking. His famous conclusion, "I think, therefore I am," ushered in the age of reason, an age of thought in which reasonable explanations for life's phenomena were going to be examined from every conceivable angle. Today we live in the twilight of that age, for the last beams of its setting sun now reflect dimly off of the foundations of truth and the great ideas of time.

Christ at the Center

Many people, myself included, can quote the words of the old song: "I don't know much about philosophy," but in spite of this fact, I'm sure that most rational people in every age have asked themselves (if only briefly) questions such as: Who am I? Why do I exist? What is my destiny? In Psalm 8, the ancient Jewish king and poet, David, posed that simple but huge question – "What is man?" I wish to explore this question, for David gives, I think, a satisfying answer.

The question itself arises because we are indeed self-aware, for unless one is crazy or in a coma, we are intimately acquainted with ourselves, no matter how much one may play around with the idea. It is possible for me to know that I am "me" and that I am here. But once we go beyond that we begin to run into other issues; our reason for being here in the first place and how we can find our purpose in life. Initially, in order to find answers to the questions that arise from the deep longings of the soul, we need to begin by knowing our Source, the Reason behind our reason.

In Psalm 8, David identifies our Source as the Creator God, and, pointing back beyond our creation, calls us to consider God's thoughts toward us – "thou art mindful of him." We began in the heart and mind of God in much the same way as babies begin in the dreams of their parents. Perhaps Descartes was wise to link thought with existence, for it is truly where we began.

"Let us make man." God says, sharing his thought with the Trinity and verbalizing his idea for his beloved creatures. "How precious are thy thoughts toward me, O God, how great is the sum of them," David declares in Psalm 139. Beyond time, before existence, God thought of us and his thoughts became blessings made real by our existence, made eternal through redemption.

"Thou visitest him," David says, because God did not think and act from a distance. He made us with his "own two hands" and the spirit of life flowed into us through his own breath. Then God came to visit, to walk and talk with man in the Garden. But, amazingly, after the sin in the Garden, God does not care to only visit, he determines to dwell with us by sending his Son, Immanuel, God-with-us, to live as one of us and then ultimately, by sending his Spirit, who indwells us forever. God's first priority in living with us was to speak to us and engage us in conversation, making us his friends. God was not alone, but we can be, and we need to know that God wishes to know us so that he can be everything to us.

This act of communication reveals a secret about our identity, particularly in the way God looks at it. I often get perturbed with people who do not believe that God speaks to us and seem to imply that "God, speaking" is some kind of product of an overstressed imagination. However, it is true that God can and sometimes does speak directly to an individual, sometimes in an audible voice. I've heard it. But we must remember that this speaking always arises from God's relationship with us, a relationship centered on communication and who he thinks we are.

God's relationship with us is built entirely on a foundation of unshakeable love and comes from his eternal delight in creating us. As Isaiah 43:1(KJV) declares, "But now thus saith the LORD that created thee, O Jacob, and he that formed thee, O Israel, Fear not: for I have redeemed thee, I have called thee by thy name; thou art mine." We are, first of all, called by God, who calls us by name. In the same way that parents name their beloved babies, God names us, and in his first creative thought towards us, he speaks our name.

Starting with this initial act of naming us, God goes on to speak more and more things to us. "Call to me and I will answer you and tell you great and unsearchable things you do not know." (Jer. 33:3) God is quite the "talker," in fact; his whole act of communication with us is wrapped up in the word "Word." God's desire to speak to us in order to express his relationship with us is a vital indication of who we are.

"Thou hast made him," David says, and herein we find the key to everything about us and to everything we may doubt or know. God made me; I come from his mind, his heart and his hands. In the first verses of Psalm 8, David reminds us that God has created the beautiful universe in which we live -- "When I consider the heavens...what is man?" Creation is a gift we are scarcely worthy of, even in the good state of Eden. Everything seems to be designed for us, everything works in a way that makes us work the right way. In Psalm 139, David says, "I praise you because I am fearfully and wonderfully made; your works are wonderful, I know that full well." He is saying that we not only exist because of God, he uniquely designs us as well. We are – as we so often tell our children – special.

In looking at Psalm 8, the difference between Descartes and David should become obvious to us. Descartes' identity was wrapped up in himself, while David's was entrenched in God. Descartes found himself in his thoughts, while David was convinced that he came from the thoughts of God. But because of the influence of Descartes' philosophy and other ideas like it, including evolutionary theory, most people today only see themselves as a product of themselves. They do not know the greater source from which they spring.

Not only that, and unacknowledged by most, sin has caused a separation between people and their Creator. "Be yourself" is not an appeal to greatness but to degradation. "Find yourself" becomes a fancy invitation to a self-made horror show. Only through acknowledging the hand of the Creator upon us, by giving up our sinful selves to the one who died to change our hopeless human condition, will we ever hope to become those whom God meant us to be.

The overarching concept or fact of who we are comes from the statement of a divine fiat made by God in Gen. 1 – "Then God said, 'Let us make man in our image, in our likeness, and let them rule over the fish of the sea and the birds of the air, over the livestock, over all the earth, and over all the creatures that move along the ground.' So God created man in his own image, in the image of God he created him; male and female he created them. God blessed them and said to them, 'Be fruitful and increase in number; fill the earth and subdue it.'" One of the first things we see here again involves communication – "let us" – a sort of discussion about our creation. We were made to both speak things and know things, things human and divine, because we arise from the eternal fellowship of the triune God. The Father declares and designs us, the Son forms us, and the Spirit breathes life into us.

The Image of God

In her book, *The Mind of the Maker*, Dorothy Sayers purposes that the creative processes of God are jointly done by the three persons of the Godhead, thus making creativity in us Trinitarian in nature. She writes, "Looking at man, he (the author of Genesis) sees in him something essentially divine, but when we turn back to see what he says about the original upon which the 'image' of God was modeled, we find only the single assumption, 'God created.' The characteristic common to God and man is apparently that: the desire and the ability to make things." She goes on throughout the book to assert that our creative acts arise from this triunal image; indeed, we could not be creative without it. (Sayers, p. 22) We are created in the image of God, and one of the ways this aspect of our creation is confirmed within us is through our ability to be creative.

The image of God is not a bit of "god-ness" within us, it is instead a sort of stamp of authenticity placed upon us by God, indicating that we came from God, we are going to God and that we shall forever be God's. As bearers of the divine image we are something like a photograph – we are not the real thing but the real thing can be clearly defined by the picture. A photograph only gives us an idea of what the real thing is like; it can never be the real thing.

Our image of God does not make us gods in any way, it only points to God, our Creator. In fact, it prevents us from ever becoming actual gods, because the image is a permanent representation fixed within us and as such cannot become the real thing in any way. Further, because we bear this image, we are not to make any images of God in any form, which is idolatry, for God Himself has made the image. We are also not to worship the image, which is to worship ourselves in a humanistic way, for God alone is to be worshiped. Our image of God is an imperfect photograph anyway, and we must remember that the only true image of God is found in Jesus Christ, who is God incarnate. He is the image *and* the real thing. "The light of the gospel of the glory of Christ, who is the image of God" is shining through him into our hearts where, after we receive Christ by grace and faith, we hold this treasure in "jars of clay."

Christ at the Center

Psalm 8 describes man in an intermediary position among created beings in which he is "a little lower than the angels" and "ruler over the works of your hands." In this hierarchy, man is not as powerful as angels, but exercises power over animals. Although created by God, neither angels nor animals bear the image of God. Angels are spiritual beings, and from the time of their creation, they serve God and reflect his glory in heavenly dimensions. Although possessing great intellectual powers, they are focused on the task of exclusively serving and praising God; everything about their existence points to the great glory of God. The angels who sinned, however, seek to disrupt God's purposes and absorb God's glory back upon themselves in eternal blackness.

The animals, which are below man in ranking, do not have souls and are purely physical beings. Because people today consider man to be animalistic, highly so, but a mere animal nonetheless, anthropomorphic traits are commonly assigned to animals, particularly pets. We must realize that animals work from instinct alone, and this instinct sometime seems very much akin to our emotions. We think this way because we have instincts, too. So we are neither angels nor animals, we are God's unique creation, man, bearing the image of god and designed to live in a physical world and destined to be drawn towards the spiritual world.

Some people believe that the image of God was completely destroyed by the fall of mankind into sin. I do not believe that this is exactly the case, for many vestiges of it remain, however twisted they may be. Scripture affirms this, for, in the Old Testament, murder is condemned because by it the image of God would be destroyed (Gen. 9:6), and in the New Testament, James says that we should not curse men "who have been made in God's likeness." Notice how both examples link the image of God with some kind of sin, showing that God still acknowledges the image he implanted at the beginning. I do not think that we could exist as human beings without it, because it still amounts to a distinguishing factor between us and the animals and the angels.

In addition, we retain distinguishing features of the image of God. We have a conscience, a sense of right and wrong, or a sense that a standard of right and wrong exists. We possess intelligence and reason, enabling us to think concretely and abstractly, making free decisions about our thoughts, something that beings without the image of God cannot do. And we can still communicate with God, howbeit in a very limited and one-sided way, as if we are using hand signals to communicate with someone who speaks a totally different language.

No doubt about it, the image of God was severely damaged by the fall; like a beautiful, fragile glass vase, toppled from a shelf and shattered into a thousand fragments, or a car which was bent and twisted in a traffic accident. It was so damaged that it no longer looks like the real thing; it has become quite obscure. The image of God, though bent by sin, is still a force within us that seeks to orient us to God. Solomon said that God has "set eternity in the hearts of men, yet they cannot fathom what God has done from beginning to end," and adds that God does this so that "men will revere him." (Ecc.3:11-14) Though marred by the fall, and bent by the blows of sin, the image of God somehow remains, cast off in a corner, waiting to be resurrected by the Gospel.

Another 17th century French philosopher, Blaise Pascal, was also intrigued by the position of man (who we are), particularly as it concerns our strained relationship with God. Pascal argues that we are wretched in and of ourselves, but we do not always see ourselves in such a pathetic way. Due to our pride, we attempt to either divert ourselves from looking squarely at our brokenness, or we make futile attempts to fix ourselves on our own. Commenting on Pascal's great work, *Pensees*, Peter Kreeft says that Pascal likened us to a weird-shaped lock, the inside mechanism of which was bent by sin and which can only be opened by an equally strangely-shaped key. (Kreeft, p. 47) It is as if we were bent inwardly back upon ourselves, for we no longer look outwards to see God and others; we only see ourselves.

Pascal writes, "Man's greatness and wretchedness are so evident that the true religion must necessarily teach us that there is in man some great principle of greatest good and...wretchedness." (Kreeft, p. 65) Pascal saw man's original great and good status, and knew that it is now hidden under a pile of sinful debris. This burden of sin drags us down and makes us miserable.

Pascal reasoned that the answer given to this dilemma must necessarily address both sides of the issue. He concludes that only Christianity can do this. He imagines God as saying, "It is I who have made you and I alone can teach you what you are." (Kreeft, p. 66) He writes, "Christianity is strange; it bids man to recognize that he is vile, and even abominable and bids him to want to be like God." (Kreeft, p. 279)

The strangely-shaped Christian key fits the strangely-bent human lock; but the key fits on purpose and not by accident. Jesus Christ, God's perfect Son and sacrifice, was broken upon the cross as he took our sins upon himself. "He was pierced for our transgressions, he was crushed for our iniquities; the punishment that bought us peace was upon him, and by his wounds we are healed." (Is. 53:5) God allowed Jesus to be bent into just the right shape to open the lock of our souls and release us into his perfectly shaped freedom.

The image of God has been rejuvenated within the heart of the Christian. Wretchedness is relieved and sin is solved. A big difference exists between ordinary fallen men and uplifted and redeemed men in whom the image of God now shines like never before. 2 Corinthians 4:6 says, "For God...made his light shine in our hearts to give us the light of the knowledge of the glory of God in the face of Christ." The road to redemption, upon which we daily walk, runs between these two extremes of wretchedness and glory. Only once safe in heaven will the image shine with its greatest, truest light – "we shall be like him, for we shall see him as he is." (1John 3:2)

We reflect the image of God in its greatest extent and purpose through our multifaceted nature – that is to say, we are one person comprised of many interrelated parts. As such, many of our characteristics are vague replications of God's; ours are finite and limited while his are infinite and eternal.

God is all knowing and wise, our knowledge grows and our wisdom varies. God has all power and strength; we are weak and crave endurance. God is everywhere present; we are locked into time and space. These multifaceted traits find their manifestation in and through our dualistic nature, which I am going to refer to our mind, body and soul. Created by the triune God, our image of God is Trinitarian in this respect – our mind, body and soul work together to make us one unique person.

The essence of man has been described as being everything from a divinely created being composed of many varying parts to a mere highly evolved animal. The church has historically taught that man is dualistic in nature, having a physical side and a spiritual side, often described as body, soul and spirit. But I prefer body, mind and soul because this description includes our ability to think and reason as a major component of our makeup. The existence of the *body* is obvious to almost everyone – just take a look in the mirror – if you dare! Created by God, we respond to God through our *souls*, which I am taking here to be the same as or incorporating the term "spirit." Our *minds*, I believe, unite the body and soul and empower us to think and reason upon their demands.

The Bible connects these three partitions as coming from and being united to the image of God. Our minds are to be coordinated with the mind of Christ: "Let this mind be in you, which was also in Christ Jesus." (Phil. 2:5) Our bodies are comprised of the same substance as Christ's body as Heb. 10:5 indicates – "a body you prepared for me." Our souls respond to and relate with God – "The Spirit himself testifies with our spirit that we are God's children." (Rom. 8:16)

These three parts reflect the Godhead's communication in unity from which we were created. The mind thinks and reasons upon the workings of the body and the intrigues of the soul. The body lives out God's gift of physical life, also being a spiritual temple in which Christ may dwell. The soul inspires the mind to think of high and godly things as the salvation of our souls brings hope to our mortal bodies. All of this is similar to the way in which the Father, Son and Holy Spirit interact in oneness.

This truth is wonderfully represented in the prayer of Jesus recorded in John 17. Jesus and the Father were united in glory before the world began; the dynamic of which was perfect united fellowship, expressed in unlimited love. While Jesus was on the earth, the disciples had experienced the sanctifying effects of this love, fellowship and glory in face-to-face communication with Jesus, but since the time had come for him to leave, Jesus asks that they would continue to be sanctified by the Word of Truth, who is the Holy Spirit. The Holy Spirit would be the manifestation to us of the eternal breath of God, providing life for our bodies, minds and souls.

Jesus prays that we would experience the unity of the Trinity in our personal lives and in the corporate life of his body, the church. He says, "I have given them the glory that you gave me, that they may be one as we are one: I in them and you in me." You see, we were created to receive and be fulfilled by this beautiful unity in our bodies, minds and souls.

MIND

The mind is often expressed as a part of either the body or the soul. Neurological function is certainly biological, controlled by the brain and nerves, while wisdom and reason are more overtly spiritual and regulated by the soul. I like to think that mind is a distinctive part of us, without which we cannot be truly human. Animals have brains, controlling their instincts and physical actions. Angels have intellect, guiding them in their service of God. We have "mind" which reasons, understands and feels and through which we uniquely express ourselves. Reason, especially, is built into us – animals do not actually think.

In 1Corinthians 2:12, Paul says that we have received the Holy Spirit in order that we may gain the ability to understand spiritual ideas, indicating that the mind is a part of the image of God as seen in Christ ("we have the mind of Christ.") The way in which Christians ought to make sense of the world comes to us through the way God sees world, not the way we interpret the world in a Christian context. But do Christians today really think about life with the mind of Christ?

Christ at the Center

    We've all seen examples of how people today do not think or use their minds to reason. Late-night talk show hosts love to exploit this woeful situation by interviewing or quizzing the frightfully ignorant "man on the street." The results are clear: people nowadays "don't know nothin'." Not only that, but postmodern people don't care – the only thing they know is that nothing can really be known, so why bother?

    In his book, *The Christian Mind*, first published in 1963, Harry Blamires twice asserts on the first page, "There is no longer a Christian mind." (Blamires, p. 3) When I first read this, I was surprised, for I have no trouble in thinking that there is no Christian mind now, but in 1963? Well, I guess all good fallacies need somewhere to begin, and as it turns out, the sixties were a prime breeding ground for secular inroads into the church. Thinking in a truly Christian way faded into the background. Replacing Christian values with a Christian *take* on values became the norm.

    In the existentialist seventies evangelicals tried to adapt the church to meet the changing needs of society and bring the church up to date. In the eighties and beyond, evangelicals tried a pragmatic approach – whatever worked and whatever looked appealing was tried. However, our thinking in all of this was suspect and, as a result, in the view of many, Christianity has become little more that just a pretty gloss to be painted over the issues of the day.

    This development raises several questions. If the Christian mind has gone missing or has been misplaced, how are we to retrieve it? If it is indeed missing in action, how must we deal with the debilitating state of affairs? If it has been stolen, how can this situation be brought to justice? A world (or a life) without a Christian mind and yet claiming to be Christian creates a confusing dichotomy. Can Christians who do not think like Christians be Christians? Blamires contends that Christians may engage in Christian practice and yet be thoroughly secular in their thinking because they do not think about life "in terms of Heaven and Hell." (Blamires, p. 4)

    And this is exactly the point at which a great watershed in Christian thinking occurs. Are we thinking in terms that are greater than our physical existence? Are we thinking in a godly way because we realize that we are truly on a journey to God? In his book, *Mere Christianity*, C.S. Lewis writes, "I would much rather say that every time you make a choice you are turning the central part of you, the part that chooses into something a little different than what it was before ... into a heavenly creature or into a hellish creature." (Lewis, p. 92) The mind thinking the way Christ would think is a mind firmly fixed on the eternal truths and therefore it interprets the actions, attitudes and events of this world through a spiritual lens. The mind thinking in a secular way, however, focuses fruitlessly on the things that will pass away.

We live in a world where almost all of life has been turned in a completely secular direction. Everything has been humanized; God has been separated from all things physical, earthly and human. Human beings and their accomplishments have been placed squarely in the center of the material universe. This kind of thinking, based on the shaky foundations laid by the faulty perceptions of truth embraced by the fallen human race, now fills the minds of many with illusive lies and hollow ideas.

At the end of the modern era, people were told that only one kind of truth existed – scientific truth – the claims of which must be empirically proven. Religious truth, particularly Christian truth was reduced to a mish-mash of personal feelings. But we have descended a step further in the post-modern world; now there is no truth upon which to think or feel. The world is full of empty people with empty minds. Thinking is a moot point, for it is impossible to arrive at the truth.

Unfortunately, the average Christian follows along with this secular pattern. He may have some feelings of goodness, expressed in attempts at better living. He is operating under the assumption that Christian ideas are those that most closely resemble truth, or in a way, just illustrate truth. His thinking is skewed in a secular direction. He has, as the Bible states, a form of godliness, the power of which he denies.

The Christian who thinks only in terms of this world, with only a Christ-like platitude or two thrown in for good measure, is most surely on the road to destruction, for "the world is passing away along with its desires." (1John 1:17) The word "desires" here means "longings"; that is, the false and illusive ideas upon which secular minds are fixed, and towards which weak Christian minds are increasingly inclined.

The Christian mind is further threatened by the idolatry of our age. We have set up many gods of every description and have placed them along side of the one true God of all. These gods may be material things, fulfilling sentiments, or the fruits of hard-fought dreams. We devote ourselves to much that lies only within the limited sphere of our earthly existence and live life in terms of passing moments filled with trivial thoughts. It is easy to fall into the trap of working mostly for what is important in the here and now, thinking that the age to come is settled and secured.

Yet, this is not true. Our life in God is but one life, for what we do here, where our thoughts lead us, lies interminably down the road to life eternal. We must have one God and one goal. We must have the same attitude or desire or fixed thought that Jesus had – to be emptied – to get rid of the ideas of this world system and to obliterate from our minds the gods of this age.

In order to begin thinking in a way that centers on Christ and is directed towards heaven, we must work on changing the focus of our thoughts. Paul's instructions in Rom. 12:1 and 2 tell us that the life which turns from the world to heaven is controlled by proper thinking. "Do not be conformed any longer to the pattern of this world, but be transformed by the renewing of your mind." When this happens we go on to "test and approve;" that is, we employ mental exercises that help us to determine what our godly actions should be.

In Colossians 1:18, Paul explains that Christ is the one who has created and redeemed us "so that in everything he might have the supremacy." We must come to this place in our lives and in our experiences where Christ has assumed first place; where we acknowledge he is over all and in all. Through prayer, we must devote everything to him so that our thoughts are fixed on the things "true, noble, right, pure, lovely and admirable." (Phil. 4:8)

Christ at the Center

I think the place where so many of us hit the wall concerning Christian thinking is mainly in the all-encompassing arena of daily life. Remember how, in Jesus' parable of the sower, the "worries of this life" rise up to choke off the life-giving word. In real life, just waking up and getting through the day distracts immeasurably from thinking on what is good and right, from seeing what is real and eternal. When reading the lives of the great saints of God, it is interesting how they realized that solving this impasse was the key to living, as Brother Lawrence said, in the "presence of God." The Apostle Paul said that he had "learned the secret of being content in every situation." (Phil. 4:11) It was to live each day -- in whatever he did both small and great -- not in his own resources, but in the power of Christ.

In 1Corinthians 10:5, Paul also talks about having an entirely Christian focus when he writes, "We demolish arguments and every pretension that sets itself up against the kingdom of God and we take captive every thought to make it obedient to Christ." Notice how controlling and guiding his thoughts towards godly concepts and outcomes strengthened his defense against secular ideas.

In order to think in a Christian way and to use our minds as Christians ought to, we must embark on a quest to develop our minds through serious reading, critical viewing and creative expression. We must train ourselves to see things in a Christ-centered light, to be "God's workmanship, created in Christ Jesus to do good works." (Eph. 2:10) The mission of our thoughts must be one that works out our "salvation in fear and trembling, for it is God who works in you ..." (Phil. 2:12,13)

BODY

The body is the physical side of man, and as such, we easily think it is our most important part. It is certainly the most obvious part, for every time one looks in a mirror a body will be there, staring back at us, for better or for worse; furthermore, the care and feeding of the body nags at us daily. Three times a day we feed our bodies, and every morning we get them ready to face the world, even if we have no where to go. And we (women, especially) certainly spend a lot of time and money making sure we are clothed properly and fashionably. Yet Jesus said, "Do not worry about your life, what you will eat or drink; or about your body, what you will wear . . ." – but we are continually consumed with these very concerns. The body, which in a very true sense is far less real than the soul, seems to be the only real thing we experience about ourselves.

When God created man, he formed the substance of his body "from the dust of the ground." 1Corinthians 15:47 says, "The first man was of the dust of the earth" and Ecclesiastes 3:20 states, "all come from the dust, and to dust all return." The word "dust" means exactly what we think it does, what mothers are very familiar with -- dirt or soil. The fact that our bodies are dust means that we are physical beings in so far as we were made with the same types of chemicals as are found in the physical world. Our chemical make-up is the same kind of thing that is found in any other physical and biological entity.

We are not spirit beings like the angels. Our bodies work in a physical way – food is transformed into energy, we reproduce via DNA, and our bodies are subject to physical forces that will ultimately wear us down and rob us of life, returning the physical body to its source, the earth.

Since our bodies are composed of the things that make up the physical world, they are completely limited by the laws of nature. A body cannot enter the spiritual dimension. A body is restricted to time, space and nature. A body cannot take on powers outside of its design. Even in the goodness of Eden, a body was never meant to be eternal or not subject to death. Therefore, when we consider our bodies, we can look no further than the here and now. This is indeed "all there is" as far as the body is concerned, yet how often we pretend that we must make it invulnerable to change and impervious to destruction!

In order to understand the best way to care for our bodies and to use them wisely, so to speak, we must stop and consider what our bodies are *for*. If our destiny is spiritual in nature, why did God bother to build a body at all? Should we ignore our bodies in pursuit of higher aspirations? Or, should we give them the greatest possible attention and make ourselves into the best possible physical specimens?

God's highest goal for the body was to make it his dwelling place on earth. Certainly, we see this in the incarnation of Christ; who became a baby, grew into a man and died a physical death. The body of Christ was a vehicle for God's glory as Col. 1:10 says, "For God was pleased to have all his fullness dwell in him."

Christ's body enabled him to live in exactly the same way we live. He ate, slept, talked, walked, and wept, to name a few actions, all because he had a body with which to do these things. Most importantly, he had to have a body that could die, for in so doing he would become our Savior – "He himself bore our sins in his body on the tree . . ." (1Pet.2:24)

We are able to understand things better if understand their origins. We need to know the purpose for which we were made. When we look at ourselves, and what the Bible teaches us about our creation, I think three things become evident: 1.) God created us for his glory; that is, so that his glory may reside within us and shine out of us, pointing others to God. Jesus said, "You are the light of the world. A city on a hill cannot be hidden." (Matt. 5:14) God planned that his glory would be shown to the world through people who walk around in physical bodies.

2.) We were created for fellowship. From the beginning, God interacted with mankind and enabled us to interact with others. Fellowship is contingent upon bodily actions such as talking, walking and eating. 3.) God created us for an eternal destiny. Eden was just the beginning of our journey. As humans, body and soul, our fate lies beyond the physical dimension. One day the body will be resurrected into its true and final form, just as the body of Jesus was the first to be resurrected in that way.

If we see ourselves as the dwelling place of God, it therefore follows that we should endeavor to make our bodies fit for the King. The well known passage from 2Cor. 6 reminds us that the body itself is a temple where the Holy Spirit lives. Jesus reminded the disciples, "You are in me and I am in you." As Christians, we are never entirely our own person. God inhabits us – wherever we go, he goes, whatever we do, he does. In this way, we are the earthly hands and feet of God, as we serve God through our bodies, and his glory shines out from us.

Now, over the years many legalistic questions have been raised over the role the body and its desires play in the Christian life. For instance, the question of what foods are proper to eat goes all the way back to New Testament times. In Acts 10, Jesus revealed to Peter specifically that we are not bound by the dietary restrictions of the law. Jesus had pronounced all foods clean. As if anticipating that controversies over food would crop up in the church, Paul warns Timothy against needlessly arguing over which foods are or are not suitable for consumption. (1Tim. 4:3-5)

It is interesting to note that this controversy and others like it are signs of the end of the age – certainly now many disagreements arise (often in the name of religion) over which foods to eat. God has given us every food item for our benefit and enjoyment. Food is one of the good and perfect gifts that comes down to us from our unchangeable God, and for this reason, we must receive our food with thanksgiving and not suspicion.

The food problem is only one example of the stress we place on the value of the physical body. Other disputed areas include what clothes we should wear, how much exercise to engage in and the role of sex in our lives. It is easy to lose track of the real reason behind our earthy existence – to be God's light and salt in this troubled world. Like Gideon's strange weapons, we are clay pots in which God's fire burns. Therefore, everything we do in our bodies must be seen in this light, as we endeavor to point others to God and not to ourselves.

Speaking to wives, Peter instructs, "Your beauty should not come from outward adornment . . . instead it should be that of your inner self, the unfading beauty of a gentle and quiet spirit..." (1Pet. 3:3,4) It was wise for Peter to address this idea to women, for we can struggle more than men do in the effort to maintain a pleasing appearance, consuming in the process undo time, energy and money. At the same time, however, we do not need to look like careless slobs. We represent Christ in every aspect of life. A happy medium must be found.

I like the way Paul confides to Timothy "physical training has some value." He is saying that we should give due place to actions which are basically beneficial to us, things like exercising, eating right and dressing neatly. Going overboard with any physical desire makes it eclipse and darken our earthy purpose of exhibiting God to others. We must find a way to like our bodies, but not love them, to respect our bodies as God's temple without giving the temple undue regard. Paul said, "Everything is permissible for me – but I will not be mastered by anything." (1Cor. 6:12)

One of the most difficult struggles we face concerning the body arises from our sexual desires -- an area in which our physical desires can truly get the better of us. In 1Cor. 6:18 Paul says, "Flee from sexual immorality. All other sins a man commits are outside of his body, but he who sins sexually sins against his own body." Because our bodies are temples for Christ, because he is in us and shown to the world through us, we cannot form sexual unions which infringe upon and degrade the testimony of God with in us. It is easy to be deceived into thinking that we can do whatever we want with our bodies; that we can be in control of our physical desires.

The great temptation of sexual sin states that whatever the negative consequences of the action may be, the physical pleasure will be greater than them all. But in the end, this is an empty promise, and our lives will be forever scarred by the lingering effects of "the pleasures of sin for a season." The Holy Spirit has come to make his home within us; consequently, he is pleased only when sex is used in the divine order of marriage, when a home is made for others under his sacred blessing.

Our bodies were created as physical units and accordingly will biologically decay when we die. After death, what we know, experience and visualize will no longer have anything to do with the physical world. Physicality will end with a resounding finality. When the soul departs, nothing is left but the pile of dirt we began with. This decay, however, is not the final word on what happens to us as personal beings; it is only the terminal point of the physical body. The resurrection is coming, during which our bodies will be transformed into very different things – a sort of "super-physical" thing.

The resurrection will come for all bodies; it is an indication that the physical, which once existed, is ending and something far greater, something fit for God's new creation is beginning. If the physical dies, it rises again. Paul says that we know that Jesus had a real physical body because he arose from the grave – "If there is no resurrection of the dead, then not even Christ has been raised." (1Cor. 15:13)

Further on in this passage of Scripture, Paul compares our present bodies with our future ones. We are now very much like a seed; we are just a little promise of what we will become. In the same way that a seemingly dead seed is put into the ground, covered with dirt and eventually springs up as a little green plant, we also die and are put into the ground, only to come back as living beings.

When we rise again we will be something much greater, something much better than what we are now, something which will never die again. As children of Adam, we have inherited his dusty framework, but when we become God's children, we receive a new destiny and a heavenly body fit for it. The new body, designed for heaven, will reverse the limitations of this physical world.

SOUL

The soul is the immaterial, non-physical part of man; even though it has no physical substance, it is real and once created by God lives on forever. It is the internal spiritual part of man, which connects us forever with God and the eternal. The soul was placed within man at the time of his creation and as such is an integral part of the image of God possessed by every person. We respond to God through the life of the soul; if it is dead in sin, there is no response on our part to God, however, if it has been made alive through Christ it is once again in tune with the Creator.

The word "soul" in the Old Testament means life, the breath of life, or a living thing. One could say it is a "life-force;" if this is not taken to mean a mystical force but a real thing. The soul was given to us to be our connection with the spiritual realm. Through the soul we love and worship God – it is our life in God. Deuteronomy 6:5 says, "Love the Lord your God with all your heart and with all your soul and with all your strength," and Jesus, echoing this verse in Mark 12:30, calls it the "most important" commandment and adds "mind" as another component with which we express our devotion to God.

Every part of us needs to be united in the expression of uncompromising love for God, but the soul is the primary conduit for this love. In the life of the Christian, the soul was once dead in sin, its original breath extinguished, but through salvation from Christ it has received new life. In 1Peter 1:8-9, Peter says that we love Christ even thought we have never seen him because we are receiving the salvation of our souls. "We love him because he first loved us." (1Jn. 4:19) This love comes through the soul's connection to God; a connection that Christ made for us when came down from heaven and died for us to bring our souls back into relationship with God.

The soul is God's property and it operates under his jurisdiction. Ezekiel 18:4 is a simple statement from God – "Every living soul belongs to me." When we die, our souls go to God. Ecclesiastes 12:7 says, "and the dust (our bodies made from dirt) returns to the ground it came from and the spirit returns to God who gave it." The life of the soul centers around our connection with God. The great tragedy of the human story is that this connection was shattered early on in the relationship between God and man. In fact, the verse in Ezekiel goes on to say, "the soul who sins is the one who will die," echoing God's warning to Adam and Eve – "when you eat of it, you will surely die." (Gen. 2:17)

Earlier I said that at the time when mankind fell into sin the image of God was bent back upon itself so that it was no longer directed towards God but focused on self instead. The death of the soul was the event that bent the image of God into its distorted shape. The life of the soul was snuffed out and an empty hollow existence took its place. We found ourselves in the position where, if we ever again wanted to be reunited with the life of God, our souls would need to be resurrected from the dead.

All of mankind goes about in a sinful state of existence. Romans 3:23 declares "All have sinned and fall short of the glory of God." As such, our souls are in a perpetual death-state, a condition in which we are separated from God who is the only source of spiritual and physical life. A person who has no spiritual life, no soul-life, even while having physical life, wanders around like a ghost. He is an empty promise of what he could have been.

This degraded spiritual life drags the mind down with it as people cease to think or stimulate their minds. They become "empty selves;" people characterized by actions and values which paralyze the life of the mind and concentrate instead on the passions of the body. (Moreland, p.88) The great dilemma of mankind is not merely that we neglected to find ways to do the worthy things which should be done or that we neglected to think the profound thoughts we should have thought, but, more significantly, that we failed to reconnect our soul-life with God. Dead in sin, we have become dead in everything else.

The pathway leading to reconnection with God was laid down by God himself, who in Christ and by his death opened the door to reconciliation. "God was reconciling the world to himself in Christ," 1Corinthians 5:19 says, and further explains, "God made him who knew no sin to be sin for us so that in him we might become the righteousness of God." (v. 21) In its natural sinful state, the soul is alienated from God, but somehow still longs for connection with God. Since God has reached down from heaven to rescue us, the highest goal of our lives now becomes seeking this reconciliation; living the life in God that connects us to Christ and continues on into glory.

In the book of Psalms, David often reflects upon the state of the believer's soul. He says that our souls can feel "cast down," weary, and troubled. He also says that the soul can be joyful and forgiven and, as such, may find great delight in God and his word. Whatever our state in life, in whatever it takes to properly cope with life, our souls must be constantly oriented toward God. If our souls are not focused on God and are not nourished by the Word, sad, withered Christians will seek the kingdom of God in futility.

In Psalm 42, David poses this question, "Why are you downcast, oh my soul? Why so disturbed within me?" His subsequent answer reveals the life of focus we must possess – "Put your hope in God, for I will yet praise him, my Savior and my God." The life concentrated on God produces a life of worship and praise, centered on not only God's redemption of the soul, but that of the mind and body as well. In the book of Revelation, we learn that the focus of our heavenly praise will not be on the grandeur of God and Heaven but on "the Lamb who was slain." Salvation of the soul is the eternal end of man; it is the only thing that gives our lives any meaning at all. "He has delivered us from such a deadly peril and he will deliver us. On him we have set our hope..." (2Cor. 1:10)

When we think about who we are, it is necessary to look beyond ourselves to who we were meant to be – it is one of those things where less is more. As John the Baptist said, "He must become greater; I must become less." On the other hand, because we are naturally bent towards selfishness and sin, when we adopt Descartes' self-centered philosophy and others like it, we end up adopting an empty, twisted existence. If we think empty thoughts not focused on God, but on ourselves, we will end up lost and confused and feeling as if our lives are worthless.

We must change our view of ourselves to correspond with God's analysis as Paul confessed in Rom. 7:18, "I know that within me dwells no good thing." True life and existence can only be expressed as it stands in relationship with God. Perhaps Christians should say, "I am God's – therefore I am." God's Word says, "You are not your own; you were bought with a price," and "your life is hid with Christ in God." (1Cor. 6:20 and Col. 3:3)

At first glance, we may think that this kind of existence greatly limits who we are and what we can do. Living in God and doing the things that honor God seems to be a boxed-in condition, but this is not really so because it is the very existence for which we were created – it is our eternal destiny – to know God and be known by him. Christ is central to our lives. Our bodies, minds and souls ought to have nothing better to do and nothing greater to be than what God desires for us. God made us and redeemed us and he desires nothing less than to be our all-in-all.

Bibliography – Man

    Lawhead, William F. *The Philosophical Journey: An Interactive Approach*. 3rd. ed. New York: McGraw-Hill, 2006. 63-70. Print.

    Sayers, Dorothy L. *The Mind of the Maker*. San Francisco: HarperCollinsPublishers, 1979. Print.

    Kreeft, Peter. *Christianity for Modern Pagans: Pascal's Pensees Edited, Outlined and Explained*. San Francisco: Ignatius Press, 1993. Print.

    Blamires, Harry. *The Christian Mind*. Study Guide Edition. Colorado Springs, CO: Purposeful Design Publications, 1997. Print.

    Lewis, C. S. *Mere Christianity and The Screwtape Letters: Complete in One Volume*. revised and amplified ed. San Francisco: HarperCollinsPublishers, 2000. Print.

    Moreland, J. P. *Love Your God With All Your Mind*. Colorado Springs, CO: NavPress, 1997. Print.

Chapter 7- SIN: The Heart of What We Do

"Therefore, there is now no condemnation for those who are **in Christ Jesus**, because through Christ Jesus the law of the Spirit of life set me free from the law of sin and death." (Rom. 8:1,2)

Before my first child was born, I heard much sage advice from those bastions of baby-knowledge – the mothers of toddlers. (Motherhood will make you very wise very fast.) "Beware the terrible-two's," they foretold, "Your sweet baby will turn into an obnoxious monster!" I was treated to reports of tiny foot stamping, unending pathetic tears and the inevitable, unceasing repetition of the word "No!" "Well," I thought, "at least all that is two years away."

And so it was. The day came when (at about the age of 18 months) my son sat in high chair and as I was feeding him his lunch, he looked me square in the eye and with a diabolical grin on his face, he spit his food right back at me! Even though I knew that day would come, I was shocked. Could my son be *sinning*? Well, I concluded that he was, for without a moment's hesitation, he did it again!

I'll never forget the panic that rose up in my heart that day. "It all begins here," I thought, "here where what I now do about my child's sin will set us on a path of either self-destruction or self-discipline." Feeling horrible, I realized that I needed to implement my first disciplinary action. (Don't worry, he got over it, and I do not think he tried that little stunt again.)

What an insight I gained that day into the heart of God, who, coming into the Garden on that evening so long ago, knew that everything was forever altered, that sin was now a fixed reality upon the earth. He came knowing that punishing the sin would break his heart and claim his child. Romans 5:12 teaches us this dismal fact about the sin in the Garden –"and in this way death came to all men, because all sinned." To be there on the day when sin begins is a horrible position to be in; to see, as it were, one drop of ink staining a bowl of pure water black, to see sin making its devious and unwelcome entrance, corrupting us all.

Now, I reacted to my son's sin the way I did because I had been raised with a healthy Biblical respect for sin. I knew that our sin comes from our first parents; that we all have a sinful nature and that Christ died for our sins. This is a fundamental and traditional (i.e. orthodox) teaching of the church. "I believe in the forgiveness of sins," the creeds declare, for sins do exist and the can and must be forgiven. How did I know these things? I knew them because they had been pointed out to me; I had been informed by my Christian parents that I had fallen short of God's standard of optimal righteousness. I was disobedient. Romans 3:23 declares that I am not alone – "for all have sinned and fall short of the glory of God…" We do not come close to God's standard, his righteous Law.

Sin is lawlessness. It happens when we break laws, ignore laws or create false laws out of the faulty resources of our sinful hearts. Paul speaks to this in Romans 7 when he writes, "Yet if it had not been for the law, I would not have known sin." He goes on expound on the conflict this stirs up in our lives; the conflict between the fact that the law shows us the right thing to do, but our sinful nature always seems to pick the wrong thing to do. He concludes that only the love of Christ can redeem us from this maddening conflict.

The Law (consisting of the Ten Commandments and their auxiliaries as given to Moses and recorded in Exodus and Leviticus), is a standard of righteousness, and as such, it is a guidebook for correct behavior. The message that comes across from the Law is one of: "live this way and you will be blessed." Moses reiterates this truth again and again in his farewell speech in the book of Deuteronomy – obeying the laws are essential to living the good life, the life which we were all meant to live. But what really happened? What influence did the Law ultimately have?

Instead of pointing out how great things could be, it only showed how terrible we are. Back in Romans 7, Paul says that the sinfulness pointed out by the Law "produced death in me through what was good, so that through the commandment sin might become utterly sinful." James says that if one "keeps the whole law, but fails in one point has become accountable for all of it." (James 2:10) So the Law, intrinsically good as it is (for it is spiritual and comes from God) plays the ominous role of lifting up an insurmountable standard of righteousness and holiness. It sets forth rules we cannot keep, for they were broken long ago. As sinners, it lies beyond our power to obey these rules on our own.

In Galatians 3:24, Paul says "the Law was put in charge to lead us to Christ." It was established by God to point out our need for a Savior. The sins from which we need so desperately to be saved have come into sharp focus through the overpowering lens of God's holy law. The Law made us see our sin and long for a solution. In Psalm 51, David declares, "For I know my transgressions and my sin is always before me." No doubt David had broken many commandments, but in reference to the situation he is writing about here, he had broken "Thou shalt not kill" and "thou shalt not covet thy neighbor's wife" specifically.

He asks God to cleanse him and create a clean heart within him because he knows he needs a Savior, not a ritual as prescribed by the Law, for he says, "You do not delight in sacrifice, or I would bring it...the sacrifices of God are a broken spirit." The thing we learn about sin through the vehicle of the Law is that God has a standard, but because of our sin nature we will never achieve it, so we are left with one alternative: to plead for redemption.

But the Law is not just the Mosaic Law, although that appears to be the fullest expression of God's standard. The Law includes what C.S. Lewis, in his book, *Mere Christianity*, calls the "natural law;" the law that everyone seems to know, but cannot seem to keep. (Lewis, p.4,5) It is the standard of right and wrong, which many recognize but not all obey. At the same time, we are distressingly ignorant of the source of our knowledge of this law. In the same way that sin just seems to show up within us, the concept of the difference between right and wrong automatically appears along side of it. Facing this odd fact about himself, Job, who lived long before the Mosaic Law, declared, "My ears heard of you" (he knew about God's righteous standard,) and "therefore, I despise myself," (he also saw his sin nature.)

When we, like Job, look at ourselves – who we really are and why we do (or do not do) what we do, we encounter a curious dichotomy in our person; that is: 1.) We are made in the image of God, and 2.) We are sinners. These two contrasting traits define *who we are* – we are beings in turmoil, for the great war between Heaven and Hell rages on inside of each one of us. Paul says that this situation is truly a war; "For in my inner being I delight in God's Law; but I see another law at work in the members of my body, waging war against the law of my mind and making me a prisoner of the law of sin at work within my members." (Rom. 7:22,23) As Christians, we are conflicted, knowing right, doing wrong, learning truth, but thinking falsehood.

If we look back at that fateful day in Eden when mankind fell into sin, we see that a standard was clearly evident. God gave one command – do not eat the fruit growing on the Tree of the Knowledge of Good and Evil. (Gen. 2:17) It seems like an easy command to obey, for the garden had plenty of other trees loaded with delicious fruit. But sinister forces were at work. The first sinner, Satan, sought miserable company.

Knowing only good, man might not have questioned this command (remember, evil was irrelevant and unknown) had not the serpent brought up the topic. Adam and Eve might have wandered around the Garden for quite a while without giving a second thought to the tree and its implications. But when Satan spoke his lie, which resounded into the goodness of the Garden, something changed. For the first time, something evil came along to stand in contrast to the goodness. For the first time, Adam and Eve caught a glimpse of the opposite of good.

Our sin may have indeed come from outside of us, but we let it in, to our eternal dismay. A standard was raised in Eden, and tempted, we fell short of it. The standard (as all standards do) revealed that something could go wrong or that something is wrong. First of all, it showed what was wrong with Satan – he lied and aspired to God's authority – and secondly, it showed what was wrong with us, for it revealed our concupiscence.

Concupiscence is an old theological term that describes the three great temptations to sin that are brought to bear upon our souls. They are, in the old words of the KJV, "the lust of the flesh, and the lust of the eyes and the pride of life." The Apostle John teaches in 1John 2 that these three things constitute the system upon which our world is based, a diabolical system that goes back to the day of the fall into sin. "For everything in the world – the cravings of sinful man, the lust of his eyes and the boasting of what he has and does – comes not from the Father but from the world. The world and its desires pass away, but the man who does the will of God lives forever." (1John 2:16, 17)

Just as Eve saw that the fruit was beautiful, desired it and knew that it would make her worldly-wise, so we are also tempted in these three ways, albeit with different objects and ideas. The world-system exerts a great influence over us, as the three temptations confront us every day. What will we **see** that we will wrongfully desire? What will we **want** to gratify our bodies or satisfy our selfish tendencies? What will come along to make us unjustly **proud** of ourselves? Each day these desires press down upon our souls. In these moments, we must remember that what categorizes this world is nowhere to be found in heaven. We are going to heaven; as the Apostle John said "the world is passing away" and, in turn, we are passing from the sinful world into a sinless one.

So you see, as Christians in this world, two realities of sin confront us. One is the ancient pervasive system of evil and wickedness that has its grip on the entire planet. The other is the stubborn sin nature in our souls, which are redeemed, but not yet chronologically put to rights. This is the same conflicting situation in which Adam and Eve found themselves as, after the Fall, they "through Eden made their solitary way," as Milton put it.

The human race consisted of two people; the entire race of human beings had sinned. They faced the discouraging prospect that their dismal condition would be passed on to their children. "In sorrow thou shalt bring forth children," (Gen. 3:16, KJV) God had said to Eve, and this sadness would arise not so much from pain in labor, (which is bad enough, I can tell you!) as it would come from the knowledge that her children would be, like herself, sinners, doomed to die.

The Bible says that sin entered the world through Adam and that, as such, it kept on being passed down from generation to generation. It is easy to think of sin as some kind of genetic marker, yet that would only allow for sin in the body, triggered by a biological code. The Bible teaches that sin corrupts the body, but the body itself is not sinful thing. However, it is a biological thing that can be impacted by sin.

Paul instructs us to "not let sin reign in your mortal body so that you obey its evil desires. Do not offer the parts of your body to sin..." (Rom. 6:12,13) Something outside of the body influences us to use our body parts for sin; it is not the body in and of itself that is sinful. Paul uses the words "obey" and "offer," indicating willful actions. The will causes us to make decisions based on our desires. The will is a part of us, in fact, a part of the image of God, and all people participate in it, yet it was somehow permanently altered when Adam and Eve sinned. Something about the will was bent in Eden. We will usually make bad decisions, as it were, for our desires come from a deadly directive.

We often ask ourselves the question "What if sin had not come to earth?" But perhaps a better question would be "What if sin had not entered heaven?" It is almost impossible to imagine how any being, living in a perfect environment, could consciously make any kind of turning away from it. But such is the power of pride, the first sin. "Your heart became proud," Ezek. 28:17 says.

In *Paradise Lost*, John Milton expresses Satan's thoughts in these words:

"...And me preferring
His utmost power with adverse power uppos'd
In dubious battle on the plains of Heaven,
And shook his throne. What though the field be lost?
All is not lost; the unconquerable will ...
That glory never shall his wrath or might
Exhort from me..." (Milton, p. 14)

The point where sin begins is the exact point at which the will begins to turn. A will cannot be pre-set; it must be free to choose. Otherwise, it is not a will at all, but a fixation or an illusion. God created beings with wills for he did not wish to surround himself with robots – angelic or human. The will is the force behind the adoration or the animosity we give to God; we choose to love or plot to hate. Sin bends the will so that it can no longer incline itself toward God.

Sin, even one sin, always has permanent negative results. The first group of beings who sinned, the angels, made one decision – to follow God or to follow Satan – and that one decision sealed their fate. Death -- separation from God -- permanently descended upon the evil ones.

Likewise, sin, and thereby death, resulting from Adam's decision, came permanently to all people. "Therefore, just as sin entered the world through one man, and death through sin, and in this way death came to all men, because all sinned." (Rom. 5:12) But because people, unlike angels, operate under the constraints of time, sin keeps coming; it keeps passing down to people as they are born. In both cases, everything changes at one particular point, but the way the ensuing consequences are carried out is different for people than for angels. For both, however, sin persists until it is destroyed.

Now, about all we know about the final fate of the sinful angels is that they will be sentenced to death in the Lake of Fire (Mt. 25:41), as is fitting, for the ultimate consequence of all sin is death. All beings were created eternal; eternally we will live or die. We know that God made a way for humans to be redeemed through the sacrifice of his son, Jesus Christ, so that in Christ, people can be carried over the gap existing between them and God.

Sin is the separation, but the Cross is the bridge uniting us with God and the means for making right what went wrong. Col. 2:13 and 14 says, "When you were dead in your sins...God made you alive with Christ. He forgave us all our sins...he took it away nailing it to the cross." The next verse explains that the Cross also proclaimed God's victory over Satan and the evil angels – "And having disarmed the powers and authorities, he made a public spectacle of them, triumphing over them by the cross." The Cross of Christ defeats all sin.

Yet, curiously enough, Christians still sin, and struggle with sin and worry about sin. Redeemed, but not ultimately perfected, we face our biggest challenge in living a life of holiness while in a state of incompleteness. In this condition, sin can still "rule in our earthly members" and "wage war against the soul." How we deal with this conflict is at the heart of what the Gospel teaches us about Christian living – what Christians should do.

I have often observed that Christians generally respond to sin in two very opposite ways: 1.) They fail to see how serious it is, or 2.) They become overly concerned with it. Obviously, sin is one of the facts of the Christian life. Paul's famous statement that he "does what he should not do" can be echoed by all of us. Paul says, "I know that nothing good lives in me, that is in my sinful nature." (Rom. 7:18) The Apostle James declares that "we all stumble in many ways," (James 3:2) and the Apostle John explains this truth – "if we claim to be without sin, we deceive ourselves and the truth is not in us." (1John 1:8)

We all sin; it is no secret. As humans, we still struggle with the tattered remnants of our fallen nature, and our biggest challenge arises when we are forced to deal head-on with it. Will we face sin and correct our behavior, or will we ignore it or downplay it and continue in unhealthy ways?

Some of us are quick to dismiss the reality and results of sin. The Apostle John speaks very forthrightly to people who "claim they have not sinned" by calling them "liars." (1John 1:10) These people try to do away with the reality of sin by pretending that it does not exist -- at least not in their lives. The Apostle Peter mentions people who develop bad habits because they have "forgotten that [they were cleansed] from past sins." (2Pet.1:9) Ananias and Sapphira (Acts 5) took such a casual attitude to the sin of dishonesty that they were unafraid to lie to the Apostle Peter, but afterwards they paid the price when the Holy Spirit struck them dead.

These are examples from the past, which serve as warnings to us, but it is amazing to see how many people in the church today who do not seem to care about their wrongdoings. Little lies, and the passive neglect of Godly things, words of gossip and harmful distractions abound at every turn. When momentarily revealed, they are somehow quickly swept into dusty corners. "All unrighteousness is sin," the Bible declares; (1John 5:17) all shortcomings need to be acknowledged and confessed, for, if they linger, they will grow larger and larger and cause trouble for everyone. Why does the church today "have a form of godliness and deny its power?" (2 Tim. 3:5) I suggest it is because those forgotten sins have added up and built something very much like gunk in a car's engine. Just like a damaged car, the church has no power.

When I was growing up in the church, I remember hearing a great deal of talk about legalism versus grace. Christians felt bogged down by rules and felt that their sins (breaking the rules) were not forgiven. But grace, we were told, sets us free from sin, and living in the freedom of grace, we do not have to feel as if we are in bondage to sin and broken rules. Now, I am not trying to say that the gospel of grace is over-rated or harmful. I feel that the popular conception of grace today has arisen from of lack of understanding.

People who know me are often surprised to hear that even though I was raised in an extremely legalistic church tradition, I never had a bit of trouble grasping the concept of grace. Legalism and grace are not mutually exclusive. Legalism had to do with how we acted, not how we were saved. Legalistic Christians worry more about whether or not they are good Christians, not whether or not they *are* Christians.

The Bible clearly teaches that salvation comes to us by grace through the faith that God gives. (Eph. 2:8,9) God's grace abounds to forgive all our sin, but I think a misunderstanding of this idea (grace lets me live the Christian life without rules) inadvertently led to a false conclusion. People were told that they were saved by a grace sufficient to cover every one of their sins. Sin had been dealt with; but Christians began to see this as "if sin is dealt with, I don't have to deal with it."

Therefore, a laxness developed about sin. The question was posed, "If we live under grace and not the Law, why should we keep laws; or, to what degree should we keep laws?" Then, an attitude of "if we are forgiven, why worry?" developed. In this way, I believe, apathy took over for legalism in the evangelical church.

Influenced by post-modern thinking, Christians are looking for an answer to sin that appeals to them personally. Seeing sins as completely taken care of somehow rids people of any responsibility for sinful actions. Many have chosen this as the form of truth they will follow, even if they do not fully understand it. Sin goes on while believers relax in sloppy grace – once saved, always saved, no worries and no rules.

The opposite fact, that Christians stress over their sins and are overly concerned with them, has become, I feel, less of a problem in the church today, due to the pervasive emphasis placed on grace. But some still struggle in this area. They often think along these lines: by their good actions they are earning points with God, but somehow, their sins are erasing the points as fast as God can put them up.

Consequently, some Christians struggle with an oppressive feeling of condemnation. They do not feel as if they are forgiven from their sins. It is as if they like the idea that God took away the heavy weight of their sin, but they, for some strange and unknown reason, continue to hold on to sin and allow it to weigh them down. They are unable to forgive themselves.

Perhaps they do not grasp the idea of what really happens when we receive salvation from our sins. First, each and every one of our sins, past, present and future sins, go completely away. The "washing of the water through the Word" dissolves them. (Eph. 5:26) Secondly, our old sinful selves die, and God gives us a brand-new spiritual life. We no longer act, think or operate in our old ways, because sin and self-rule are dead and gone. Thirdly, we live in a new dynamic that is worlds apart from the old life. Psalm 103:12 says, "as far as the east is from the west, so far has he removed our transgressions from us."

God's forgiveness changes us completely. If we are holding on to old, tired sins, or fretting over forgiveness we do not feel, it is, no doubt, because our old friends the world, the flesh and the devil have pointed us in the wrong direction. We have been forced to remember what God forgets. This is why God tells us that "his mercies are new every morning," for each and every day, forgiveness begins again.

Remember, Jesus said, "If the Son shall make you free, you will be free indeed," and "there is no fear in love," John explains, "for perfect love casts out fear." As Christians, we are perfectly loved by the Son of God, who by his death and resurrection set us free from sin and death. Forgiven from the power and torment of sin, we rest and walk with God in a life that is unbounded, not bound.

When it comes to the issue of sin, we need to live in the reality of what we know about it, otherwise uncertainties will take over and spread like disease. The solution for both groups – the apathetical sinners, and sinful point-earners – is found by learning to understand the Biblical concepts of forgiveness and confession. 1John 1:9 says "If we confess our sins, he is faithful and just and will forgive us our sins and purify us from all unrighteousness." We confess and God forgives.

Confession is an admission of our wrongdoing. It is stating forthrightly exactly what has been done wrong. It needs to be done with a penitent heart, with feelings of genuine sorrow and regret over the transgression. Just a simple statement of confession can clear the mind and pacify the soul. It is simple, yet profound.

One of the most stirring accounts of confession I have ever read was in an article in *Christianity Today* written by Christian author and speaker, Becky Tirabassi. She tells how, as she traveled around the United States speaking primarily in Christian colleges, she began to make calls for confession. The response was amazing, as in place after place, young people responded by tearfully confessing their sins. Having gone to a Christian college myself, I am not so much surprised that there were sins to confess, but that they had long gone un-confessed. These young Christians, beset in many different ways by the world, the flesh and the devil, were just waiting, longing for someone to come along and remind them, or even tell them, of God's way to reconciliation and peace – the journey of confession.

Young people today, including Christian young people, are participants in the post-modern worldview, where emphasis is placed on how one feels, and what the meaning is, and making personal choices about truth. But confession sidesteps all this by pointing us to one particular point – what exactly have I done wrong? It is the action, not our feelings, with which Christ is concerned. One could beat around the feeling-bush all day, so to speak, without ever getting to the heart of the matter – admitting an actual act to be wrong in the eyes of God. Adjusting our feelings never makes us feel forgiven, only confession does.

Once our sins are spoken of in the presence of God, a great release and freedom descends upon our souls. Figuratively, the ball is kicked out of our court, as God, and God alone, now truly forgives. "Against you, and you only have I sinned," David declares, "...so that you are proved right when you speak and justified when you judge." (Psalm 51:4) In his book, *Confessions*, St. Augustine also quotes from Psalm 51, ("have mercy upon me according to thy great mercy,") and prayerfully observes, "...for Thy name's sake, and in no point deserting what Thou hast begun, supply what is imperfect in me. This then is the fruit of my confession – the confession not of what I have been, but of what I am – in that I confess not only before you, with inward exultation yet trembling, with inward sorrow, yet with hope as well." (p. 175)

St. Augustine believed that confession presupposed a life of confession. Throughout the book, he masterfully paints a picture of the journey of the Christian life in which confession of sin is combined with confession of faith. Our sinful hearts, through the admission of guilt, may only find rest, redemption and restoration in God. "For Thou hast made us for thyself," he writes, "and our hearts are restless till they rest in Thee." (St. Augustine, p. 3)

He goes on to say that when we call out to God, seeking his forgiveness, we are inviting God to come to us. But, (he thinks), if God fills heaven and earth, how can he come to our tiny sinful hearts? It is by grace, Augustine concludes: "The house of the soul is too small to receive thee: let it be enclosed by thee. It is in ruins: do thou repair it." (St. Augustine, p. 5)

Christ at the Center

Only when we, like St. Augustine, realize that grace is life, and not just the spark of life, will we be able to life the way we should. Paul says in Galatians 2:20, 21, "The life I live in the body, I live by faith in the Son of God, who loved me and gave himself for me. I do not set aside the grace of God . . ." He means that in order to live the life of confession or faith, we must operate under the jurisdiction of grace, for when we decide whether or not to do good, it is only by and through grace that anything can be accomplished at all. When we regularly confess sin, we are forgiven, and in a way, in that moment, we experience fresh grace, allowing us to live in peace.

Maybe it our vague familiarity with the Catholic Church's tradition of confession has soured the evangelical church concerning the practice of public confession of sins. The passage from the Catholic Catechism on confession seems to combine Biblical ideas with church traditions. After one confesses their sins to a priest, in keeping with the Church's power "to bind and loose," the priest intercedes for his/her forgiveness. Then the priest prescribes a regimen of penance designed to right the wrongs perpetuated by the sin. (Catechism, p.402 - 407)

Overall, this process appears to require people to make a lot of judgments about the sin. Since it also requires a certain amount to time and effort, perhaps people began to think it not worth their while and, in addition, perhaps they did not think that so many human opinions should be brought to bear upon their sin. And non-Catholics especially may have felt that they did not need to confess their sins to others, because we can all pray for forgiveness on our own.

I feel that in Matt. 18 Jesus was telling his disciples that as leaders (and indeed all leaders) in the coming era of the church they would be called upon to make judgment calls. They could say, for example, "Yes, we feel that such-and-such is sin as the Bible defines it," and then go on to enact discipline as necessary. But as to the specific sin, even when confessed to the people sinned against; must be confessed one-on-one to God, who alone, ultimately, forgives.

In addition, the Bible says we are to "confess your sins to each other and pray for each other;" (James 5:16) and, if we, while worshiping, remember an altercation, we are to "leave your gift there in front of the altar…go and be reconciled to your brother." (Mt. 5:25) We are under obligation to confess sins in the presence of other Christians, as this clears the air, so to speak, and strengthens the ties of fellowship. Secret sins tear down the church; confessed sins build it up.

I think this is the lesson that so powerfully came over the college students I mentioned earlier. They came, they saw their failures, and confessed their sins. By doing so, they received and felt the freedom of grace. So many times we come, we see, but neglect to confess, and continue to feel the depressing condemnation of law. One thing is missing – the simple public statement – "I was wrong."

Now, when our sins are confessed to God, he immediately forgives them, as explained in 1Jn. 1:9: "If we confess our sins, he is faithful and just and will forgive us our sins and purify us from all unrighteousness." The forgiveness God directs toward us, so often unlike ours to our fellow man, is total and it never fails or falls apart. We tend to remember past wrongs, but God forgets when he forgives. In the book of Jeremiah, God makes this promise to Israel, who had greatly sinned against him – "For I will forgive their wickedness and will remember their sins no more." This promise is repeated for us in the New Testament in Heb. 10:17, emphasizing to us that God always forgives and forgets.

If anyone is entitled to hold on to a laundry list of incriminating failures, faults and deceptions, it is a holy, just and omniscient God, but because he loves us, the grace he extends to us is such that our sins are no longer held in his memory. This is grace at its highest, love at its fullest, and hope at its greatest extent. When Mary was told that she would be the mother of the Son of God, her heart did not so much rejoice in fact that the Messiah was finally coming, but in the realization that the mercy of God would be personally given to her. Likewise, the mercy of forgiveness sets our spirits free from the weight of sin, in order that we may rejoice as Mary did.

Salvation For All?

A major issue affecting our view of sin today centers around the questions of: "Who can be saved?" and "How is one saved?" Today's postmodern pluralist view would suggest that all of the world's religions are salvic, that is to say, in some form or another they provide a path to redemption which can exist quite independent of Christianity. (Hick, et.al. p. 17) A faithful follower of another belief system is believed to be able to receive mercy from a loving God.

A less liberal approach to this idea, called inclusivism, basically contends that all religions reveal some sort of saving grace which can be activated by acquiescence to Christ, or the religious acts of those who follow another religion can lay the foundation for receiving the saving benefits of the gospel. (Hick, et.al. p. 96)

Lesslie Newbigin compellingly argues for the inclusivist approach in his book *The Gospel in a Pluralistic Society*, in which he relates that when he was an Anglican missionary in India, he noticed much spiritual awareness and deep religious sincerity among his Indian friends. He became reluctant to believe that all who die in their sins without Christ suffer eternal condemnation. He felt that, as we live our lives in the tension operating between the great love and grace of God and the "appalling sin of the world," we need to become aware that God may have ways to save the lost, no idea of the method of which is given to us in this life. (Newbigin, p.175, 176) In other words, God can work to save the lost in ways unknown to us.

Newbigin also held to a free-will interpretation of salvation; that the grace of God operating in the soul of a man could "evoke some response – however feeble, fitful, and flawed." (Newbigin. p. 175) This groundbreaking view, developed by Newbigin at the end of the modern era, has come to be widely accepted in some evangelical circles today. But pluralistic inclusivism seems to address the idea of salvation over the idea of sin, so the question is raised – what does sin have to do with salvation?

Christ at the Center

The Bible reveals some definite facts about sin and salvation and, at the same time, alludes to truths that now lie beyond our comprehension. First, let's look at what we do know:

1. The Bible considers sin to be a universal condition. Sin came into the world through Adam and Eve's rebellion and was consequently passed on to all human beings. (Rom. 5:12)

2. This internal sin (also called the sin nature) separates us from God, a condition that the Bible calls spiritual death. Eph.2: 1 declares, "You were dead in your transgression and sins in which you used to live..." We initially live our lives in a state of soul-death. The passage in Ephesians goes on to explain that our souls can come alive again through the application of the gospel message – "God made us alive with Christ."

3. People can be led to the knowledge of God through the revelation of nature and through the human conscience and reason. Romans 1:19 and 20 say that "what may be known about God is plain to them...God's invisible qualities...have been clearly seen, being understood from what has been made..." Knowing about God, however, does not necessarily constitute salvation.

4. Sinful people generally do not seek God because their sins draw them away from God. (Ps. 53:3 – "everyone has turned away, they have together become corrupt.") Jesus, however, came to earth "to seek and save those who were lost." (Luke 19:10) He is the one who ultimately seeks sinners, but sinners may feel drawn to God – "no one can come to me, unless the Father who sent me draws him." (John 6:44)

5. God has commissioned Christians to spread the gospel of salvation from sin to every place and person on the planet. Redeemed people, interacting with sinful people, spread the message of salvation. Our commandment to do so was given in Christ's last statement while here on earth: "Go and make disciples of all nations." (Mt. 28:19)

Now, let's look at some of the biblical ideas which are harder to comprehend:

1. Isaiah prophesizes that nations other than Israel, who do not know God, will be drawn to God (Isa. 55), but this could simply mean that that gospel would go out to the nations of the world after the death and resurrection of Christ. This passage

also contains the phrase "my thoughts are not your thoughts, neither are your ways my ways, declares the Lord." It is always wise to remember that we do not know every aspect of God's plan to save the lost, but this should not stop us from spreading the good news whenever we can.

2. God is working to reconcile the world to himself, to right the wrongs, as it were, to bring people back into good relationships with him, (2Cor.5), and in so doing he is "not counting men's sins against them." This portrays how God is forgiving the sins of those who come to him through Christ, for "the blood of Jesus Christ cleanses us from all sin." (1John) Christians are said to be God's "ambassadors" in this endeavor, but the questions arises – can God reconcile sinners without the ministry of saints? I have heard stories of people coming to faith through a vision of Christ or by the ministry of angels. God is certainly able to reveal himself in these ways.

3. In Romans 11, Paul says that even though Israel rejected the person and message of Jesus in New Testament times, they will eventually accept Jesus as their Messiah. At that point, "all Israel will be saved," and God will "take away their sins." Will God forgive the sins of an entire nation? Paul references this as a "mystery," a spiritual truth that cannot be fully comprehended by us while we are here on earth.

So the question we are faced with is this: What will God do with sinners in the time period after Christ who did not get a chance to hear the gospel and, in addition, what will happen to the people who lived before Christ and had no contact with the Jews? I believe that this is a question that we can only raise and not answer.

The question revolves more around sin than salvation. In order to be with God forever, one's sins must be eradicated. As pluralism may wrongly suggest, people do not merely need be saved from themselves. No, they must be saved from sin, and the salvation from sin only comes through Jesus Christ. "There is no other name under heaven," Peter asserts, "by which we must be saved." (Acts 4:12)

God has every miracle at his disposal with which to save the lost, miracles that he may choose to use in ways that we do not understand -- but this truth runs through it all -- all people who are saved and will be saved will be redeemed through Christ alone. When reflecting on this great truth, Paul wrote a poem of praise, found at the end of Romans 11. "How unsearchable his judgments," he says, and "who has known the mind of the Lord?" He triumphantly declares, "For from him and through him and to him are all things." God alone knows the extent of his grace.

Just as there was a day when sin began, there will be a day when sin ends. The prophet Daniel writes that a time will come "to put an end to sin." (Dan. 9:24) Jesus said that the gospel, the solution to the problem of sin, "will be preached in the whole world, as a testimony to all nations, and then the end will come." (Mt. 24:14) David predicts, "The wicked shall be turned into Hell, and all the nations that forget God." (Ps. 9:17 KJV)

God will forgive and forget. Indeed, he will wipe out the sins of those who receive his grace in Christ, but, by contrast, some will forget him. Even though the truth of God has been clearly revealed to mankind, some will refuse to see. They will go to their sorry and disastrous end, unknown and unremembered by God.

In his book, *The Jesus I Never Knew*, Philip Yancey writes, "Jesus never met a disease he could not cure... But he did meet skeptics he could not convince and sinners he could not convert. Forgiveness of sins requires an act of will on the receiver's part, and some who heard Jesus' strongest words about grace and forgiveness turned away unrepentant." In the final analysis, salvation requires a willingness to be saved. Most who turn away from God do so because they do not wish to seek him, and even those who are very much in the dark about God remain there because they are enslaved and deceived by Satan, the would-be ruler of this fallen world.

But those who are known by God will come to the joyful place where are sins are forgotten by God and are buried forever in a deep, deep sea on the day when sin ends. This is, as Peter said, "the coming of the salvation that is ready to be revealed in the last time." We call it redemption, the day when the old world is abolished and everything begins again, perfectly free, perfectly good, never to fail again.

Bibliography – Sin

Lewis, C. S. *Mere Christianity and The Screwtape Letters: Complete in One Volume*. revised and amplified ed. San Francisco: HarperCollinsPublishers, 2000. Print.

Milton, John. *Paradise Lost*. New York: Barnes and Noble Books, 2004. Print.

Tirabassi, Becky. "Young, Restless, and Ready for Revival." *Christianity Today* 28 Dec. 2007: n. pag. Web. 18 May 2010. http://christianitytoday.com/ct/2007/december/32.46.html

Augustine, Saint. *Confessions: Books I-XIII*. Indianapolis: Hackett Publishing Company, Inc., 1993. Print.

Catechism of the Catholic Church. New York: Doubleday, 1995. Print.

Hick, John, Clark H. Pinnock, Alister E. McGrath, R. Douglas Geivette, and W. Gary Phillips. *Four Views on Salvation in a Pluralistic World*. Grand Rapids, MI: Zondervan, 1996. Print.

Newbigin, Leslie. *The Gospel in a Pluralistic Society*. Grand Rapids, MI: Wm. B. Eerdmans Publishing Co., 1989. Print.

Yancey, Philip. *The Jesus I Never Knew*. Grand Rapids, MI: Zondervan, 1995. Print.

Chapter 8-FALL . . . AND REDEMPTION: What's Wrong and How It Gets Right

"For as in Adam all die, **so in Christ** all will be made alive." 1Cor.15:22

In order to understand what happened and why at the time of the fall of man, we need to review a couple of fundamental truths about creation. The first truth is that **time** was *created*. It has a beginning; God speaks into the void and time instantly proceeds, unrelenting, ever forward. Time has a middle, or turning point, which is the death and resurrection of Jesus Christ. Finally, time will end when "death is swallowed up in victory" and time flows back into eternity. If one imagines eternity as a circle, time is a line within the circle, or perhaps a line segment, since lines, according to geometry (I think!) go infinitely in opposite directions. So, we experience a time-line in eternity. The eternal God surrounds it, overshadows it and knows "the end from the beginning."

As it has often been said, time is history, spelled "His-story." Part of God's eternity is time, so he sees everything as **now**; we see events as past, present or future. Therefore, when we talk about the events of the Creation, the Fall, and Redemption, we see or anticipate the passage of time. God does not; for him it is all part of the whole, an immediate and eternal reality. We feel disjointed because we are separating things now, but one day all things will be reunited and made whole – as Colossians 1:20 says, Christ will "reconcile to himself all things."

If we take anything that has happened in history, we can put it into one of the three main stops along the time line created at the beginning; that is, events are related to either: 1.) Creation, 2.) The Fall, or 3.) Redemption. This theme is repeated throughout the Bible. Man is created sinless, he sins and falls from goodness; he is redeemed and can be restored. Time keeps repeating these processes over and over, although within the context of our lifetimes, most of the emphasis of the lessons of history is placed on the fall and its consequences. But if we want to experience life as God intended, we need to be aware of the reality of all three states. As a human being, I proceed from a perfect creation, I am a victim of the fall into sin so it discolors everything I do, but Christ has redeemed me by his blood, and this redemption has built into it an eternal dynamic waiting to be fulfilled in me.

Another thing to remember about Creation is that it was *whole* – complete, perfect (in the sense of being as good as it could be) and done in a certain way so that everything *worked*. Mankind, at the time of their making, constituted the absolute epitome of all the amazing works of God. As perfect, complete and good beings, they lived in a perfect, complete and good world. Mankind was made in the image of God, as revealed in Gen.1: 26, when God said, "Let us make man in our image, in our likeness."

Although our physical makeup has a lot to do with this, (Jesus, as God, had a human body just like ours, or, more precisely, ours is just like his,) the *imago dei* also precludes our spiritual side. We have souls – a spiritual dimension, and furthermore, we have intellect, something which somehow connects the two. We also recognize our own being, we are self-aware, and we possess emotions even as our Creator God does. The image of God, as originally given, was great. God had made a physical/spiritual being, whose chief end was to "enjoy him forever," to reflect the glory of God back upon him. Most profoundly, we were to be friends of God as we freely communicated with him and shared in his love.

In Ecclesiastes 3:11, Solomon shares the most profound truth known about the nature of mankind; "he has also set eternity in the hearts of men," that is to say, we have a connection to God which was built into us at the time of Creation. The connection was physical, mental, emotional, and spiritual. We could, in innocence and perfection look upon the face of God and see ourselves reflected there. Certainly, man fell from a great, great height.

But before we visit the Garden of Eden, the scene of the fall of mankind, we need to establish a precedent concerning the ones who were the first to fall: Lucifer and his angelic followers. The Bible doesn't say much about it, but from 2Pet. 2:4, we know it is an accepted fact – "God did not spare angels when they sinned." The most direct statement on the topic is found in the words of Jesus, "I saw Satan fall as lightning from heaven." This is quite possibly the event referred to in Isa. 14:12: "how art thou fallen from Heaven, oh Lucifer, Son of the Morning!" The account that follows tells of a powerful being who sets out in pride to exalt himself above God, and who is consequently thrown down to earth by God.

The book of Job, the oldest story in the Bible, precludes that Satan roams the earth, for in Job 1:7, Satan tells God that he has been wandering about on the earth. Two things seem to set the scene for Gen. 3: 1.) God calls his creation complete, good and without fault, and it appears that 2.) Satan sees this and chooses to be filled with pride instead of glorifying God. When he does this, some of the other angelic beings choose to abandon God and follow him.

Almost as if he is the director of a play, God sets the scene in the Garden of Eden for a drama to be played out which will determine the destiny of man. Some argue that Eden and the events that took place there are allegorical. They merely represent man's digression into sin and out of goodness. But I think Eden was **real**, although it was certainly very *different*. Eden seems to be a sort of heaven-on-earth, a place where the physical and the spiritual crossed in some way now unknown to us. Just because talking snakes and trees of power are not usually a part of our everyday lives doesn't mean they never could have existed. Eden was, I think, a sort of "test case."

God, being sovereign, is free to set things up as he wills. The nation of Israel, for example, was such an entity, as Isa. 43:1 reveals, "But now this is what the Lord says – he who created you, O Jacob, he who formed you, O Israel." The chapter goes on in detail to explain how Israel's history is full of specific events that reveal God's plan not only for Israel, but also through them for the whole world as well. These events take place because Israel is God's special tool to reveal God's redemption to the rest of the nations. Eden seems to have had a similar purpose.

We are told in Gen. 2: 8, "the Lord God planted a garden in the east, in Eden..." God put together a kind of laboratory/arboretum, the size of which is unknown to us. God set man down to live and work in this beautiful, unique place. Eden was a platform for displaying the perfection of God, but it was different, it was singular. Here, Adam sets off on his God-given quest to be a farmer/naturalist; he cultivates the garden and names the animals. We do not know how long Adam lived this way, on his own, yet with God.

As God brought the animals to him to receive their names, however, one glaring discrepancy came to light. Adam found that he was alone in the world for he had no female counterpart. In response to man's need, God creates woman, beautiful and self-assured, the last and crowning glory of all created things. Now Adam and Eve are united by God in perfect communication and purpose, and the world is theirs.

Once again, we have no way of knowing how long Adam and Eve lived in their perfect environment; a beautiful, unique place, Eden, within a perfect cosmos. Maybe it took them a long time to find the center of the garden where the mighty trees grew, but I am sure that once they did, they were filled with awe – these were no ordinary trees. In fact, the tree of life appears again, eternal, on the banks of a river in Heaven. "On each side of the river stood the tree of life, bearing 12 crops of fruit, yielding its fruit every month. And the leaves of the tree are for the healing of the nations." (Rev. 22:2) At the close of time, a tree possessing the power of God's creative life will represent healing and eternal life for all peoples of the world.

But something else moves in the trees of the Garden, something sinister and real – Satan has overcome the snake as the paradigm shifts in Paradise. Adam and Eve no doubt knew they had come to a turning point, a momentous day, an encounter with destiny. No wonder Eve sensed a longing, a curiosity, a question hanging, mysteriously in the air. Sometimes I'm afraid we do not give Eve enough credit – as God's good creation, I'm sure she was brilliant, but she never had heard a lie; she had never thought of anything other than the truth.

Eve knew the truth, for she had spoken with God. Remember, every word which God speaks is never forgotten; they are impressed eternally upon the mind, as Ps. 119:89 says,

"Your word, O Lord is eternal; it stands firm in the heavens." So what did Eve do, if she knew the truth so well? She turned; and as she did so, she heard the first words of contradiction, "Did God really say . . ."

What a strange question the snake enquired of Eve – Were they excluded from eating fruit from any tree growing in the Garden? Eve knew God's exact words as given in Gen. 2:16,17, "You are free to eat from any tree in the Garden, but you must not eat from the tree of the knowledge of good and evil, for when you eat of it you will surely die." Where had the snake been? Was he unaware of God's mandate? How odd this question was, echoing loudly, barely discordant, upon the stillness of the perfect truth she had always known. Startled, she turned a little more – Wait! (she felt), and then she said, "We may eat fruit from the trees in the Garden, but God did say, 'You must not eat fruit from the tree that is in the middle of the Garden, and you must not touch it, or you will die!" (Gen. 3:3)

So far, so good: Eve knows better than to eat the fruit that God, by his Word, had forbidden. We shouldn't be so hard on Eve for throwing in the "don't touch it" part. After all, she possessed reason, she could think about things, and clearly, she thought that it would be impossible to eat what one did not touch. I believe that here it is revealed that mankind did indeed have free will. They knew enough about the truth to think about it. They knew they could analyze God's words and apply them to their situation. They could choose because they could reason.

Now the serpent/Satan utters his great lie, the first and ultimate lie, "You shall not surely die." How these words reverberated, like a jangle of drums, across the quiet meadow. Oh, Adam and Eve knew what death was. Life in the Garden depended on death, how else would they know to fear it? By contrast, their lives were precious to God for the *imago dei* was emblazoned upon their souls – they knew they were eternal. The great lie rose as a cloud to dim the brightness of this fire – not to surely die, not to be as the mouse caught and consumed by the cat, not to be scattered as fallen leaves beneath a tree!

Still Eve turned to hear these misleading words, "For God knows that when you eat of it, your eyes will be opened and you will be like God, knowing good and evil." Now no question remains, for the air of Eden is alive with unbearable discord, the overwhelmingly loud explosion of a further lie. Never forget that this first lie was told to a woman, and it has followed her, unrelenting, like a horrible, haunting ghost, through the succession of years – *you will be like God*! Like God, she who bears life may also control life! She can *know* -- oh the power of knowing right from wrong, good from evil; to be the one in possession of a discernment that leads to absolute knowledge – like God, no longer his confidant, but his equal – now here was life in transcendence and all she had to do was reach out and touch it!

Turning to face the tree, even as the wind in the leaves whispered, "Beware," she sees the fruit and thinks three mind-shattering thoughts. These three ideas will change the course of history, for they constitute the foundation of all evil: 1.) I can determine what's good for me, 2.) 'Looking good' trumps 'being good', and 3.) By my own reason, I can decide what is true. Thousands of years later, the Apostle John reveals the pervasive implications which came from Eve's faulty line of reasoning, "For everything in the world – the cravings of sinful man, the lust of his eyes and the boasting of what he has and does – comes not from the Father but from the world. The world and its desires pass away, but the man who does the will of God lives forever." (1John 2:16,17)

Yes, God's first command was truth, and disobedience to it results in death, a passing away into oblivion, as the forbidden fruit consumes us with eternal emptiness. The temptation in the Garden was not merely about plucking a piece of fruit and eating it. It was about the lies that were told about the fruit, about the faulty reasoning that went far beyond the fruit into questioning the words of God, which resulted in an act of willful disobedience. If Adam and Eve questioned these simple words of God, there would be no end to what they could denounce and doubt, and so it has been. For the last time Eve turns (she has come 180 degrees now,) and stands with her back towards God. Against her own better judgment, she touches the fruit, picks it and eats it. Paradise goes silent.

But what about Adam? Much conjecture, everything from "co-conspirator" to "innocent victim," has been made over his role. In Genesis 3:17, God declares him guilty –"you...ate from the tree about which I commanded you, 'You must not eat of it.'" In Romans 5:12-14, Paul says, "sin came into the world through one man," and then goes on to refer to this act as the "transgression of Adam." But, later in 1Timothy 2:14, Paul says that Adam was "not deceived." So what did Adam do?

If we look carefully at the account of Genesis 3, one thing stands out about Adam's behavior. He didn't say or do anything; he was silent. I think this is significant because in the rest of the passage, before and after the eating of the fruit, several specific conversations are recorded. The snake talks to Eve, Eve talks to the snake, Adam and Eve talk to God, and God delivers precise edicts to Adam, Eve and the snake. Why is Adam silent, if he is not fooled by Satan's lies? By rights, he should have been shouting, "Don't eat it Eve, remember God's command!"

This is just a thought, but maybe Adam's sin was silence, or apathy. He just failed to do the right thing when confronted with a crisis. Genesis 3:6 plainly stated that Adam was with Eve, so he heard every word of the fateful dialogue between Satan and his wife. He could have said something or grabbed Eve by the hand and pulled her away before the fruit was picked and eaten. As James 4:17 says, "Anyone, then, who knows the good he ought to do, and doesn't do it, sins."

Between Adam and Eve we see the two great categories of sin – the sins of commission and the sins of omission, that is, the sins willfully and deliberately committed, and the ones resulting from neglect and self-adsorption. Eve did the wrong thing; Adam failed to do the right thing. Yet, they both ended up doing the same thing as they disobeyed God's command.

Together guilty, they immediately become aware of their nakedness and feel ashamed. Imagine their surprise at this unexpected consequence, a feeling they couldn't account for or reference, a guilty conscience. They turn away from the tree in a panic, the fruit forgotten, searching desperately for an alibi. The snake quietly slithers away, going to hide for the few hours of secrecy still afforded to it.

Christ at the Center

Picture the scene in the Garden that afternoon. The sun is hotter, too hot, perhaps. The insects swarm, no longer delightful, the wind merely annoys. Together they decide to sew fig leaves together to make clothes. I can just imagine this activity! To this day, men and women have totally different ideas about how to do things. No doubt, this little sewing session was the stage for the world's first argument!

But in the evening, faithfully, God comes. Even in their darkest hour, God does not abandon Adam and Eve. He calls out to them, wishing to restore the broken connection, all the while knowing the infinite pain he himself will suffer to reconnect humanity with Heaven. "Where are you?" God inquires. This question comes in one way or another to us all. Joshua told the Israelites to "choose for yourselves this day whom you will serve," (Josh. 24:15), and Jesus remarked, "He who is not with me is against me." (Mt. 12:30) The moment of truth comes, the "jig is up," the consequences for sin are about to be doled out.

First, the snake, as an animal, is debased; from being "more crafty than any of the wild animals" it descends to being "cursed...above all livestock and all wild animals." Now it will have no legs and will crawl upon the dusty ground. Women will forever be frightened by snakes, and snakes will have cause to be frightening.

God presses his point further however, addressing the evil being who possessed the snake and used it as his degrading tool. The power and influence of Satan may bring harm, misery and sorrow to mankind, but one person, born from a woman, will purposefully and finally defeat him by crushing his head, as it were, therein bringing death to death itself. This is the first promise of redemption.

Secondly, the woman is told that two things will forever after mark her existence: 1.) Pain in childbirth, and 2. Subordination to her husband. Remember, it was desire for control that swayed Eve's mind. In pride, she had seized upon the opportunity afforded her by the snake to rule her world. Once deceived, she tried to gain the advantage in the fight to the top, a fight that never should have begun. Humiliated, she now finds her life spinning out of control.

Thirdly, Adam is told that the free abundance of the Garden is now lost to him. He must continually work and work hard to cultivate plants and produce food. The ground itself will be uncooperative; some plants will mutate into stubborn and vile weeds, hindering his efforts. Not only that, but this very soil of hardship will open up to receive him when he dies. He will ultimately return to the dry dust of his genesis. As Solomon mournfully observed, "all come from the dust, and to dust all return." (Ecc. 3:20) Imagine the dreary cloud that fell on Adam and Eve's hearts as they grasped the bitter reality of God's prophetic words – "for when you eat of it, you will surely die."

Finally, Adam and Eve are exiled from the Garden, God's special and perfect portion of Heaven on Earth. They are estranged from the heavenly sphere within the context of this life. From now on, everything in life is only physical and cursed at that. They leave Paradise behind, never to return on their own, for the way is closed off by a mighty angel's flaming sword.

But as they walk away, Adam and Eve wear the skins of a sacrificed lamb. The shame of their nakedness is covered, but shame still tears at their hearts. The sacrifice of another lamb, the Lamb of God, is destined to remove that shame forever and reopen the gates to Paradise. The story of the world now turns to redemption – "For as in Adam all die, so now in Christ shall all be made alive." (1Cor5. 15:22)

After Adam and Eve leave the Garden, sin continues to characterize their lives and the lives of their descendants for many generations over a long period of time. Genesis 3-5 describe man's complete and utter decent into evil until God becomes so weary of mankind's disgusting actions that he sends the judgment of the Flood. Nothing gives a more accurate description of the true fallen nature of man than his state before the Flood – "every inclination of the thoughts of his heart was only evil all the time." (Gen. 6:5)

The question is often raised, "Why did God create a world where evil, pain, suffering and death could occur?" If God is perfect and good, why are imperfect and bad things happening all around us every day? Something is very wrong and doesn't sit right with us; perhaps it is because of our sinful, twisted viewpoint that we blame God (who has never sinned) for these discrepancies and not ourselves who sin daily.

We want perfection and lash out at God for not providing it. We want to be happy and understand our existence, but not being assured of these things, we demand an explanation from God. It seems that something used to be right, but now it has all gone horribly wrong. I like the way Peter Kreeft and Ronald Tacelli describe this discomforting feeling. "We behave as if we remember Eden and can't recapture it, like kings and queens dressed in rags who are wandering the world in search of their thrones." (Kreeft, p. 135) We seem to remember Paradise and long to live there again. In the meantime, we sulk around, mad at God for conditions we have caused.

And then, on top of these questions, we add the real clincher, "Why did God create us with free will if we were going to end up choosing to sin?" Then we get all hot and bothered about being-or-not-being-robots, when all along it is our free will that even allows us to debate these issues! Yes, we had free will, and yes, we made the wrong choice, but God had made a way out of the mess that brings us back to him. All of this, the good and the bad, is the reality of redemption.

Let me give you an illustration that may help us think through the "because of free will man sins – and how can God allow that – so how can he be good" problem. This illustration is from my own experience, and like all illustrations, it may fall short, but I have a point. I am a quilter, and over approximately the last 30 years I have made so many quilts that I have lost track of how many I've made and who all has one; (however, those who do not have a quilt like to remind me of their plight!)

I like to say that I am a *real* quilter, but not a purist. I sew the little pieces of fabric together with my sewing machine, but I do all the quilting **by hand**. (In case you are unaware, quilting means sewing the 3 quilt sections – pieced top, batting, and backing – together by making tiny, tiny stitches (by hand!) through all 3 layers.) I have spent hundreds of hours and taken thousands of tiny stitches in order to create my special quilt-creations. I pour a lot of myself into them, and spend a lot of the quilting time praying for the person who will receive the quilt.

Christ at the Center

When I first started quilting, I decided that my quilts would be used in my home and by my children, and not stored away or hung on walls. In taking this position, I conceded that my quilts could wear out and bad things could happen to them. A child could spill hot chocolate all over one, or the cat, taking a comfortable nap, could leave one covered with cat-hair. The quilt on my bed, the one I am sitting on (purists never sit on quilts) as I write this is 20 years old. Pieces are wearing thin and colors are fading, but I have put it on my bed every summer for all these years. Sadly, I may have to retire it at the end of this summer.

When I made the decision to use the quilts, I knew that disasters could occur, and certainly, they have – like the time one of them, (old and on its last legs, fortunately), was used as a bed for a litter of kittens. Now that was a disaster! To make the quilts and then allow them to be used was to invite the possibility of problems. But on the other side, we all have enjoyed many hours of warmth and comfort and beauty from the quilts because, in some strange way, they are made with love.

Now, do you see how this is like God and his creation? He makes a beautiful, perfect world. But he takes a risk – man can choose. A world where no-sin exists is also a world where sin can exist. (Kreeft, p.51) So, tempted, man fell and a disaster occurred. If this were all we knew of the situation, it would have been a total disaster, the end of everything.

We often forget that God himself is intimately acquainted with the pain and suffering caused by the fall. In Gen. 6, as God observes the evil on the earth he is grieved that he ever made mankind, and "his heart was filled with pain." Jesus mourns over Jerusalem as he senses the crushing trauma caused by the evil influences there. Sin broke God's heart, and it still does. Yet, God loves and the power of his love is far greater than the power of sin, death, suffering or pain. This love is freely given to us; God does not hide it nor keep it secret, for it is through redemption the questions we ask about sin and its consequences are resolved.

Christ at the Center

In order to solve the problem of sin and man's hopeless condition, God sent Jesus, his Son, to bear the penalty of sin, death. He died on the cross to bring about redemption. Redemption cost God dearly in the death of his Son. When we question the pain, suffering and death in this world, we must bear in mind that God suffered and he was innocent. We, perhaps, deserve our woes, but Jesus did not.

He did what he did out of his great love for us, to bring about God's greatest longing and desire – to have the world reconciled to him. Ephesians 2 explains that we were "dead in [our] transgressions and sins," (because that sin in the Garden sent the penalty of death crashing down on us all,) but due to God's overwhelming love, God has now made us alive with Christ through grace and has "raised us up in Christ."

This truth is central to our life in Christ, so, to seal the amazing story of redemption upon the heart of every Christian, Jesus instituted the practice of baptism. It represents our death in sin and our hopeless state as we are held under the water. Yet while there, we are covered by the water in the same way as we are covered by the blood of Christ, "shed for the remission of sins," for just as water makes us clean, so Christ's blood "cleanses us from all unrighteousness." Then we come up from the water, dripping wet and *changed*, showing that we are already resurrected to live an unending life with Christ.

Baptism is called a **seal;** we are in a way impressed with it indelibly upon our hearts. From the day we are baptized, we are all living symbols of redemption. Once baptized, we, as Paul said, "bear on my body the marks of Jesus." We show the world our identity in Christ when we live lives totally devoted to him, completely drowned, yet completely set free to finally live.

After Genesis 3, the Bible becomes the story of redemption-in-time; that is, how God arranges events in this world to bring about the coming of the Christ, the redeemer. Time is really all about the story of redemption. Gal. 4:4,5 says, "when the *time* had fully come, God sent his Son...to *redeem* those under the law." We get to wondering, however, why God took such a long time to get around to sending Jesus, and why it now seems to be taking so long for the world's final redemption to be put in place.

Christ at the Center

Why didn't God just send Jesus to die the very day Adam sinned? Why weren't things restored to perfection *as soon as possible*?

God created time; he had a plan for it, complete in every way from day one. God always sees time as a whole within eternity; he sees it in its entirety and from every angle, something we cannot do. Solomon points this out in Ecc. 3, when he proposes that even though we have this sense of the eternal within us, try as we might, we cannot comprehend it. A disconnect has come between our perspective on life and God's. We keep seeing things vanish into time as if they were falling into a deep pit.

As Solomon goes on to say, by contrast, "everything God does will endure forever – nothing can be added to it and nothing taken from it." Then he answers the question that naturally follows, "Why? Why does God work that way?" Solomon answers, "God does it so that men will revere him." You see, everything in our lives, everything in history, as a whole, is all about all the glory belonging to and going to God.

Since he can use time as he wishes, he has reasons for causing redemption to unfold within the confines of time. As far as the actual fact of redemption is concerned, it is an eternal reality of God, for Jesus is called the Lamb slain from the foundation of the world. Adam's sin was always taken care of, as far as God is concerned. In Titus 1:2, Paul says that his faith was promised before the world began.

In Hebrews 2:9, 10, we learn that the death of Jesus for all mankind brings "many sons into glory," but Jesus had to be human in order to be a suitable sacrifice, and therefore he had to be born as a man, becoming our "brother," so to speak. God chose to have this event unfold in the passage of time, coming to fulfillment at exactly the right time. The "many sons" are those to be found in the "great multitude that no one could count" which the Apostle John sees in his vision of heaven in Rev. 7. They come from "every nation, tribe, people and language," and they cry out, "Salvation belongs to our God who sits on the throne and to the Lamb."

They sing about redemption, and, clearly, God wishes for many people to be there to sing the redemption song, many people from many time periods and places. As God created this world with myriad natural diversity, so also heaven will be filled many different people who are his "new creations in Christ," who bring eternal glory to him as the creation does today.

Now, let's go back to the Garden of Eden, God's specially created place where he placed Heaven on Earth. Nothing that God creates is ever truly lost, (unless a choice is made to turn away from God.) Eden will one day be restored, but then it will fill the Earth. "The earth will be full of the knowledge of the Lord as the waters cover the sea." (Isa. 11:9)

When God created he knew sin would happen, however, he also knew that the final outcome would be better than, much greater than, man's original state, good and complete as it was. Somehow, in a way now only known to God, redemption would bring about the greatest glory. It is as if some long-lost pretty thing, ground down and ruined by the dust, will someday be found, but found to be beautiful, precious and incredibly valuable. You see, through faith, we behold this treasure today. It is very real, yet somehow just beyond our grasp.

1Corinthians 15 describes how this ultimate reality will be played out. Adam and Eve's sin truly did bring about our death and separation from God. We could no longer walk hand in hand with God and behold his face, so clearly reflected in our own. This reflection was dimmed and clouded over, as mankind was estranged from his Creator. We hold this fragile image in our human bodies, which die and undergo decay.

However, as partakers of the *imago dei*, we have souls, destined to live forever. When Christ died for us, and we, by faith, accept this gift of salvation, he first liberates our fallen souls. We are set free to live a new spiritual life. But redemption was not designed to end there; our bodies will be redeemed. Although we enter the grave as sorry mortals, overtaken by the disaster caused by death, we will, by God's power, emerge from the grave as immortal victors, forever changed to bring the greatest glory to God. We are "sown a mortal body and raised a heavenly body," (v. 44) and "just as we have borne the likeness of the earthly man, so shall we bear the likeness of the man from heaven." (v. 49)

It's not only us who will be changed, but every created thing will also be renewed because sin touched everything. Romans 8:19 tells us that the "creation waits in eager anticipation for the sons of God to be revealed." Outside of any choice on its part, (for man chose to sin,) the natural world was forced into a weary cycle of decay, corruption and death. In this upside-down state it actually "groans" for its redemption and ours. The original creation will one day be obliterated by fire (2Pet. 3:10), but something new and better will arise from the ashes. Redemption will not only make things right, it will make things better.

As mortals, we cannot comprehend this new world. Things will operate under an entirely new paradigm. In fact, the Biblical authors only mention it – they seem to just throw the idea out there – "But in keeping with his promise, we are looking forward to a new heaven and a new earth, the home of righteousness." (1Pet. 3:13) Incomprehensible, hidden, known only by faith, the redemption calls us, "You are going home," it whispers, home to Heaven, where we will once again walk with God and forever behold his face.

Bibliography – Fall and Redemption

Miller, Donald. *Searching for God Knows What*. Nashville, TN: Thomas Nelson, 2004. Print.

Kreeft, Peter, and Ronald K. Tacelli. *Handbook of Christian Apologetics*. Downer's Grove, IL: InterVarsity Press, 1994. Print.

Christ at the Center

Part 3 – Who We Become

Chapter 9-THE CHRISTIAN: In Christ and Christ In Us

"Therefore, if anyone is **in Christ** he is a new creation; the old has gone, the new has come!" 2Cor.5:17

Every year the Pew forum on religion and public life conducts a survey on the religious beliefs of Americans. The respondents are broken down into groups falling along the denominational lines within Christianity, as well as broader groups such as the major world religions and cultic movements. The 2008 survey revealed that a great many people, (Evangelicals included), express very unclear and ambivalent ideas about their faith. For example, there is a strong indication across the board that many feel that there are many ways to God, and other faiths, besides one's own, may lead to God. Members of religious faiths also express the surprising notion that there may not even be a God after all! They also contend that the tenants of their respective religions are up for personal interpretation; a perception which I like to call (in relation to evangelicals) "Christian relativism."

So, what is a Christian, then, or who is a Christian in this day of religious pluralism? What sets them apart from their global neighbors? Is there anything left of the radical differences between them and those surrounding them, which sent them, in ancient times, rejoicing to their deaths? Is fuzzy Christianity worthy of the name "Christian" at all?

From the very day the church began – the day of Pentecost – Christians were noticeably different. When people suddenly started speaking in languages they had never learned, it was certainly startling. (Not to mention, in addition to that, the sight of burning flames of fire hovering over their heads was indeed shocking!) The world sat up and took notice that day – here were individuals who were radically different, distinctively changed, bearers of God Himself. God the Holy Spirit had come to earth, not to visit, but to possess men, to distinguish them from their contemporaries as "God-like." The name "Christian," given to believers early on, means "little Christs." It clearly indicated their unique status as people who belong to God, who have been touched by God, who have somehow taken on Christ-like characteristics.

In 1Peter 2:9-12, Peter is reminding Christians of their position in Christ – "But you are a chosen people, a royal priesthood, a holy nation, a people belonging to God." This rush of metaphor speaks to the overwhelming realization of how amazing it is to be God's child. From nothing, the Christian has been raised to everything. The purpose of this salvation, coming as it does from the heart of God, is to give glory to God, so that the holy nation of Christians will return a never-ending song of praise to God. As Christians share the gospel message with others, more join in the song that will echo around the world until the day Christ returns.

Peter reminds his readers that being a Christian means a distinctive existence of walking against the tide of evil and standing up for truth even when all alone. He encourages Christians to "live such good lives among the pagans that, though they accuse you of doing wrong, they may see your good deeds and glorify God." This passage is prophetic; because for the next 300 years or so, this was the lot of almost every true believer. At that time, many a Christian lived a life of Godly character, was wrongfully accused for it, and eventually died a martyr's death. No confusion existed about who was or who was not a Christian. The way to God was clearly marked and uncompromised. Christians did not die for a good cause; they died for all that was and always will be good.

Writing in the mid-second century, Justin Martyr questioned the civil authorities of his day as to why they were persecuting Christians merely because they were called "Christian." He says that when you think about it, it is a glorious name, a name worthy of high regard. "Indeed, so far at least as one may judge from the name we are accused of, we are most excellent people." He is saying that even if you thought Jesus was just a well-known ex-carpenter who died for his beliefs, even that is worthy of high praise. But if Jesus was more, which indeed he is, then the name is elevated even higher ("the name that is above every name") and those who bear that name are citizens of Heaven along with Christ.

Justin Martyr further argues that Christians would not purposely deny their faith, because they seek to please God, not men, and in this life they are on their way to God. He writes, "For impelled by the desire of the eternal and pure life, we seek the abode that is with God, the Father and Creator of all and hasten to confess our faith…" Christians live in anticipation of a heavenly kingdom, he says, and this longing supersedes any desire to further the interests of earthy kingdoms. Christians will die for Christ in this life, knowing a better life awaits.

In the ancient Church, Christianity was certainly distinctive. Christ's words – "By this all men will know that you are my disciples, if you love one another" (John 13:35) – were an unmistakable mark of distinction. Interestingly enough, their lives in Christ were lived out on ordinary days, in ordinary jobs, moving among common people. They were not persecuted just because they preached on street corners. The testimony of their lives penetrated society like yeast infiltrates dough, just as Jesus predicted in his parable.

The simple faith of the first generations of Christians was deceptively modest, for their underlying great strength was the power of God lived out in everyday life. It was steady power, not explosive power. The challenge for each succeeding generation of Christians has been to sincerely live this kind of life – the life of "Christ in you, the hope of glory." (Col. 1:27)

But in today's world, the distinctiveness of Christianity has been blurred into an eerie sameness with society. On ordinary days, we live as ordinary people, reserving Christianity for special circumstances, whatever we interpret those to be. In many ways, this situation came about due to a "sacred-secular split" imposed upon us by various philosophical ideologies that arose 100-200 years ago in the western world.

In her book, *Total Truth*, Nancy Pearcy explains that any value requiring faith is sent to the mysterious, relativistic "upper story" of opinion, while facts, (those provable by scientific naturalism), become the only basis of truth available to modern man. In this post-modern world, even facts are fuzzy, and truth is what you make it. Many Christians are influenced by these worldviews, and as such, are bound to take a shaky stand when it comes to truth. Couple this with a general lack of Biblical understanding so prevalent in today's churches, and we have Christians who scarcely know what to live for, much less die for. How, then, are Christians different? What should we look like?

The Bible speaks to many traits characteristic of a Christian. However, the portrait of a Christian is far more easily painted on canvas than photographed in real life, as it were. But to narrow it down, to get at the heart of who a Christian is and what he is like, I would like to explore four fundamental principles that ought to characterize a genuine Christian.

First of all, a Christian is **redeemed**. This concept encompasses not only our experience of salvation, but also our life in Christ and our position in glory. 1Corinthians 6:20 explains that we have been "bought with a price," which is, of course, the "precious blood of Christ," shed on the cross to ransom our souls. (1Pet. 1:18,19) If we think of the Christian life as a journey, as we should, this is the starting off point. It is the place where God gives us spiritual life, enabling us to walk with him. Redemption both sets us free from the tyranny of sin, and also frees and forgives us from our consuming guilt. The newly redeemed take up a new name – Christian – one of Christ's own.

I love the way the book *Pilgrim's Progress* gives such a truthful representation of a Christian's walk through this world. Surrounded by challenges without and within, Pilgrim steadily winds his way to the City of God. This is a picture of our "everyday redemption" – the constant call to come along with Christ wherever we may be going. Jesus issued this call in Luke 9:23, "If anyone would come after me, let him deny himself and take up his cross daily and follow me." This "following after" is the redemption others see; the light in a dark world, the life well lived because it is not our own life after all.

The culmination of redemption will be our arrival in glory, an event that every believer looks forward to with unending hope and vigilance. 2Corinthians 4: 16-18 describes our state of longing – "Therefore we do not lose heart. Though outwardly we are wasting away, yet inwardly we are being renewed day by day. For our light and momentary troubles are achieving for us an eternal weight of glory that far outweighs them all; so we fix our eyes not on what is seen, but on what is not seen, for what is seen is temporary, but what is unseen is eternal." In his perceptive exposition on these verses entitled, "The Weight of Glory," C. S. Lewis says, "The sense that in this universe we are treated as strangers, the longing to be acknowledged, to meet with some response, to bridge some chasm that yawns between us and reality, is part of our inconsolable secret. And surely, from this point of view, the promise of glory, in the sense described, becomes highly relevant to our deep desire. For glory means good report with God, response, acknowledgement, and welcome into the heart of things. The door on which we have been knocking all our lives will open at last."

A mistake that many Christians make is thinking that redemption, as part of salvation, is a momentary experience. We forget that redemption, once begun by God, goes on and on, as it were, and leads us upward in our journey. Redemption is eternal, and as such, is constantly at work, constantly bringing us forward and upward. Living as someone who is redeemed is not so much living as one who is saved, but as one who is being saved.

Second, a Christian possesses a **new and different nature**, miraculously given to him by God, which supersedes the old sinful nature received as a result of the fall. "If anyone is in Christ, he is a new creation; the old is gone, the new has come!" (2Cor.5:17) This nature is the core of who we are – ransomed, set free and eternally righteous. But our human nature has kept some of its scars. Bound by time, as we exist in it, we have not yet escaped from sin's lingering influence. Each one of us can say with the Apostle Paul, "What a wretched man I am! Who will rescue me from this body of death?" (Rom. 7:24)

Sin, and our bodies, and our lives are a part of our earthly existence. The life of eternity offers us so much more, but deep inside we know that, in so many ways, we are stuck here – stuck in the mud of desires, distractions and disturbing events. Any kind of material wealth seems to bog us down further, for it adds

Christ at the Center

to the burden of *things* to our already soggy existence. No wonder as Paul looked around himself he asked to be rescued.

Of course, Paul was a bit quicker than we are to arrive at the liberating answer: "Thanks be to God – through Jesus Christ our Lord!" (v.25) To the Christian, Christ is everything; he is the quiet center around which all of life turns. Everything else is just extra, trivial or just basic to survival. Life, both here and forever, is centered in Christ and lived through our new nature, which always looks beyond the temporal to the eternal. In this respect, and in this respect alone, the Christian should follow the overused modern maxim "be yourself."

We should not be merely exhibiting the pleasant traits of a happy person, but we should be living as one whose life goes far beyond personality and is true to our eternal redeemed nature. This nature is simple and pure and does not get bogged down by the here and now. It is heavenly minded *and* earthly good, to alter the old phrase, because only Christ working through us can accomplish any good in this world as we are his hands and feet to do his will.

Third, the Christian is **a citizen of God's kingdom**. We live under the loving dominion of Christ our ruler. Our lives are not ours to control; we were "bought at a price." (1Cor. 6:20) The phrase, "your kingdom come," which Jesus instructs us to pray is not really about asking God to help us accomplish kingdom-building tasks on our own. We do not establish the kingdom – the Father does – and we desire to be his humble servants in this process. To this end, the Christian devotes his life and activity; as the motto of Wheaton College so succinctly puts it – "for Christ and his Kingdom."

In his book, *The Sermon on the Mount*, Clarence Jordan makes this thought-provoking statement concerning the way Christians should view their lives in this world. "They shall see God *now*; it is not a matter of waiting until we get to heaven." (Jordan, p. 20) He explains that this "seeing" includes our being able to make sense of God's Word and his works and to recognize our place, our role, in the kingdom.

Remember how the prophet Isaiah, when describing his encounter with God, simply says, "I saw the Lord." (Isa. 6) This dramatic vision of God, which comes to all true believers, sets us off on our journey down the kingdom road along which we are guided by the Word of God and empowered by the Spirit of God to do the work of God. And remember, Jesus said that we would be able to do "greater works" than his.

As citizens of God's kingdom, Christians focus on Christ, the King. Our mission is to be agents and facilitators of the kingdom to the ends of the earth. Our attitudes should always be humble, desiring only God's will in this life and in the world. Our lives are sacred, because the kingdom is not of this world, but heavenly. Planted in our hearts by faith, the small mustard seed of the kingdom springs into life, and one by one through us all, it fills the earth. The life of righteousness, holiness and purity – the Christian life -- is the life lived by kingdom citizens.

I need to stop and clarify here that not all believers have viewed the kingdom as a real and enduring paradigm for all Christians in all times and places. In fact, I was raised in a fundamentalist tradition called "dispensationalism" which held that the kingdom was not for Christians, really, it was more for the Jews only, to be granted to them on some future, yet to be determined date. Consequently, Christians given to this view disregarded or spiritualized all of the N.T. kingdom doctrine; it just didn't apply.

But I have come to realize that the kingdom is *real*, in that almost frightful way that spiritual things are real, and if we do not live our lives in the reality of God's kingdom, we will be living without a focus, without a goal. Speaking of his Father's kingdom, Jesus said, "But seek first his kingdom, and his righteousness . . ." (Matt. 6:33) In the dispensationalist tradition the fundamentalists were looking long and hard for righteousness, but never bothered with finding the kingdom. They didn't see that one does not really exist without the other, and as a result, their "kingdom-building" activities (which they called "evangelism") such as they were, often times turned inward upon themselves, not outward to the world.

As Christians, we are strangers in the cosmos of this fallen world because we, like Abraham, seek the city of God where he forever reigns. But as a *different* sort of people, we stand out.

Kindness and truth, purity of heart, and poverty of spirit, indicate our true identity. On our way to the heavenly city, as we see it coming closer day by day, we know that we are traveling home.

Finally, although much more could be said, a Christian **fully embraces truth.** John 8:32 says, "You will know the truth and the truth will set you free." Consider for a moment the story surrounding the events taking place when Jesus spoke these famous words. A blind man had been healed and the rulers of the temple were stubbornly trying to explain it away. Their first obstacle was Jesus himself -- who was he and where did he come from? Furthermore, where did he get his authority and power? In their unbelief, they did not see that Jesus came from Heaven; that God had come to earth bringing truth with him.

They were unchanged, unfazed by the blinding light of truth that blazed around them in the temple that day, but the man born blind saw the truth. He was changed not only in his eyes, but in his heart as well, for truth had captured his heart and become a light to guide him from then on out. When he said, "Lord, I believe," and bowed and worshiped Christ, he spoke a creed echoed by all Christians – "I will stand for truth; God's truth."

Jesus instructed his disciples to be "in the world and not of it," because the great enemy of truth, Satan, deviously operates in our world-system, twisting the truth into unrecognizable shapes. In this arena, the Christian is vulnerable – what is true, really, which ideas can be trusted? Much of what we hear sounds so good and so right, making it difficult, then, for many Christians to discern correctness. Remember, Jesus said we walk a narrow path. Truth is skinny because it is absolute; it is either-or, it is real or false.

In the classic verse from John 8 quoted above, Jesus says, "you will *know* the truth." I believe this is the point of departure for many Christians. They do not *know* very much. They listen to many sermons and lessons, they read much well-intentioned Christian literature; but *knowing* something, something that can change your comfortable life, well, that's difficult. (It's too much like school; one may say, "You mean I have to know this stuff, like there's going to be a quiz or something?")

I reply, yes, the Christian life is like one long test, a test we want to pass and not fail, and it all depends on whether or not we know the right and true answers. It is more of an entrance exam, really, judging our aptitude for heaven. Do we want to live life only in terms of earthly ideals, or do we want to strive for eternal rewards?

In Matthew 13, one of Christ's most shocking parables is told. It is striking to the core of Christianity because it is a tale we would rather not hear, a truth we would rather not know. I call it the parable of the "75% solution," but it is usually known as the parable of the sower. In this story, Jesus tells the story of a farmer, who, on a typical spring day, goes out to plant some seeds. At first everything seems to be going well, nothing alarming crops up immediately.

But as the sower sows, his troubles multiply and three things go wrong: 1.) Some seeds fall on the path and are eaten by birds, 2.) Some of them spring up in rocky soil and then quickly die, and 3.) Some of the young plants are choked by noxious weeds. At the end of the day, only a quarter of the seeds sprout, grow and thrive; the others, the 75%, vanish, never to live, never to grow. Jesus explains that this story illustrates the reactions people have when hearing the kingdom message, and as it turns out, they are mostly negative reactions -- which can initially appear positive!

During my life as a Christian, I have seen the virulent 75% solution do its destructive work. I can point to cases of Christians who became Christians, who acted like Christians, who ended up, well, *ending*; somehow unaccounted for at the end of the day. Of course, only God knows the status of these people, but for all intents and purposes, as it were, they do seem to vanish from the narrow way. I ask myself, "What happened to these people? Where did they end up? Why was faith so hard or so shallow that it was abandoned?" And then I ask the hardest question of all, "Why are so many people affected this way?"

Recently I observed a particularly poignant case of the 75% solution. A young college student, who had attended a Christian college and who came from a Christian home, turned on God, and went so far as to doubt the existence of God and walked away from the Christian life. I do not wonder so much how or why this happened, because the power of evil is great, but I wonder in this case, how does this person *feel*? How can one suddenly live a life without God – a life where one could no longer pray, a life where an eternal future is held forfeit?

I think that what happened here is at the root of so many trapped in the 75% solution; that is, being a Christian was confused with practicing Christianity. If a person only *practices Christianity*, one can be a selfish as one wants. The level of personal involvement in living the Christian life can be carefully controlled. Eventually, selfishness takes over, and the 'Christian life' is lived on merely human terms. Lived under these conditions, God is no longer needed.

However, when one lives the life of *being a Christian*, something of an amazing contradiction happens. First, we die ("except a grain of wheat falls into the ground and dies" Jesus observes [John 12:24]) and then we live. We express this truth by our baptism. Sin is put to death by the sacrifice of Jesus on the cross, and our faith in this raises us up to the new and greater life that comes from Christ's resurrection.

The genuine Christian life is lived separate from ourselves and completely for God. Christ is daily at the center of our existence, our every breath. It produces a magnified existence, for, as Matt. 13:20 indicates, the fruit of our Christian influence can be as much a 100% more than we could ever generate on our own.

The world is searching for this type of Christian, the one whose "life is hid with Christ in God." In a world where Christians increasingly have difficulty expressing what they believe, or even holding on to what they believe, it is time for us to declare that being a Christian in the real world is the end of business as usual. It is the end of preconceived notions about what Christianity teaches, and time for confidence in what it teaches. The end has come for empty Christian rituals and traditions and codes of conduct.

The time has come instead to live "sacramentally" and "redemptively." (Briefly, this means that we must recognize and live out the innate power found in our baptism and through communion, which causes us to do God's kingdom work of setting the world to rights by his gracious love.) If Christians are to stand out in this world, instead of blending in, it will be not be because they are strangely different, but because they are gloriously different.

God makes himself known to the world in real life – through our lives. So, if Christians are indeed "little-Christs," the world must see that we are in Christ and our lives are just extensions of the life of Christ, the life-giver. This is what Jesus meant when he said, "I am the vine, you are the branches…apart from me you can do nothing." (Jn. 15:5)

Bibliography – The Christian

Gorski, Eric. "Americans: My Faith isn't the only way." *Californian* 24 June 2008: A-1, A-4. Print.

"U. S. Religious Landscape Survey: Views of One's Religion as the One True Faith." *The Pew Forum on Religion and Public Life*. Pew Research Center, Feb. 2008. Web. 17 May 2010. <http://religions.pewforum.org/pdf/comparison-Views+of+One%27s+Religion+as+the+One+True+Faith.pdf>.

Justin Martyr. *The First Apology of Justin Martyr.* (ebook)

Pearcey, Nancy. *Total Truth: Liberating Christianity from its Cultural Captivity*. Study Guide ed. Wheaton, IL:: Crossway Books, 2005. Print.

Lewis, C. S. "The Weight of Glory." Preached originally as a sermon in the Church of St. Mary the Virgin, Oxford. 8 June 1942, published in Theology, November 1941, and by the S.P.C.K, 1942. Retrieved online a http://www.verber.com/mark/xian/weight-of-glory.pdft.

Jordan, Clarence. *Sermon on the Mount*. Koinonia ed. Valley Forge, PA: Judson Press, 1970. Print.

Chapter 10-CHRISTIAN VIRTUE: Christianity from the Inside Out

"[God] has committed to us the message of reconciliation. We are therefore Christ's ambassadors, **as though God were making his appeal through us**. We implore you on Christ's behalf: Be reconciled to God." 2Cor.5: 19,20

When looking at the Christian life and the characteristics which identify us, it crucial that we consider the one thing which is most obviously seen or not seen by those outside of our faith, and that is: Christian character. I am reminded of a remark our pastor made at the funeral of a fellow church-member: "his was truly the life well-lived." And how true that was – this man had been the humble servant of all, and especially of Christ. He had lived a virtuous life, a life to which we must all aspire.

Fundamentally, certain characteristics constitute such a life, and they are exhibited to others by the overall condition of our character of life. These spiritual qualities are known as the theological virtues – faith, hope and love. (I will address the other four virtues in a later chapter.) As Christians, we live our lives energized by these three great truths, for they form the core of who we are and how we behave. Furthermore, a Christian is defined by his mission; that is to say, his life as governed by the three virtues will result in a life of service to God and others.

When I began to think about the life of virtue, I realized that an understanding of faith, hope and love is fundamental to a life lived with Christ at the center. It is the realization of the most profound concept in Christianity – "Christ in you, the hope of glory." It is neither easy nor serendipitous, but difficult and the stone upon which many stumble. The life of faith, hope and love may not be easily seen or felt, but when it is, it eclipses all other human interactions and lives beyond life itself.

Recently, in my reading, I came across two very similar quotes about the faulty image of Christ reflected by many Christians today. When discussing why people reject the Christian faith, Peter Kreeft says, "perhaps they are not rejecting

Christ at the Center

Christianity, but Christians," and Dr. Hugh Ross comments that modern day scientists tend to reject theistic ideas (even when there is overwhelming evidence in their favor) because they see "not so much the deficiency of evidence for the Christian faith, but rather the deficiencies of Christians." (Ross, p. 136) Christianity stands today at a crossroads; will those who claim to be Christians be distinctively Christ-like or will they simply blend in with everyone else?

It appears that many have chosen to blend in. A recent study conducted by Christianity Today and Zondervan Publishers noted that contemporary Christians seem to fall into five categories – Active, Professing, Liturgical, Private and Cultural Christians. Only the first two groups focused on Christ as being the key to their faith; the others claimed an esoteric kind of belief in God as the center of their spiritual life. (Even the second group, Professing Christians, is less than wholehearted, believing in salvation through Jesus, but also being reluctant to share this truth with the world at large.) It is here that these erstwhile Christians blend in, disappearing into a faithless, hopeless and loveless society, having no spiritual purposes, and no noticeable differences from any other belief system.

This state of affairs reminds me of the famous Rea family story about the naked ladies shirt. Silky shirts with intricate patterns on the fabric were popular in the 1970's, and one Sunday, my husband, (who was the pastor's son), wore one of these shirts to church. His sister, sitting behind him, focused on the shirt for a moment, and noticed, to her utter shock and horror, that the pattern on the shirt concealed the forms of naked ladies! (He has never lived down this error in clothing selection!)

The lesson for us here is to realize that when Christians start to blend in, all sorts of evils begin to evidence themselves, and Christianity becomes powerless. But the life of purity, the life that influences the world through its mission for good, is distinctively based on the three great virtues and causes our life in Christ to be visible to the world.

In its definition of **faith**, the Catholic Catechism strongly links it with *belief*, thereby meaning that we do not just believe in God and truth, but that belief is, in and of itself, the entire body of Christian truth. (Catechism, p. 498) Faith plants our feet on the ground, and in order to do so, our faith must be complete. Our belief system must cover all aspects of Christianity in order to function. If we are shaky in some areas, and rigidly firm in others, or misguided in others, we will be uncertain about our faith. This ambivalence will not evidence our faith to others.

Consequently, the virtue of faith grows through knowledge. James explains that the test of faith produces patience, which in turn, makes us "mature and complete, not lacking anything." (James 1:4) He goes on to say that if we are deficient in patient faith, we need to ask for wisdom. Knowing the truth gives us confidence to live our faith, and therefore we must be able to profess, or articulate our faith.

If we cannot explain our belief system to others, we not only look silly, become worthless also. Our faith has no value to us or to anyone else. Paul paints an interesting picture of this when he says Hymenaeus and Alexander "shipwrecked their faith," (1Tim. 1:19) Because they could not accept certain foundational truths, their faith and lives fell to pieces. We do not pick and choose our beliefs, but grow through the instruction given by the Holy Spirit into an ever-increasing knowledge base through which the virtuous life is lived.

Once again, we see that we are on a journey, during which our faith grows and expands. When addressing the church in Thessalonica, Paul remarks, "your faith is growing more and more, and the love of everyone of you has for each other is increasing." (2Thes. 1:3) Faith lays the foundation for works of love. Loving deeds, or charity, can only arise from a firm foundation of faith.

We only do what we know how to do; what we are convinced of through the Scriptures is the right thing to do. Our faith has trouble growing if we are unclear about what we believe. Romans 10:17 says that faith comes initially by hearing the message of salvation. We can compare this to the seed from which a plant grows; in fact, Jesus said we should have "faith like a mustard seed." A seed is powerful, it has potential energy, if you will; however, it is not the seed but the plant that produces the fruit. Faith must grow, and as Paul says, growth comes from the "words of Christ."

Faith, growing through the Word, is the fuel for the Christian life. It gives us strength to fight through trials. Hebrews 10:38 says, by way of a quotation from the Old Testament, "But my righteous one will live by faith." The next chapter, chapter 11, the gallery of faith, goes on to describe life after life lived by the explosive power of faith. We are invited to join this "great cloud of witnesses" in the life-long race of faith, during which we are transfixed on the goal of not just getting to be *with Christ*, but being *like Christ*.

As we run, we are transformed. At the end of his life, Paul said, "I have fought the good fight, I have finished the race, I have kept the faith." (2Tim. 4:7) Notice that keeping the faith – what we started with in Christ, what his word grew in us -- is exactly what helps us to finish strong. "What overcomes the world?" John asks. It is our faith; everything that we believe.

As we journey through life, through its trials and setbacks, uncertainties and often irritating sameness, we are made steady by **hope**. Hope is the firm realization that a better existence awaits us; that everything here is not cause for our eternal happiness. Life goes up and down, but hope never changes. Hebrews 6:17-20 teaches us that people may change, (for example, they may fail to keep their promises), but God made an unchanging promise to us, which is the promise of eternal life. "We have this hope as an anchor for the soul," the passage states. Hope doesn't change; it is like a ship's anchor that ties a ship down in a storm. The ship may toss back and forth, but it won't sink.

I think that hope is the most neglected and misunderstood of the three great virtues, because we think of it in the sense of *wishing*. We wish for better circumstances, but our wishes are insignificant. We try to fix contrary things ourselves, forgetting that fixing things is outside of our jurisdiction. Our faith is small, and our hope wavers. "Hope does not disappoint," Paul says. When we lose hope, or waver in hope, our efforts to fix our problems disappoint us because what we do doesn't really work.

Hope, on the other hand, does not so much fix problems, as it enables us to live well in the middle of them, for hope, once we discover it, is huge. Something that "anchors the soul" must be great because the soul contains the image of God, and even fallen and redeemed, it is the greatest of all created things.

And yet how feeble our souls can be, how uncertain, how trivial. God sent us hope in his Son to give us that firm center around which all of life turns. In Col. 1:26&27, Paul says that the concept of hope is foundational to the great mystery of salvation – the overwhelming truth that we can scarcely grasp – that Christ is *in us*, and he is the *hope of glory*. Hope is steady because it comes with Christ who comes into us.

The hope in us, the hope in Christ, is fixed on heaven. One day we will have more than Christ-in-us, which is overwhelming enough; we will be with Christ and behold his face. This is why Paul says that this hope of glory carries a greater weight, it is *bigger*, than the burden of trials we now face. (2Cor. 4:16-18) As for our trials, God promises to wipe away all our tears and cast into oblivion the troubles that caused them in the first place. The heavenly reality of redemption is so far beyond us that it makes it difficult to describe.

Notice how Paul says the troubles are "light" and the glory is "heavy." From an earthly perspective, it should be the other way around, for the troubles seem to be heavy and the glory is deemed light or ethereal. But lightness is not the nature of hope. It is one of those things not of this world; an unchangeable thing. It is a certainty *beyond real* or *more real* than any earthly experience. As C.S. Lewis contends in many of his writings, and particularly in *The Great Divorce*, heaven will be our deepest desire made real, it will be hope given substance, the ultimate destination of the journey with God, which becomes the eternity with God.

We have our hope because the **love** of God has been poured into our hearts through Jesus. Now we need to pour that love into the lives of others. The virtue of love used to be called "charity," a word that emphasizes the actions of love. Charity more clearly depicts what love *does* – it thinks of others, focuses on others and helps others. When evangelicals abandoned the word charity, (perhaps only because it was archaic) we lost the sense of urgency to action it involved.

We turned instead to *feel* love, but love is not a feeling, in fact, any feelings associated with love arise from grace, for real love is undeserved. In 1John 3:18, the Apostle John says, "Dear children, let us not love with words or tongue, but with actions in truth." A person who loves works and labors long, and in doing so does not look for rewards or accolades. Charity is its own reward; it is the crown cast at Jesus' feet. "We love, because he first loved us."

All the New Testament teaching about love centers on Christ's comment about the Greatest Commandment. "The most important [commandment], answered Jesus, is this, 'Hear, O Israel, the Lord our God, the Lord is one. Love the Lord your God with all your heart, and with all your soul and with all your mind and with all your strength.' The second is this: 'Love your neighbor as yourself.' There is no commandment greater that these." (Mark 12:29-31) This statement referred back to two Old Testament passages: 1.) Deut. 6:4, 5 – "Hear, O Israel: the Lord our God, the Lord is one. Love the Lord your God with all your heart and with all your soul and with all your strength," and 2.) Lev. 19:18, "...but love your neighbor as yourself."

By way of their simplicity, these two commands appear to stand out in sharp contrast from the seemingly endless tedium of the Jewish law. Love God. Love others. Everything depends on it; nothing else truly matters. As the ruler who inquired of Jesus concerning the greatest commandment observed, these two commands are "more important than all burnt offerings and sacrifices."

Jesus further expands on this idea when he tells the disciples that the old commandment has become new, or taken on a new dynamic. "A new command I give you: Love one another. As I have loved you, so you must love one another." (John 13:34) At first glance, the new command seems very similar to the old, but we must notice where the love comes from. It comes from Christ, not the Law. All the love that we can ever have for others comes first from the heart of God.

Christ at the Center

In the Old Testament God says, "I have loved you with an everlasting love; I have drawn you with loving-kindness," (Jer. 31:3) and in the New Testament this same idea is expressed in 1John 4:10, "This is love: not that we loved God, but that he loved us and sent his Son as an atoning sacrifice for our sins." God performed the action that set love in motion when he sent Jesus to be our loving sacrifice. Only God is powerful enough to perform this initial deed of love.

The new command from Jesus for us to love others as he loved us makes love the basis for our mission. Love propels us out into the world to unselfishly do "greater things than these" – that is, the loving deeds done collectively by the church will amount to something greater than the miracles and ministry of Christ. The kingdom of God is built by love in the concrete actions of service to others. Love seems to grow by "doing" like our muscles grow by exercise. Paul prays that our love will "abound more and more in knowledge and depth of insight." (Phil. 1:9)

Yet, sometimes fear brings our loving actions to a screeching halt. Circumstances may put us in a place where we do not know how to proceed. Difficult people may freeze our desire to love. But most of all, our own selfishness and worldly-mindedness may stop the flow of love completely. "There is no fear in love," the Apostle John says, "for perfect love casts out fear." (1John 4:18) "My peace I leave with you, my peace I give unto you," Jesus says. (John 14:27) Peace is included with God's gracious gift of love, and when we focus on it, and not on people or circumstances, we will understand a fearless love. We will know how to act and what to do and we will not be afraid.

Love never comes from us -- though the great mistake of our age is that we are inclined to look at it in this way. Remember, "We love because he first loved us." This great unconditional love, the love that loved sinners, and that loved all that is contrary to it, is the love we have received from Jesus. Now it becomes our solitary purpose to give this love back to the world. As Christians, we are the only ones who have ever really known this unconditional love; we are the only ones who can pass it on.

Christ at the Center

In the late fourth century, Christians, both men and women, who sought a deeper life with God went out into the Egyptian desert to live as solitary hermits. They formed the first monastic movement, people who abandoned everything to live a life centered on Christ. When I first read about this, I asked myself, "Why did they go out into the desert?" -- for this was after Constantine had made Christianity the state religion and the great Roman persecution had ended. Why then did they leave favorable circumstances to live so utterly alone, so empty of possessions and company?

It was, I realized, for the sake of knowing Christ alone, to feed only on the burning flame of love that was kindled by "Christ in you, the hope of glory." Jesus said that we must abandon everything for him; we must leave houses, land and relatives and fix ourselves on him. And Paul said that he gave up everything to "know him and the fellowship of his sufferings."

Today we look at the monks and Paul and the words of Jesus with a sideways glance of suspicion. Give up everything – surely, this is symbolic, we say; it means we must be *willing* to give it up, willing to see our pleasures dimmed. But a *living sacrifice* is the key to the Christian life. In living this way, we will constantly give up everything for Christ and a sacrificial mindset will control our way of life. Jesus said, "Anyone who does not take his cross and follow me is not worthy of me. Whoever finds his life will lose it, and whoever loses his life for my sake will find it." (Matt. 10:38,39) For love alone, we too must go out into the "desert" of sin and selfishness to live a life of devotion that is alone governed by and arises from the three great virtues – faith, hope and love.

It is interesting to note that when unbelievers look at Christians, they look for this distinction. They really do not want to see someone like themselves, someone who blends in. They seem to know that Christians should be distinctively different, and when we are not, or when we fall short, they criticize.

Every day I seem to see more and more how Christians need to go "out into the desert" in order that our true character may be revealed to the world. Once again, this love does not come from us, even if we are devoted Christians. It comes from

God, who "has poured out his love into our hearts by the Holy Spirit whom he has given us." (Rom. 5:5) Love lifts us up to do what we cannot do by ourselves.

    The life of virtue is a life of mission. "Go ye into all the world," Jesus said. The love of Christ compels us, or drives us forward to share the good news with everyone, everywhere. As we go, the actions of charity become the actions of Christ himself when we do his will. The foundation of hope keeps us steady in a hostile world and fixes our goal on the greater reality of Heaven. Through hope we now know the peace we will one day possess. Faith is the body of knowledge that grows in our hearts and which we cannot keep to ourselves, but gladly must teach to others.

    At the end of his great discourse on love, (the greatest of the virtues, he concludes) Paul simply says that faith, hope and love *remain*. They last forever. They continue on into and beyond the final redemption. When the physical starry universe and our small blue planet burns away, faith, hope and love, in the end, shine on.

    Peter tells us to keep the end of all things in mind as we live "holy and godly lives." The fervent fires of redemption will try whatever we build or accomplish in this life and only the gold, silver and precious gems of virtue will remain. We have been granted a treasure box within our souls, filled with the jewels of virtue, shining now by grace, shining forever, transformed by glory – the only lasting things in heaven or earth, the only things worth our time and attention.

Christ at the Center

Bibliography – Christian Virtue

Kreeft, Peter, and Ronald K. Tacelli. *Handbook of Christian Apologetics*. Downer's Grove, IL: InterVarsity Press, 1994. Print.

Ross, Ph.D., Hugh. *The Creator and the Cosmos*. 3rd. Colorado Springs, CO: Navpress, 2001. Print.

"5 Kinds of Christians." *Leadership Journal* 01 Oct. 2007: n. pag. Web. 18 May 2009. <http://www.christianitytoday.com/global/printer.html?/le/2007/fall

Catechism of the Catholic Church. New York: Doubleday, 1995. Print.

Gonzalez, Justo L. *The Story of Christianity: The Early Church to the Present Day*, Prince Press, 1999. Print.

Chapter 11-PRAYER: Communication Between Heaven and Earth

"We have not stopped praying for you and **asking God to fill you** with the knowledge of his will through all spiritual wisdom and understanding." Col.1:9

Isn't it strange that the most necessary part of the Christian life – prayer – is also the most neglected? As James 4:2 so succinctly states, "You do not have, because you do not ask God." When beginning a discussion on prayer, this thought is the most striking; we think of it first, because it is a problem touching us all. Jesus summed it up best in Matt. 26:40 when he, in despair, said to his disciples, "Could you men not keep watch with me for 1 hour?...Watch and pray so that you will not fall into temptation. The spirit is willing, but the body is weak." Over and over again, we find ourselves caught in the disciples' dilemma; we have plenty to pray about, plenty of needs to sort out with God, but so very often we "fall asleep" in various ways.

During World War II, the BBC, when broadcasting into Nazi-occupied European countries, identified itself as "London calling." Those two words symbolized hope to thousands of people caught in the uncertainties and tragedies of war. "London calling" is also the title of a famous anti-war song from the late 70's performed by the British punk-rock group The Clash. Basically, the lyrics of the song make very little sense, as far as I can tell, but some sort of existentialist concern seems to be expressed as to the horrors of nuclear war. Either way, the phrase has come to symbolize truth (or something close to it) calling out in a war-torn world. When we think of prayer, we begin with "God calling" – God trying to make contact with us, the exiles of war.

Prayer is face-to-face communication with God, the give and take of thought, ideas, questions and instructions. Prayer begins with "God calling." He begins the conversation and we are compelled to respond.

God got into the habit of walking and talking with us back in the Garden and he still desires to do so. Before the sin in the

Christ at the Center

Garden, Adam and Eve walked and talked openly with God, but after they sinned, the voice of God calls out to them without a response, because they are hiding, ashamed and silenced. Many Christians suppose that we are the ones to begin the process of prayer, but since we are the ones hiding in shame, God must be the first to open the conversation.

He does so by listening for our voices. Psalm 34:6 says, "This poor man cried and the Lord heard him," and verse 15, "the eyes of the Lord are on the righteous and his ears are attentive to their cry." When we respond to God he delivers us from shame, as verse 5 explains, "Those who look to him are radiant, their faces are never covered with shame." Prayer makes our relationship with God *work*.

Our first responsibility in prayer is confession. This is not to say that, in any given prayer, confession must occur first, but that it must be a part of our prayers. Psalm 51:17 says, "a broken and contrite heart, O God, you will not despise," and 1John 1:9 tells us, "If we confess our sins, he is faithful and just and will forgive us our sins." In order to speak with God, we must come out of hiding and step into the light of forgiveness. Then we will feel set free, like a window has been opened on Heaven, but prayer will be a burden if we are beset by sins.

Essentially, all sins revolve around selfishness, which can severely limit the effectiveness of our prayers. James 4:3 says, "When you ask, you do not receive, because you ask with wrong motives, that you may spend what you get on your pleasures." This brings up a curious paradox of prayer – how can I tell if I am asking for what I need as opposed to what I want? Here we must realize that, when we pray, it is not only we alone who pray, but the Holy Spirit prays also. Ephesians 6:18 says, "Pray in the Spirit on all occasions with all kinds of prayers and requests." We not only pray to the Father in the name of Jesus, but in conjunction with the Spirit as well.

Prayer focuses on building relationships through communication; in prayer we participate in a filial relationship, that is, the communication is between a father and a child. We go to God as a child goes to a parent and asks for favors, and as a child, we long for the parent's love and attention. On God's part, he leans down to hear us, he works to help us, and we are always at the center of his heart. At his Son's request, God the Father has given us the Holy Spirit to be with us and help us in every way. The Spirit guides us into knowing and doing what is right as opposed to following our natural tendency to do what is selfish. In this way we can pray for God's will and not our own.

On the other hand, sometimes life seems to spin so entirely out of control that we have no idea what we want, selfish or not. Even when we cannot formulate words for our requests, or do not know which way to turn, the Holy Spirit prays to the Father for us within the perfect relationship of the trinity itself. Romans 8:26 and 27 explains this incredible truth; "We do not know what we ought to pray for, but the Spirit himself intercedes for us with groans that words cannot express. And he who searches our hearts knows the mind of the Spirit, because the Spirit intercedes for the saints in accordance with God's will."

Often I have not known what to pray for, or what to say, or even if what I ask for is appropriate. I'm sure every Christian has felt this way, and that's what makes these verses so special to all of us. When I can't pray, God prays for me. When I'm so distraught that I cannot articulate my thoughts, God expresses them for me. When a situation seems impossible to navigate – the Holy Spirit knows the way through it, and he cares enough to ask the Father to show me the way. As humans, we repeatedly face these kinds of situations. How troubled we would be if we did not know the reality of the Comforter's prayers, how hopeless and adrift our thoughts would remain!

But Christian prayer displays, above all, **hope**. 1John 5:14&15 states, "This is the confidence we have in approaching God: that if we ask anything according to his will, he hears us. And we know that he hears us – whatever we ask -- we know that we have what we asked of him." As God's children, we can live in the confidence of knowing that God has our best interests at heart.

As well as dealing with uncertainties in prayer, we also find ourselves surrounded by numerous distractions. The disciples slept, Martha cooked dinner, and Job was beset by a world of trouble. We work, or go to school, or take care of babies and so on; yet 1Thes. 5:16&17 states, "Be joyful always, pray continually." How can we do this when our lives are full of sorrows and obligations?

In the 17th century, a monk living in Paris, France asked himself the same questions. His assignment in the monastery was to be a cook (kitchen duty), and every mother can tell you how distracting that can be! Yet, Brother Lawrence determined to live his life in the presence of God, in constant communication with God, in order to be the reflection of God. His story is told in the little book, *The Practice of the Presence of God*, which contains his letters and reminiscences.

At first glance, it is easy to dismiss Brother Lawrence's devotion to a life of prayer as an extension of his life as a monk. If all Christians were monastic (we are inclined to observe), all of us would have plenty of time to pray and the perpetual reminder to do so! But Brother Lawrence was not taking time – or lots of time – to pray; he was living prayer out; he never stopped; it became the life within his duties. We tend to look at it the other way: prayer is a duty in life, and as a result, we feel guilty if this duty is neglected or mundane. Prayer-as-life, however, fills us with vitality because it is a connection to God as relevant as breathing; in fact, perhaps this is why we use the expression "breathe a prayer."

Another encouraging lesson from Brother Lawrence's story is that it took him ten years before he even came close to living this type of life of prayer, but he never gave up. In one of his letters he says, "Let it be your business to keep your mind in the presence of the Lord. If your mind sometimes wanders and withdraws itself from him, do not become upset. Trouble and disquiet (worry) serve rather to distract the mind than to re-collect it." In other words, he had learned not to beat himself up over his failures, so he just kept trying.

Brother Lawrence practiced a life of prayer in the presence of God for forty years. He was rather like I imagine the Old Testament saint, Enoch, to be – the day came when he set out on his prayer-walk with God and just kept walking – all the way into the presence of God! Before that day came, though, he had to set out anew every morning. This is what we are called to do in Eph. 3:17-19 as Paul prays, ". . . that you may have power…to **grasp** how wide and long and high and deep in the love of Christ, and to **know** this love…that you may be **filled** to the measure of all the fullness of God." When this concept is worked out in us by the power of the Holy Spirit, when we day-by-day grasp and know and are filled, we can live the kind of life God intended for us, the life-in-prayer.

A helpful technique that I have learned is to pray immediately upon thinking of a situation or person that needs prayer. In this way, I pray throughout the day. This discipline guards the motives of my heart to always be in tune with God so that I am always ready to pray. I have found that this habit helps me to think about everything that goes on in any given day more from a godly perspective than my own, and I worry less because I am inclined to turn problems over to God right away. I try to live in the spirit of Psalm 55:17 -- "Evening, morning and noon I cry out in distress, and he hears my voice."

Another idea about prayer that has been very helpful to me is to always pray in specific terms. I don't feel that we ought to "beat around the bush" or trip ourselves up with a host of self-apologetic "if-it's-your-will-Lord's" or to ask God merely to "bless" this, that or the other thing. God knows exactly what's going on in our lives, and he has a detailed plan for every event and circumstance. God wants us to care as much about our lives as he does. He wants us to trust him implicitly. He wants us to tell him exactly what is going on, because he cares about every detail.

James points to the prophet Elijah as setting a good example for us – he prayed that it would not rain and it didn't; he prayed that it would rain and it did. But a word of caution – be careful what your pray for – God will not forget a word you say – like the time I prayed for between $300.00 and $400.00, and God graciously gave me $350.00!

Many Christians who are overly concerned about praying in God's will worry that if we inadvertently ask for something contrary to it, God will sort of smack us over the head about it. The Lord's Prayer does say, "Thy will be done;" however, I believe this is to teach us the foundation on which all prayer is laid. We pray in the realm of God's will in the context of living in his Kingdom, where his will is constantly being done. The will of God does not in any way depend on us, nor on what we ask for. God works forever as he wills.

In the humble lessons of prayer, we will eventually come to the place where our will, our desire, is for our lives to be lived as he wishes. Once again we see how communication with God leads us into the life lived totally in him. Like Jesus we will say, "Here I am, I have come to do your will." (Heb. 10:9)

The life of prayer is one of unrelenting focus. In Luke 18 Jesus tells a parable about a woman who kept asking (we would say "bugging") a judge to grant her justice in a case someone had against her. She kept asking and asking, and although the judge was unmoved at first, he finally granted her request because she *just kept asking*! The Bible says that Jesus told this story with one specific purpose in mind: that we would "always pray and not give up."

This lesson on prayer is hard to learn because often it seems that God is not paying attention to us. Time goes by and goes by and nothing happens. Bothersome circumstances and people seem impervious to change. Yet God instructs us to keep on asking – "Ask and it will be given to you, seek and you will find; knock and the door will be opened to you." (Matt. 6:7) Notice the time and effort expressed in this verse. Prayer is not a piece of cake; it is a journey, often a long and difficult one. We press on in prayer, one step at a time, stepping (that is, asking) again and again. "Never give up," God tells us – why? It is because we are walking *on his road*, his will.

In the introduction to his amazing book, *With Christ in the School of Prayer*, Andrew Murray writes, "If there is one thing I think the Church needs to learn, it is that God means prayer to have an answer." We become so self-deprecating when it comes to prayer that we often feel as if (a.) we won't get an answer, (b.) we don't deserve one, or (c.) if we do, it will surely be a long time coming. It's almost as if prayer has been reduced to a multiple-choice test that we're hoping to pass.

We must remember that we do not pray in fear, but in confidence. "Let us then approach the throne of grace with confidence," states Heb. 4:16, and this passage goes on to say that an answer will be provided (*"receive* mercy" and *"find* grace.") Like every area of the Christian life, we grow in our level of confidence in prayer. New situations or changing needs cause us to climb higher and farther in our prayer journey. God is constantly trying to get us to realize that he always hears and answers prayer. As C.S. Lewis observed about prayer, "It doesn't changes God, it changes me."

It is astounding how suddenly and poignantly these changes can come. I think this is true because prayer is all about communication – we talk to God and he *actually talks back*! When it happens, we literally stop in our tracks. Suddenly everything in our world is eclipsed by the greatness of God. We wake up from the routine of prayer to the ringing alarm clock of the limitless power of prayer.

Last week I had one of those moments. While shopping in the grocery store, (a very mundane task were it not for the frightful prices), I realized that my daughter was somewhere on her flight from Indianapolis to Los Angeles, so as I pushed my cart down the aisle, I prayed for her safety. As I thought this prayer, I suddenly began to cry, which is uncharacteristic of me. I was struck by a realization from God with the force of an ocean wave – I pray because events outside of my control are not outside of God's control. I saw his greatness in the care he always gives to us; as we constantly ask, he constantly answers.

When I got home from the store, a trivial thing happened; I realized that I had lost one of the earrings I was wearing. This was vexing, because, first of all -- *what if someone saw me like that!* – and, secondly, I had lost another earring a couple of days earlier. It was as if a vortex had opened up in the earring-space-time universe! So, I prayed about it – I've said prayers about such things ever since I was a child – God is in control of everything, after all. Within a few minutes of praying this simple prayer, I found not one, but both earrings.

That in and of itself was moving, (with God, there are no small lessons), but what I learned later was staggering. When I was praying for my daughter earlier, her plane had to make an emergency landing, complete with ambulances and fire trucks, during which, fortunately, everything turned out to be ok. In response to this odd combination of petitions, and to show me his concern and providence over **all** events, great and small -- *God answered*!

But how quickly we forget, and looking back at the prayerless, slumbering disciples we are quick to criticize, especially when they fell back asleep after being shaken awake by *God*! When it comes to us, however, so little has changed. God's Word instructs us to: "Be joyful in hope, patient in affliction, faithful in prayer," and 2 Thess. 3:13 says, "Never tire of doing what is right."

Moving toward these goals is part of the journey of prayer. Years after the incident in the Garden of Gethsemane, the Apostle John wrote, "...we have confidence before God and receive from him anything we ask because we obey his commands and do what pleases him." (1Jn. 3:21&22) He goes on to say that our assurance in prayer comes from the Holy Spirit. Over the years, John had learned that the power to persevere in prayer came from his partnership in prayer with the Holy Spirit, which produced the confidence he had that God answers.

Another disciple who was in the garden that night, Peter, instructs us to "be clear-minded and self-controlled so that you can pray." (1Pet.4:7) In the garden, he was anything but clear-minded and self-controlled, waving swords around and all, but over time, he learned the lessons of the journey of prayer.

Our dilemma in prayer – that it is at once so needed and that we so often neglect it – can be resolved if we, like Peter and John and Enoch and Brother Lawrence, continue on in our journey with God. We "walk" through our failures, misconceptions and distractions as he calls us on to higher and greater goals. Remember, he walks with us and prays for us in all our difficult times. We, in turn, must keep walking, keep turning the corners and keep listening for "God calling," until the day when we finally walk into Heaven and speak face-to-face with God.

Bibliography – Prayer

"The Practice of the Presence of God by Brother Lawrence." *Practice God's Presence*. Light Heart, n.d. Web. 08 May 2009. <http://practicegodspresence.com/brotherlawrence/practicegodspresence08

Murray, Andrew. *With Christ in the School of Prayer*. New York: Hurst & Company, Print.

"Quotes by C. S. Lewis." *Good Reads*. Good Reads, Inc., 2010. Web. 18 May 2010. <http://www.goodreads.com/author/quotes/1069006.C_S_Lewis>.

Christ at the Center

Part 4 – Life in the Body of Christ

Chapter 12-THE CHURCH: Christianity Together

"But you have come ... to the church of the firstborn, whose names are written in heaven. You have come to God, the judge of all men, to the spirits of righteous men made perfect, **to Jesus the mediator** of a new covenant..." Heb. 12:22-24

[author's note – Since I first wrote this, I have changed churches, and what a refreshing change it has been! But I am keeping the language I originally used in order to point out some of the important challenges faced today by the evangelical church in general.]

I live in a community that has grown quite rapidly over the last 25 years or so. When we moved here back in the late 1980's, we had the choice of going to about 5 churches. Not being Catholic and not desiring to remain Baptist, we chose a "community church" which was and still it loosely connected with a reformed denomination. It was sort of a 'general' church with friendly people, opportunities to serve, and a pretty good sermon to listen to every Sunday. (At that point in time, I must admit that I was looking at church with some fairly typical modern-Western-evangelical ideas.)

Now, after a cursory glance at the current phone book, I see 54 churches listed, further divided into 36 denominations or categories. I would venture to say, however, that a few things are pretty much the same in each one; there are a lot of friendly people, plenty of opportunities to serve, and an interesting sermon to listen to every week. I'll bet that almost every evangelical church in my area is very much the same, just bearing a different name.

But the modern, Western ways of doing church are beginning to lose their luster and many people, like me, are growing restless. Why do we keep on doing church the same old way? Why do we keep repeating the same old denominational church-speak? Is anything about church even Biblical anymore?

Christ at the Center

In his book, *The Present-Future*, Reggie McNeal illustrates this demise by suggesting that churches should actually hire unbelievers to visit on Sundays in order to provide some unbiased feedback. He says to ask them, "Would you come back if you were not paid to do so?" He then adds, rather cynically, "(I know a lot of church staff who would answer 'No' to that one!)" And how true that is! Even people who earn their living by working at a church are disillusioned – I know how that feels!

Over the last year or so, I have gone on a pilgrimage of sorts, to see if I could discover what is missing or wrong or skewed or whatever it is about my church and other evangelical churches as well. I first visited an Episcopal church, where I experienced liturgy for the first time. I saw that it was not empty and repetitious, as I had always heard, but that it was engaging and full of life. I went to a Catholic mass, and was struck by the thought that we as Protestants and Evangelicals owe them so much for their faithful preservation of foundational Christian truth. I went to a house church where experiencing worship was like going back in time, a pure experience of the first century intimacy which is still relevant, if not necessary, for today.

Certainly all three of my experiences were radically different from my evangelical experience nowadays and my early fundamentalist tradition. But it was not the differences I was after; I was not looking for the exotic or even something new to me, although it did seem that all three of my experiences were radically different from what I experience Sunday after Sunday, for what I found was not so much different as it was *meaningful*.

I believe that meaning is the primary ingredient missing from many evangelical churches. Everything we "do" in church needs to be infused with meaning, otherwise it will not be remembered, and consequently, not acted upon. My experience also pointed me in the direction of something timeless; that is, it is neither outdated nor contemporary. It fits everywhere and everyone, at any time.

As I have thought about my pilgrimage, (as opposed to my Sunday after Sunday experience), I noticed several factors common to the churches I visited which are missing, different or changed in my church. I think that these characteristics can reveal places where improvement can and should be made. These things are sensations, in a way, or ideas that seemed to be expressed. Remember, I did not spend a lot of time in these places and did not make a detailed study of what was going on. However, I believe God sent me on my pilgrimage and it became almost larger than life, for it was time for me to see some things I had never seen before, or to see them in a new light.

I cannot speak for every evangelical church or pastor; so remember that I am addressing problems here that seem to be evident in many instances. As the advertising disclaimer says, "individual results may vary." I can only speak specifically about my church; however, I feel it is quite typical of the situation in many evangelical churches in America.

To begin with, I felt an overarching **sense of community and unity**, not just within each particular church, but directed toward the larger body or denomination, and beyond that, toward the Christian church as a whole in the world as well. In evangelical churches, we seem to talk about this relationship, but it does not seem to be foundational, that is to say, a living out the idea of the Church as being one and working toward the unity Christ desires of us. Jesus said, "May they be brought to complete unity to let the world know that you sent me and have loved them." (John 17:23) We seem to hold to the concept of unity far more in theory than in practice. How much richer our church experience would be if we could freely interact and learn from each other!

I grew up in a Baptist denomination which was separatist, meaning that they believed that they should not "fellowship" with churches in other evangelical denominations (even Baptist ones), and certainly not with other Protestants, and never with Catholics. The justification for this was that some area or other of doctrine or practice in the other churches was wrong in some way. These churches were also perceived as associating themselves with unbelievers in a direct or indirect way. Of course, this line of reasoning is based on some heavy "judgementalism" and self-aggrandizement – "we have a corner on the truth."

Christ at the Center

What first clued me in to the fatal flaw in this argument were the words of Jesus in John 17:20, 21 -- "My prayer is not for them (the disciples) alone. I pray also for those who will believe in me through their message, that all of them may be one, Father, just as you are in me and I am in you." My church group believed that they should exhibit unity among themselves and within each individual church body. The concept of unity was to be practiced by a church, not among other churches in other denominations. But it always worried me that the prayer of Jesus was on behalf of all churches in all places and times, and my group was ignoring that fact.

When I finally came to my day of reckoning with this passage of Scripture, I had to walk away from the separatist movement. Unity is unity for all Christians, not just one group or church. I often say (in jest) that it will be something to see the looks on the faces of these Baptists when they wake up "on that great gettin' up mornin'" with a Catholic on one side of their mansion in Heaven and a charismatic on the other! That will be a lesson on unity better learned this side of glory.

When churches live in unity, when they realize it is the glue that both holds them together and to Christ, they live in a sense of community. A church that lives in community expresses three characteristics:1.) Shared experiences, 2.) Meaningful dialogue and 3.) Servant-attitudes. We can see Jesus revealing his desire for the church to exhibit these traits in the Upper Room discourse. He prays, "May they be brought to complete unity." (John 17:23)

Shared experiences are events or characteristics, which the church has without fail; they happen regularly and thereby, draw people together. Jesus says (John 14:4-6) he will unite his followers into one way or one truth leading to Heaven and eternal life. The Holy Spirit will indwell them all (14:16) and give them all the ability to understand the same thing – the truth about the words Christ has spoken. They will together face persecution (15:20) and show unending reciprocal love (13:34) by demonstrating the love of God to the world.

Meaningful dialogue indicates free, open and respectful communication between God and the Church, between churches and between members in churches. The Holy Spirit (14:25) is the catalyst of these conversations as he instructs believers about the truth and helps them to remember the words of Jesus. He will further empower them to be testimony to love and truth. He will enlighten believers with the ability to understand and share the truth – "but when he, the Spirit of truth comes, he will guide you into all truth." (16:13)

Servant-attitudes are expressed collectively through a desire on each individual's part to live a life of giving to others. In the John 13 passage, Jesus performs a powerful drama illustrating the centrality of servant attitudes and actions. Instead of waiting for the house servant to wash the disciples' feet, and not waiting for the disciples to get the idea to act, Jesus gets a towel and a bucket of water and performs the hospitable, yet humbling, task himself. He says, "I have set an example that you should do as I have done for you."

Later he adds that even though we have servant's hearts, in this new dynamic of unity, we act toward him and toward others as friends. We go beyond being servants (just carrying out tasks) to being friends who care and love and express those feelings in kind deeds.

One of the things that struck me about the churches I visited was that they **practiced traditions** that provided a platform for establishing unity. The traditions were teaching tools, not random rituals. In evangelical churches, we have largely removed these traditions or changed them so much that their power is greatly diminished. We are ignorant because we have not learned truth through things that were meant to be Biblical object lessons. We are victims of too much change.

For many years, I looked around my church and wondered, "How can we fix this? What program really works?" Now I see that we need to go back to the *things that do not change*, the things that are Biblical. These things are reflected in the historical traditions, sacraments and creeds of the church. They form the church's connection to its past and its future. Many of us evangelicals experience an alienation from our true mission because change has swept us away from the touchstones of who we really are.

Christ at the Center

The most common excuse I hear for the failure to follow traditions or repeat creeds is that people who do these things are only going through the motions. They are mouthing "vain repetitions" and performing empty rituals. But let's get something straight – Jesus said that the pagans were the ones doing the "babbling." (Matt. 6:7) For all his criticism of the Pharisees, Jesus did not say that "church people" were mumbling worthless things. He never slammed genuine Jewish tradition, for he respected the acts themselves. Matthew 5:17 says, "Do not think that I have come to abolish the Law or the Prophets; I have not come to abolish them but to fulfill them." Jesus read Scripture in the synagogue and participated in various feasts.

What Jesus repeatedly warns against is having a bad heart-attitude. When performing a religious *rite*, our hearts must be *right*. Matthew 5:8 declares, "Blessed are the pure in heart, for they will see God." If our hearts are not right, we will be engaging in an empty waste of time, but it we are in tune with God, our worship experience will have true meaning and we will grow in our relationship with God.

All orthodox Christian churches agree that Jesus established two rituals, often called **sacraments**, which were to be integral marks of who the church is and what the gospel means, namely, baptism and communion. Unfortunately, over the years the church has bickered over how these sacraments are performed and exactly how significant they are. This is unfortunate, because all of the arguing has muddied the waters, especially for evangelicals who have inherited the watered-down versions of once powerful traditions. We didn't know what to make of them, so we made little of them. Therefore, we need to examine what is Biblical about the sacraments – what *does not change* – in order to find the foundation to which we must return.

When Jesus came to John the Baptist to be baptized, John refuses to do so at first, thinking that he is unworthy and such a step is unnecessary. But Jesus says that it is necessary, or, "proper to fulfill all righteousness" (Matt. 3:15), that is, to accomplish what was right. Following the baptism, God proclaimed, in an audible voice, "This is my Son, whom I love, with him I am well-pleased." (v. 17) For the Christian, baptism also comes with the same proclamation; we are God's children. When disciples of all nations come to faith, they are baptized first as Christ commissioned us. In so doing, their identity as Christians is immediately proclaimed.

Baptism also indicates the power and presence of the Holy Spirit in each individual Christian's life, and thereby, in the Church as a whole. Jesus said, "John baptized with water, but...you will be baptized with the Holy Spirit." (Acts 1:5) Just as the Holy Spirit, appearing in the form of a dove, descended on Christ at the time of his baptism, so all Christians will be baptized, covered, filled with the Holy Spirit in their souls. The Apostle Paul says that the baptism of the Holy Spirit is what makes the church Christ's living body – "For we were all baptized by one Spirit into one body." (1Cor. 12:13)

An interesting little story from Acts 19 illustrates how important it is for us to realize that baptism goes beyond a water ritual used as a mark of identification to becoming an ignition point for the power of the Holy Spirit. Paul had met some believers at Ephesus who had accepted the message of John the Baptist to repent and had been baptized with John's baptism. Paul called it a "baptism of repentance." He then tells them the Gospel story – the truth about Jesus – and consequently they are baptized in water in the name of Jesus. They also receive and display the gift of the Holy Spirit. They were only halfway right at first, but baptism makes them whole. They are identified with Jesus, not John, and display the powerful results of baptism by the Holy Spirit.

Perhaps Paul was thinking about this incident when he scolded the church at Corinth for being divided and arguing over points of doctrine. They seemed to be choosing up sides based upon whose interpretation of Scripture they happened to agree with. Paul points back to baptism as the foundation of true faith. "Were you baptized in the name of Paul?" he asks. (1Cor.2:13) In other words, when we start making what influential Christians say (good or bad) about the Bible the basis for our faith, we find ourselves on a slippery slope.

Christ at the Center

Paul goes on to explain that we are baptized *in Christ*. He is the source of all wisdom and truth through the ministry of the Holy Spirit. In this way, baptism is the springboard into the world of truth, but truth does not come from what people say – it comes from God.

The problem of divisions and taking sides has certainly been brought to bear upon the evangelical church. We have denominations of every flavor and writings expressing myriad points of view. What this does is turn our attention away from Christ and on to Christians, so that we lose focus on the *things that do not change*. Paul tells us, "Set your minds on things above, not on earthly things. For you died, and your life is now hidden with Christ in God." (Col. 3:2,3)

Where, exactly, did we die and where were we hid? It was in the water of baptism, where the Holy Spirit, who alone leads us into all truth, covered us. Evangelical Christians need to return to the centrality of Scripture that is made real and understandable to us by the Holy Spirit. The evangelical church must return to the one in whom we were baptized, the one in whom our identity was established, and recognize and remember the power of our baptism.

The second sacrament we need to examine is **communion** also known as "the Eucharist" in Catholic, Orthodox and Anglican churches. I was puzzled when I first learned that "Eucharist" means "thanksgiving." I thought it meant either "sacrifice" or "remembrance." Growing up in a Baptist church, the emphasis of communion was on remembering Christ's death and confession of sin. (Here I am supposing we confessed our sins – certainly it was never done *out loud*.) "Thanksgiving," on the other hand, was a holiday in November.

The idea of thanksgiving comes, first of all, from the fact that during the Last Supper Jesus offered prayers of thanks for the bread and wine. "Jesus took bread, gave thanks and broke it...then he took the cup, gave thanks and offered it to them..." (Mark 14:22,23) The thanks is given not only for the gift of physical food from the Father, but also for the gift of the Son of God who is the living bread and the true vine. Communion arises from a thankful heart that remembers the grace of God.

Christ at the Center

An account of the events of the Lord's Supper is given by Matthew, Mark and Luke, while John concentrates on the sermon and prayer given after the meal. Later in the New Testament, Paul gives an account of a special revelation about communion, which he received in a vision from Christ. These accounts are very precise and take us step by step through what was, to the disciples, a startling change in the ancient tradition of the Passover. Imagine the significance of having a centuries-old celebration suddenly transfused with a whole new meaning!

When Jesus singled out these two elements of the old Passover he created a living tradition that would transcend time and place. It was to become nourishment for the very life-blood of the church. It is now what we are all about – we are partakers of the body and blood of Christ and are truly and forever alive.

After the Protestant reformation, three viewpoints (more or less) on the degree of reality of the bread and wine in relationship to the body and blood of Christ emerged with the many denominations of the church. The Catholic Church continued to hold to transubstantiation, the belief that the bread and wine, in a miraculous way, become the actual body and blood of Christ, but retain the actual chemical qualities of bread and wine, not flesh and blood.

The second view, called consubstantiation, is held by the Lutherans, and, in a variety of ways (I use the word "variety" to simplify things) by the Anglicans and Orthodox as well. It says that the body and blood of Christ are present in the elements, but we cannot and should not attempt to give and explanation for how this works. This is a variation of the Real Presence view, which states that the bread and wine change to the body and blood of Christ through the power of the Holy Spirit who is living in people of faith. The Catholic view is a form of Real Presence, but the difference between the Protestant and Catholic views is that the Protestants do not worship the elements as the Catholics do.

Thirdly, most evangelicals and fundamentalists believe that the elements of communion are only symbolic, that is, the bread and wine (or the more conservative choice, grape juice) are representations of the body and blood of Jesus. Eating and drinking them symbolizes our union with Christ. In this view, the purpose of the Communion service is to remember the death of Christ and look forward to his return.

Of course, being raised a Baptist, I grew up with the symbolic tradition where communion was observed in a simple and solemn manner about once a month. Yet, for years, I struggled to find the *meaning* in communion; I often felt as if I were only going through the motions. There was always one thing I could not reconcile the Biblical passages about communion with my actual experience – simply that the Bible never says communion is symbolic.

In the Gospels, Jesus says, "This *is* my body and this *is* my blood." He also says in John 6:55, "For my flesh is real food and my blood is real drink." 1Corinthians 10:16 says that the cup is the blood of Christ and the bread is the body of Christ in which the church participates together. No matter how hard I tried, I couldn't really find a Scriptural basis for the communion elements being just symbols. So what are they, really, and exactly how significant is communion? What should we believe?

I'll never forget the first time I thought, "But what if the bread and wine really are (in some way) the body and blood of Christ? What happens if they really are *real*?" And I literally stopped dead in my tracks, because, if they were real, how then could I touch them? *They would be holy* and I would have to fall on my face before God!

Since that day, I have been terrified by the casual attitude of evangelicals toward communion. There have been times when I have observed it and expected to see fire fall from heaven and not in a good way. For example, one Sunday the verses from 1Corinthians 11 were read, warning against such attitudes, and we proceeded to observe a completely casual communion during which people served themselves and not one prayer was uttered, neither of confession nor thanksgiving!

I believe that our preponderance for not taking communion seriously is the greatest hindrance to the revelation of the Holy Spirit's power in evangelical churches today. 1Corinthians 11:29 says, "For anyone who eats and drinks without recognizing the *body of the Lord* eats and drinks judgment on himself." Even if we say that the elements are merely symbols, we still need to be serious, reverently applying to our lives the infinite meaning of redemption through the cross. (And maybe, along the way, we can lose the grape juice and find the matzos, too.) But a further step is needed. We must get to the place where we realize that we are taking into ourselves the very life of Christ as provided by his eternal sacrifice for our sins.

As evangelicals, we tend to get nervous about attaching such profound powers to ordinary bread and wine. After saying that Jesus and his divine message can be compared to a stone that people trip over, Peter says that Christians are "a chosen people, a royal priesthood, a holy nation" (1Pet. 2:9); in other words, we are different, too, like a rock one trips on because it is out of place in the middle of the road. I like the way the King James Version says that we are "peculiar people;" we are just plain odd.

People who claim to take in the body and blood of Christ are peculiar. In fact, the Roman pagans thought the early Christians were cannibals or that they were offering human sacrifices. Indeed, the sacraments are unusual and defy human and (in our day) modern explanations. Baptism and communion are to be practiced consistently by the church in all times and in all places. They should be neither updated nor diminished because they are sacred activities that bring us spiritual life and unity. I agree with C.S. Lewis: "There are three things that spread the Christ-life to us: baptism, belief, and that mysterious action which different Christians call by different names – Holy Communion, the Mass, the Lord's Supper...I cannot myself see why these things should be the conductors of the new kind of life...But though I cannot see why it should be so, I can tell you why it is so...He [Jesus] taught his followers that the new life was communicated this way." (Lewis, p.61,62)

I do not think, however, that baptism and communion provide us with salvation in the sense that participating in these activities brings us saving grace itself. The Bible teaches that salvation comes by the grace of God through faith and not though works of any kind. But I think that, through the power of the Holy Spirit, the sacraments are far more important to spiritual life than we evangelicals have been lead to believe.

They are steps along the trail of grace on which the journey of salvation takes place; a trail that begins at the moment of belief. Evangelicals would do well to wake up the fact that salvation does not begin and end at one specific moment in time. It is more like a journey that winds its way to the gates of Heaven. Jesus said he was "the Way," not "the green light." Baptism sets us off on our journey in the power of the Holy Spirit. Communion continuously nourishes us with Christ, who was sacrificed for us.

Another activity that demonstrates unity among the church is memorizing and reciting **creeds**. Historically, Christians have articulated their faith through creeds from Christianity's earliest times. They are succinct poetic statements of belief, packed with meaning. If you look hard enough you can find the very first creeds tucked away here and there in the New Testament. 1Tim. 3:16 is one of my favorites: "Beyond all question the mystery of godliness is great: He appeared in a body, was vindicated by the Spirit, was seen by angels, was preached among the nations, was believed on in the world, was taken up into glory."

Some others are: Eph. 4:3-6 -- one Lord, one faith, one baptism -- and 1John 2:12-14 -- I write unto you, dear children, etc. Jesus gave his followers creeds such at the Beatitudes and the Lord's Prayer. The New Testament writers were familiar with creeds because there are many of them tucked away in the Old Testament as well. They are short statements designed to remind Israel of God's power such as Deut. 26:5-9: "My father was a wandering Aramean..." (Webber, p.44,45)

Many evangelicals are familiar with one of the oldest creeds: the Apostle's Creed. It begins; "I believe in God the Father Almighty, and in Jesus Christ, his only Son." It was written to take a stand against Gnosticism, the belief that Jesus was only divine or mystical and not fully human also. This creed and others came about because the church wanted its members to know and recognize a common belief. As the Catholic Catechism explains, "Communion in faith needs a common language of faith, normative for all, and uniting all in the same confession of faith." (Catechism, p. 58)

In other words, we all need to be on the same page. The creeds are mini-apologies or short statements of fundamental beliefs that could be easily repeated from memory. They serve to unite worshipers in oneness of belief when they are recited out loud together during church services.

However, in today's typical evangelical church service, one would be hard pressed to hear any declaration of a creed, historic or Scriptural. The excuse commonly given is that Christians can now use the Bible to articulate their faith. The idea is one of "we don't need to repeat a creed because we can read what the Bible says." But, as many of us are aware, plenty of Christians are walking around today that would be unable to give a short summary statement of their faith because they haven't a clue as to what the Bible actually says. They can repeat the creed of the United States -- the Pledge of Allegiance – in their sleep, but the Apostle's Creed or the Nicene Creed are mysteries to them.

I once heard a pastor say that he does not like to repeat creeds and such in the church service because repeating things is a fruitless activity. He didn't think that repeating a statement together has any value. So, in this spirit, we don't repeat things in church anymore (except the endless refrains of praise songs.) Repeating things can certainly become monotonous. (How many times were you *not* thinking about the Pledge when you said it at school?)

However, repeating something can engrave a truth or an idea upon one's heart. For example, every American over the age of 6 knows about "liberty and justice for all" and feels entitled to it! What would happen if Christians felt the same way about "the forgiveness of sins, the resurrection of the body and the life everlasting?!"

I believe the evangelical church needs to return to teaching and repeating creeds because they connect us with: 1.) Our past, as we recognize our heritage, 2.) Christians around the world, as we confess the same faith in Christ, and 3.) Our fellow church members, as we see and hear those around us repeating the same words of belief. I have observed that many Catholics or Lutherans are consistent in articulating their faith, because they are constantly reminded of its structure.

On the other hand, evangelicals can be all over the place about what they believe because they are unfamiliar with the basic principles expressed in a creed. In addition, many evangelicals also express a materialistic, self-centered attitude toward church, centering on the experience of the moment. Creeds can provide an anchor for this post-modern ambivalence by connecting the past – what the church has historically confessed to be true – with the present – what believers need to know to be true no matter what they experience.

The same idea should be applied to all we do in a worship service – prayer, singing, and Scripture reading. These things are tools that help us learn about God and grow in our faith. I will look at them in further detail in the next chapter. They are not, on the one hand, empty rituals, or, on the other hand, entertainment segments. They are connections to God and introductions to Heaven. The Holy Spirit is the one who takes the truths expressed in all phases of worship and applies them to our hearts. He does this in order to reveal God's love and redemption to the world through the body of Christ, the Church. Jesus said that we are like a city on a hill. We are a group of people through whom words and actions point others to God.

The Greek word translated "church" is "*ekklesia*," meaning "to call out of." It is used in the book of Acts to refer to the Old Testament gathering together of the Jewish people for religious assemblies. They had been called out of Egypt to be God's people, very much as the first Christians saw themselves as being called out of their world order.

When the gift of the Holy Spirit was given to them on Pentecost, they received God's permanent power, which went far beyond any human bond or goal. The Holy Spirit made the "gathering," spiritual, mystical and timeless. The church became a living entity, destined to fill the earth. All Christians receive this unity through the Holy Spirit. 1Corinthians 12:12 explains that the church is like a living body. Each part is related to the other and all the parts work together because "we were all baptized by one Spirit into one body." Jesus plainly says, "you know him [the Holy Spirit] for he lives with you and will be in you." (John 14:17) We have the eternal life of the Spirit, providing unity for all believers in all times and places.

The powerful life of the Holy Spirit goes beyond a nice peaceful feeling inside an individual Christian's heart or a sense of fellowship between believers, although these are legitimate feelings. One of the greatest failings among today's evangelicals is that we have not figured out the significance of our greatest gift – the Holy Spirit. We are like a girl who receives an engagement ring from her fiancée only to leave it in the box and say that it's a nice thing to own. No, it has been my experience that girls with engagement rings are living in the joy of being engaged, for they dance about and make sure the ring is within everyone's optimum view! It's sort of larger-than-life. In the same way, the church needs to take the Holy Spirit out of the box and show his power to the world.

Jesus' parting words, spoken just seconds before he disappeared into the clouds, were, "But you will receive power when the Holy Spirit comes on you." (Acts 1:8) This power was an unending life-force, destined to spread like wildfire around the globe. But somehow our "engagement rings" got put back in the box ("the love of most will grow cold" – Matt. 24:12), and we now hardly know why we have the gift of the Holy Spirit, nor what to do with him. Perhaps receiving power from God will disturb our orderly, impotent lives, for fire from Heaven just might burn away our toys.

Living out the life of the Holy Spirit is more than waking up to the amazing power that lies within us. We all have "potential" because we were made in the image of God and our salvation frees us up to realize it. We must grasp the fact that the Holy Spirit unites the church into something that is supernatural, not natural, real, and not symbolic. The Apostle Paul tries to put this all-encompassing truth into words when he says in Eph. 3 that it is like a mystery – a truth so profound it is difficult to always hold on to. He writes, "This mystery is that through the gospel the Gentiles are heirs together with Israel, members together of one body, and sharers together in the promise of Christ Jesus."

Christ at the Center

He asks God to fill them "to the measure of the fullness of God," and goes on to add that "the power at work within us," (the Holy Spirit) is given "glory in the church and in Christ Jesus throughout all generations." But how often this glory is veiled in our churches by all the trivial stuff we do and all the unchangeable things that we neglect.

I figure I have been a member of seven churches so far in my life. Five were Baptist, one is Reformed (loosely), and one was non-denominational. That one, though not perfect, was truly special, not because of all the things they "got right," or the great preaching, or all the college students who gave it an amazing vitality. It was because they lived out a consistent principle of pointing to Heaven in everything they did. Other churches in my experience have pointed to a denomination, a dogma, a person, or nowhere in general, but this church pointed to Heaven where the *ekklesia* will gather, never to part again.

If I could be like Martin Luther, and nail my 95 theses to the church door, I would just tack up an arrow, an arrow pointing up. For, you see, that is where our attention must turn, off of ourselves, off of our struggles, off of all the things we do and up to Jesus, seated in Heavenly places with God. We must fix our gaze Heavenward, where the children of God will gather, finally together, finally home.

Bibliography – Church

McNeal, Reggie. *The Present Future: Six Tough Questions for the Church*. San Francisco: John Wiley & Sons, Inc., 2003. Print.

Loutzenhiser. "Communion/Eucharist." 02 Sept. 2007. Online Posting to *CCEL International Discussion Room*. Web. 17 May 2010.

Lewis, C. S. *Mere Christianity and The Screwtape Letters: Complete in One Volume*. revised and amplified ed. San Francisco: HarperCollinsPublishers, 2000. Print.

Webber, Robert. *Ancient Future Worship*. Grand Rapids, MI: Baker Publishing Co., 2008. Print.

Morland, J. P. *Kingdom Triangle*. Grand Rapids, MI: Zondervan, 2007. Print.

Chapter 13-WORSHIP: The Connection Between Heaven and Earth

"In a loud voice they sang, '**Worthy is the Lamb** who was slain, to receive power and wealth and wisdom and strength and honor and glory and praise!'" Rev.5:12

It is spring; and, within these last couple of days, the Singing Bird is back and, naturally, singing. I am referring to a bird that returns to our neighborhood each year, and has not yet, by the grace of God, been ensnared by my cat, Bob. Every morning this bird starts singing at about 5 A.M. and continues at it all day long. The trouble is I get up at 6 A.M, never before. The song of this bird is pervasive and somehow linked to the sunrise, maybe even the pre-sunrise, and as the days grow longer and longer, it sings earlier and earlier.

Every year I forget about Singing Bird, and how it will awaken me at dawn, how it was created to sing, to do what the Creator intended it to do. Even though on many a spring morning, I wish that Singing Bird would shut-up-and-go-back-to-sleep; I love to listen to Singing Bird's anthem of praise. He gladly does what he was meant to do; he participates in the glory of God. (Eventually, Singing Bird moved on, but I always remember him with joy!)

An old hymn says, "This is my Father's world, the birds their carols raise; the morning light, the lily white, declare their Maker's praise." The desire to praise God is written into nature, as each created thing, in its own way, reflects the glory of God. So why is it then, that we who were made in the image of God, who as individual Christians, bear the glory of God in our very being, have so much trouble with praise and worship? And why does so much of this trouble have to do with music?

Many evangelical churches are facing a crisis today, because by trying to solve one problem (making church services appealing to contemporary society,) we created another much larger problem – the demise of worship itself. We have lost sight of what worship is, and who worships and how.

Christ at the Center

In spite of pastors and worship directors who attempt to downplay or outright ignore the issue, the "worship wars" rage on. Like any war, the heart of the issue is the heart itself. Are the hearts of those who gather to worship living and beating in tune with the Father's glory, or are they seeking personal glory or promoting the glory of performers on a stage? Sunday after Sunday, evangelical churches offer nothing in the way of true worship to their members; Sunday after Sunday, Christians feel that they're missing out on something – if only they could put their finger on what it is…

In the same way, (figuratively speaking) that Martin Luther woke up one day and realized that the Bible or the church wasn't doing what they were supposed to do, we need to wake up and realize that the worship service isn't doing what it's supposed to do. We desperately need a revolution in worship. I am not talking about making old-fashioned, fuddy-duddy worship appealing to young people, as this has been tried and is failing, even with the young people. No, I am talking about "old folks" like me, who have pretty much been cheated out of worship for our entire lives, stepping up and saying that we will no longer be patronized by the "traditional" service, nor frustrated by the "contemporary" service; we wish to be transformed within the context of a genuine worship service.

The sense that something is missing from worship, or even perhaps that something has been stolen, is growing among evangelicals today. (At this point, by "worship" I mean what goes on in church on Sunday morning.) The experience is dull, familiar and boring. It doesn't seem to lift us up to Heaven, nor compel us, as servants of Christ, to go out into the world with the Good News. We seem to be stuck in neutral.

Fr. Alexander Schmemann, an Orthodox theologian, attributes this ambivalence to the modern sacred/secular split. What's done in church (and he is referring to *liturgy*) has become a Sunday ritual; it has no bearing on real-life on Monday. As we attempt to contemporize worship, it becomes less of an experience that reinforces a spiritual difference from the world, and more of an experience that is so much like the world that our souls can gain no value from it.

Christ at the Center

An old saying goes, "Familiarity breeds contempt" and that is exactly what is happening now in many evangelical churches. Being contemporary just for the sake of it has bred a generation (or two) of empty-hearted Christians. It's not just contemporary services that have fallen into the rut; the traditional ones are hollow as well. I call these two extremes "hymn-singing church" and "praise-band church;" during my lifetime I have experienced both. Some churches I have attended do neither very well.

"Hymn-singing church" put a lot of emphasis on, well, singing hymns. Good ones and bad ones, and in this precise order: doxology, short prayer, hymn, hymn, Scripture reading, long prayer, hymn, announcements, offering, hymn, sermon (long), hymn. In this setting, one only needs to get involved with the singing; otherwise, the lack of participation will be obvious to all. But the individual churchgoer rarely prays, reads Scripture, or in anyway speaks aloud. Communion is served once a month, but an individual worshiper receives it in silence. But the hymns, at least, if they were good ones, had meaning, and one could participate in that meaning.

"Praise-band church" put a lot of emphasis on, well, the praise band. By its very nature, (as it is perceived by our culture) a band is all about performance, and a performance is exactly what it delivers. Now the worshipers are excused from singing, the fabulous praise band will do that for us. The band plays so loudly that no one can be heard singing anyway, even by one's self. The last vestige of participation has been torn from us.

Not only that, but the lyrics to many praise songs are trite and repetitive, imparting very little meaning to one's soul. No one takes the time to read Scripture, a few verses will flash up on the screen during the sermon, but one does not need to use an actual Bible. As for prayer, it is the rambling, breathy sentiments of the worship leader. Communion is reduced to a little tack-on at the end of some services, often served do-it-yourself style.

Between "hymn-singing church" and "praise-band church" real worship got lost. Evangelical churches mimic the old nursery rhyme, "Jack Sprat could eat no fat, His wife could eat no lean, and so betwixt them both, they licked the platter clean."

Christ at the Center

Churches are wiped clean, clean of meaning, sincerity, spirit and truth, so clean that nothing of substance remains. How long do pastors and worship leaders think that Christians can live off an empty platter? When meaningful music, Scripture reading, earnest prayer and significant Communion are swept away, what's left? Only the pastor's sermon is left, making Sunday morning all about the words of one person. The pressure this placed on the pastor is great and soon takes its toll, as the sermon becomes as dull and lifeless as everything else.

A few years ago Matt Redman wrote a song about the deep longing for worship, clearly reflecting the lack of meaningful substance in worship and the desire to regain what was lost. It says, "I'm coming back to the heart of worship, and it's all about you, it's all about you, Jesus." This song has a point, certainly, in spite of the fact, in my opinion, that it's poorly written and goes all over the place musically. It is a sort of cry for help as in, "Help, I know something's wrong, so maybe it's selfishness or world-centeredness, or any number of "ness's" we evangelicals like to beat ourselves over the head with." But I think, if we look at Scripture, we see that even though worship is about Jesus, it's a little bit about us, too; it's about the **connection** between the church, the Bride, and Jesus, the Groom. Worship is more like a wedding than a concert.

The conversation between Jesus and the woman at the well (John 4) contains Jesus' own definition of worship. The woman, eager to get a nugget of truth from a real *Prophet*, asks, "Where should we worship?" The Samaritans worshiped on Mt. Ebal (maybe we could call that the contemporary service) and the Jews worshiped in Jerusalem (maybe we could call that the traditional service.)

It's easy to skip to the "spirit and truth" part, but first notice Jesus' comment on Jerusalem – "salvation is from the Jews." The Jerusalem worshiper at least had a focus on what he was doing. In worship, we celebrate redemption and grace where God's glory is revealed to us by the coming of his Son. Jesus said that the Samaritans were worshiping something they didn't know about, or perhaps had forgotten about, the joyful realization that a Deliverer was coming.

Christ at the Center

When the Apostle John sees a vision of worship going on in Heaven, he sees mighty angels worshiping God on His throne as well as worshiping the Lamb who was slain. John is telling us that Jesus is the Almighty God, worthy to be worshiped. Why? It goes back to salvation, as the angels and elders sing, "With your blood you purchased men for God." (Rev. 5:9)

John 4:24 says, "God is Spirit, and his worshipers must worship in spirit and in truth." As believers, God the Holy Spirit indwells us. On a personal level, God is always with me. I do not have to go to the temple, for I am the temple. Worship is personal – one on one with God, praising him for my salvation, thanking him for his blessings toward me, making my requests known in prayer, and using my voice to sing. I must do this from the heart, in truth. If I fake it, I am not telling the truth. I must enter the temple within and fall on my face before the throne in my heart where God lives. I worship in my body and soul because Jesus saved me.

I remember hearing this definition of worship when I was younger: worship is not what I say, but what I do. Worship is an action verb. Think of all the things we do while we worship: sing, pray, read, listen, speak and maybe even, write. I can do these things by myself or in a group, but they must be *done*; feelings or thoughts alone are not sufficient. It is true that our hearts need to be tuned in the right direction, but sitting in church every week trying to feel holy and feel happy and feel God is a useless endeavor. Right actions will be the natural outcome of right feelings.

During the Triumphal Entry of Christ into Jerusalem, a group of children and the disciples were excitedly praising Jesus. (Luke 19) The religious rulers were all upset and said that the people were making a scene, to which Jesus replied that if the people didn't perform the actions of praise, the rocks beside the road would! Praise and worship must be done, not merely thought or felt. The worship connection here is like a conversation – I speak to God, he speaks to me. There are no silent conversations.

One of the best definitions of worship is this simple statement that I have heard many times in my Christian experience – worship is sacrifice. The first use of the word "worship" in the Bible is found in Gen. 22:5 where Abraham says, "We will worship and then we will come back to you." The story here is about Abraham's experience when he set out at the Lord's request to literally make a sacrifice of his son, Isaac. Abraham's feelings were certainly not the center of this act of worship! I'm sure he did not feel one bit like going on this dismal journey. His faith was greater than his feelings; faith that he would do whatever God asked him to and that God would take care of the outcome.

The whole story is full of the actions that Abraham undertook. He went on a journey; he put the wood on Isaac's back and even tied Isaac down to the altar. God did not ask Abraham to do a "thought experiment" as in "what possibly would happen if I sacrificed Isaac?" This is often what we do in church on Sunday morning as we muse about how we can think higher and holier thoughts or do higher and holier deeds (should the need arise) during the coming week. No, in the spirit of true sacrifice, Abraham literally gave something up and took a risk that would change his life. So, God responded to Abraham; he completed the connection by providing a ram, a substitute, for Isaac.

This first Biblical example of worship is a tribute to God's provision of redemption. It's all about what Jesus referred to first in John 4 – salvation. Our worship centers on the provision of the sacrifice of the Lamb of God. Now, fast-forward to one of the last examples of worship in the Bible, Rev. 5, where thousands of angels sing "worthy is the Lamb who was slain," and salvation is again focused upon.

We often think of worship as a means by which our spiritual/emotional needs are met. We want to be happy, inspired, motivated, that is, we want to gain something for ourselves. Even though what we wish to gain is a good thing, worship as sacrifice means giving something up, in fact abandoning everything about ourselves to the will and power of God. As Colossians 1:18 says, "He is the head of the body, the church; he is the beginning and the firstborn from among the dead, so that in everything he might have the supremacy." If we

Christ at the Center

exchanged our selfishness in worship for abandoning ourselves to Christ alone, what a difference it would make in our lives and in worship services!

Imagine worship as "what can I give away or completely let go of?" instead of "what can I get and how good can it make me feel?" This is not a comfortable position to be in. For a while, we had a little "disclaimer" in our church bulletin that informed people that they need not join in on the singing if they felt uncomfortable doing so. Comfort! Comfort, indeed! The sacrifice of worship -- where we are emptied of ourselves in the presence of God -- causes us to be disturbed, not placated!

Perhaps we struggle most with worship when we get to the edge of this feeling. At that point, it becomes necessary to do things like confess sin, forgive others, and submit to the will of God. Look what happened to Isaiah when his path crossed God's in the temple one day. (Isaiah 6) The first thing he did was to confess his sin. Then he surrendered himself to go out to the people with God's message. Isaiah was not comfortable at all; the very real fire from the altar burned his lips. He became a sacrifice.

Hebrews 13:15 says, "Through Jesus, therefore, let us continually offer to God a sacrifice of praise, the fruit of our lips that confess his name." It does not say "the fruit of our mind that thinks about the words of the praise song." It is far more comfortable the think holy thoughts that to perform holy deeds. The actions we carry out in church on Sunday will translate into our activities during the week.

The next verse says, "And do not forget to do good and to share with others, for with such sacrifices God is pleased." The "sacrifice of praise" is directly related to the "sacrifice [with which] the God is pleased." Many Christians struggle to **live** their faith during the week because they never put anything to **death** on Sunday.

While I was looking for Bible passages relating to worship, I noticed a duality of purpose and procedure within the Scriptures specifically using the word "worship." Worship is very personal and, at the same time, it is exceedingly corporate. It is very much like a human body, as the Bible says (1Cor. 12), each individual part enables the entire body to function correctly and completely. Worship seems to work in the same way. One person/body part may be in tune with God, as it were, while the group around him is out of sync. Conversely, a group might be joyfully worshiping together while individuals in the group are distracted or disinterested. Like the human body, it works best if independent parts are united, in this case, to praise God as one.

In the Cruden's concordance, under the word "worshipped," the following people are mentioned: Abraham, Abraham's servant, Israel, Moses, Gideon, Hannah, Samuel, Saul, David, Job, a leper, a ruler, a woman, the disciples, a healed crazy guy, a healed blind man, Lydia, the 24 elders, and the angels. In addition, Adam and Eve walked with God in the Garden, and Enoch walked into eternity with God. These specific names teach us that our own personal attitudes, actions, feelings and words of praise are a very important means of connection between our Creator and us. People who go through the motions at church or only feel the feelings may fail to connect one on one with God.

God, however, is always capable of connecting one on one with us. The first part of James 4:8 says, "Come near to God and he will come near to you." Relationships with God will not deepen if people are superficially swept along with a crowd, or if (as I think happens more often) they are hanging around at the edge of the crowd, not really wishing to get involved. Confession of sin and a personal desire for change is a prerequisite for a healthy relationship with God. As James 4:8 finishes, "Wash your hands, you sinners and purify your hearts, you double-minded."

The Protestant Reformation placed a great deal of emphasis on the spiritual habits and responsibilities of the individual. The importance of the priesthood of the believer was stressed as well as the authority of Scripture in one's life. Christians were reawakened to the personal walk with God as they reconnected to the source of truth for themselves.

These kinds of personal traditions have been handed down to us as evangelical Christians, so that we now put a great deal of emphasis on the personal part of worship, to the extent that our corporate worship has become so confused that it hardly seems to matter. Also, personal worship has been reduced to mere feelings as we seek happiness instead of the positive spiritual disciplines.

I mentioned earlier that I think evangelicals are sensing that something is missing from worship – something that we are longing to regain even if we cannot identify it. The more I think about it, the more I observe and the more I read the thoughts of others, the more I am convinced (and I'm going out on an evangelical limb here) -- that what is missing is *liturgy* (or, at least something like it.) We are missing a pattern, a tradition, something on which to hang our spiritual hats on Sunday morning. It's all up to us now. We hear statements calling us to examine only the rightness of our own hearts and attitudes. We are adrift in a sea of loud music and breathy, rambling prayers.

For several years now, the evangelical church had been caught up in the "seeker-sensitive" mode of operations as we attempted, in a pragmatic way, to get people who are looking for God to show up on Sunday morning. It's interesting to note that Jesus said, "**Go ye into** all the world" – but in spite of that clear-cut indicative we interjected modern ideas, thought patterns and attitudes into the mission of the church. The results are coming back to haunt us.

In his article, "The Future Lies in the Past," (Christianity Today, Feb. '08) Chris Armstrong purposes that as the Protestants and later the Evangelicals alienated themselves from their historical past they ceased to be "true neither to Scripture nor to our theological identity as the church...[this] has allowed Evangelicals to allow the world to shape the church." No wonder we are empty when we are missing something God wants us to have – the connection with him that comes from all of us following Biblical patterns.

I always thought that the concept of liturgy went back to the time of the early Roman Catholic Church, and I had no idea of what or why certain traditions were performed and passed along. Then I found out that Christian liturgy comes from Jewish liturgy, which is detailed in the Old Testament. The traditions of the church are not random activities; they were meant to be teaching tools for the mostly illiterate churchgoers and a

Christ at the Center

continuation of the ceremony established by worshiping the one true God in a majestic manner worthy of him. They were meant to enlighten, not enslave. The roots of the church's teaching-traditions were firmly planted in Jewish practices with which the early church was very familiar.

Three Old Testament passages (1Chron. 15,16; 2Chron. 5-7; Ezra 3) describing worship in the tabernacle, the temple, and the reconstructed temple are almost identical in their descriptions of what constituted worship. First, the Ark of the Covenant is placed in a position of great honor. It contains the Law of God; the Word is given a prominent place. Second, music, both instrumental and vocal, pervades the entire ceremony. The music is skillfully performed and professionally coordinated. Third, prayers, songs and sacrifices are offered up to God and the people verbally respond to each activity. They make statements out loud, such as "Amen," "Praise the Lord," "Give thanks," and "His love endures forever."

This worship, although heartfelt and exuberant, was not contemporized or performed extemporaneously. It was deliberate and proceeded along established patterns. It was meant to draw attention to God's majesty through the richness of meaning expressed in formal, elaborate ceremony.

Christian worship arose from this rich tradition. The Scriptures continued to be read, Psalms sung, prophecies or words of instruction spoken, and responses given. The Lord's Supper was taken at almost every service where Christians met together. Eventually these things took on a distinctive Christian tone. Even in the most contemporary of church services today their vestiges remain, although very ghostlike vestiges, I'm afraid.

The significance of these procedures and patterns of tradition was primarily educational. Churchgoers were supposed to learn something from what went on in church. The memorizing of and repetition of phrases, prayers, and Bible verses are tools used for helping us to remember truth. Physical actions such as standing, kneeling, and speaking reinforce concepts in our minds and engage us. Singing revives one's soul to purely worship God and enter into the very language of

Creation. As the old hymn says, "All nature sings, and round me rings, the music of the spheres."

If we forget the *purpose* of the things we do in church, we will quickly lose sight of their *benefits*. The events of the service must be *meaningful*. When I visited an Episcopal church last year, I was overwhelmed with the meaning I saw in everything that went on. Having been told all my life that liturgical services were dry, dull, boring and meaningless, I surprised to learn that this is not true at all. I was the one who had missed out on meaning in my just-sit-there "hymn-singing" and "praise-band" churches.

Like most evangelicals, I have been a victim of "willy-nilly" worship planning. In order for the sequence of events of a worship service to be meaningful it must be implied that someone needs to determine what will be meaningful and why in each service. Since little or no planning or purpose (or so it seems) go into evangelical worship services, they become futile exercises in formality, even when they are informal; that is to say, we are doing worship services just for the sake of doing worship services – it is merely a formal activity.

The pattern of liturgy exists to remind us of the reality of our salvation – our communion with Christ through the Word and prayer. We celebrate our communion in Christ through his body and blood, and our hope of eternal life. All liturgical styles incorporate these truths to remind us of our position of completeness in Christ where we now stand in the presence of God. They take place in church – the house of God, i.e. the physical place where believers choose to gather together. All the "pieces" of liturgy are personal and corporate at the same time, so that each individual worships while the group of believers as the Bride of Christ worships.

In his work of Creation, God made rest, peace and wholeness his primary focus by instituting the Sabbath day. Sunday worship should reunite us with that day and point us to the day when we are finally united with Christ in Heaven and are at rest. In her blog, Amiee Milburn, who is Catholic, writes about how worship represents unity in Christ in glory:

Christ at the Center

> *At the Cathedral, I usually sit near the front, to one side, so that during the mass I can turn my head to see and hear the whole congregation singing, responding, and gesturing as one. It is a beautiful mass where the congregation truly is reverent, attentive, loving, responding. The voice of the congregation often sounds to me truly as one great voice, a single organ, crying out to God in love and worship.*
>
> *I turn my head so I can marvel at the wonder of it, and contemplate how this is truly a partaking in the great worship of heaven, where countless voices, a vast sea of voices, are raised as a single voice, the Bride and Body of Christ worshiping her Head as one in Heaven.*

By contrast, I have gone to church and seen just the opposite – people standing silent, maybe swaying, as mediocre music accompanied by a torrent of drumbeats swirls around them. Many talk to each other but not to God. They are all alone in a crowd, longing for something to unite them, something that will truly connect them with God, whom their souls desire. The people Amiee describes at the cathedral and other true worshipers in other settings are not isolated individuals trying to fit in. They are united in the purpose of their actions, yet each one individually comes to God and is met by God. Their actions lead them there, into a holy place.

True worship focuses on Heaven. The great longing of our hearts is to be with God. As the Apostle Paul so aptly says, "I desire to depart and be with Christ, which is better by far." (Phil. 1:23) The great longing of God's heart is to be with us, as expressed by his name announced to Mary by the angel Gabriel: "Immanuel – God with us." These two great longings unite in true worship.

But we have exchanged this truth for the lie that our longings can be met merely on the surface by what does or doesn't go on in church, and not deeply in our hearts where God by his Spirit dwells. Part of this lie is that we go "deeper" on our own, what goes on in church has very little to do with individual worship. I think that what goes on has everything to do with whether or not people worship. Empty meaningless activities, or neglecting the Biblical form for the activities, or even the lack of meaningful activities, will result in empty, dissatisfied churchgoers.

The Apostle Paul says that the natural response to the reality of God-in-us comes in the form of singing. Eph. 5:19 says, "Speak to one another with psalms, hymns and spiritual songs. Sing and make music in your heart to the Lord." Music is core around which all worship centers. Music has been here since the time of Creation; we, like Singing Bird, were made to sing.

If you have ever participated in a worship service when you really sang – a time and place where the audience was so connected to God that everyone's voices, good and bad, overflowed with praise, you know that what you experienced was a "little bit of heaven." You saw, in your heart, a glimpse of the saints and angels worshiping around the throne of God. Every week we are given the opportunity to participate in a piece of that glory, but so few of us seize the day. The "glory has departed" as we have replaced contemplative hymns and purposeful Scripture Readings with empty noise. This is not to say that "newer" forms of music have no place in worship, but like everything else, they need to have a purpose, and while we're at it, also substantial lyrics and universal "singability."

I believe that many evangelical churches are operating under an idolatrous deception – we are worshiping in a musical environment designed to make us feel good (or at least designed to make young people feel good) instead of facing our unworthiness by coming face to face with the grace of God, grace which, if we really thought about it, would bring us to our knees in humble silence. As the Bible says, "The Lord is in his holy temple; let all the earth keep silence before Him."

In Old Testament worship, the sacrifice was the culmination of worship. Singing, Scripture reading and responses of praise accompanied and proceeded the time of sacrifice. In liturgical traditions, the observance of Communion replaces the sacrifice. We remember and are thankful that Jesus Christ was sacrificed for us. We present ourselves now in an ongoing way as a living sacrifice ready to go out and be God's servants in the world. (Rom. 12:1,2)

In this way, we learn that salvation is more than a one-time experience; it is an ongoing journey of life in God. If worship is primarily experience-based, it will be hard to leave the starting point and move on. It is imperative that we "get over ourselves" as worshipers and take up our cross and follow Christ. It is time for our journey to reorient itself. It is time to get back to the heart of worship – the heart of sacrifice, the heart of selflessness, the heart of suffering. The heart of worship transcends time and place and centers in eternity.

Several passages in the Psalms describe the saints going up to house of God while singing joyful songs. We, too, are on a journey to the house of God as David, Solomon, and Ezra, together with the singers and the people celebrated so long ago. What they did and what we do now are parts of the eternal worship of Heaven.

Our eternal end is to "glorify God and enjoy him forever," as the Westminster Catechism states. In Heaven, we will not selfishly worry if the worship style suits us or not. We will all be like Singing Bird who sings just because he was created to sing. Our destiny lies in eternal worship, and it begins on Sunday.

Bibliography – Worship

Milburn Cooper, Aimee. "Liturgy and Eschatology: Making the Kingdom of God Visible Now." *Historical Christian*. Aimee Milburn Cooper, 26 June 2007. Web. 13 May 2010. <http://www.historicalchristian.com/my_weblog/alexander_schmemann>.

Milburn Cooper, Aimee. "One Body, One Voice: Praying and Worshiping Truly as One." *Historical Christian*. Aimee Milburn Cooper, 17 Jan 2008. Web. 13 May 2010. <http://www.historicalchristian.com/my_weblog/liturgy/>.

Galli, Mark. "A Deeper Relevance." *Christianity Today Magazine* May 2008: n. pag. Web. 15 May 2008. <http://www.christianitytoday.com/ct/article_print.html?id=55186>.

Armstrong, Chris. "The Future Lies in the Past." *Christianity Today* Feb. 2008: 23-29. Print.

Christ at the Center

Chapter 14-HEAVEN OR HELL: The Journey's End

"Behold, **I am coming** soon! My reward is with me, and I will give to everyone according to what he has done. I am the Alpha and the Omega, the First and the Last, the Beginning and the End." (Rev. 22:12, 13)

In the course of this book, I have looked at the Christian life as a journey; a journey of salvation where Christ must be at the center of all our concerns. Now, I wish to look at the journey itself in more detail and to examine the destination of the journey – the life eternal, where, for the Christian, Christ finally becomes in all and over all, world without end.

The Two Roads

Christ clearly stated that there are two roads in life leading to an eternal end, and each individual, according to choice, travels on either of the two roads. "Enter through the narrow gate," Jesus tells us: "for wide is the gate and broad is the road that leads to destruction and many enter through it. But small is the gate and narrow is the road that leads to life and only a few find it." (Matt. 7:13,14) Eventually, everyone is confronted with the choice of which way to proceed, and in so doing, to commit to the road that *seems right* or the road that was *made right* through the sacrifice of Christ.

When I began to think about the paradigm of the two ways, I immediately thought of its most famous representation, found in John Bunyan's classic book, *The Pilgrim's Progress*. In fact, I believe that a great deal of our perceptions about life on the Way have come from this book, especially when we think of all the obstacles and setbacks which come our way. The most interesting part of Christian's journey is not that, once through the Wicket Gate, he stays firmly on the path, but that he periodically **departs** due to the choices he makes.

At the outset of his journey, as he struggles to stay on the path, Evangelist says to him, "Thou has begun to reject the council of the Most High, and to draw back thy foot from the Way of Peace, even almost to the hazarding of thy Perdition."

Christ at the Center

(Bunyan, p. 27) Even though at this point Christian had already entered the salvation-gate, he was not perfected and he still had choices to make. He needed to learn to live his life in and through the strength of Christ who would help him to carry on.

Galatians 2:20 says, "The life I live in the body, I live by faith in the Son of God, who loved me and gave himself for me." Paul is telling us that, as Christians, we have our whole lives to be lived by saving grace, not just one act of repentance to be decided on. "I do not set aside the grace of God," he adds, because he realizes that he carries on through the grace daily given to him in Christ. "Surely goodness and love will follow me all the days of my life," David declares; and in this fashion, he hopes to enter the house of the Lord at the end of the road governed by grace.

One of my favorite books is *The Great Divorce* by C.S. Lewis – but this was not always the case, for, when I first read it, I didn't understand it at all. I was far too much a fundamentalist; I did not yet know that salvation was a journey. I did not realize that in this life we travel either on the road to Heaven or on the road to Hell. Yet the longer I walked with Jesus (even in the old fundamentalist way), the more I learned, the more I saw, I gradually came to see the road I was on and had been on for so many years. Grace had put me there, in spite of my ignorance. When this realization came, I suddenly could see that the characters in Lewis' purgatory represented real people on a real road; people whose actions and attitudes lead them to Heaven where everything changes or condemn them to wander forever the endless sameness of the streets of Hell.

In the preface to *The Great Divorce*, C.S. Lewis writes: "We are not living in a world where all roads are radii of a circle and where all, if followed long enough, will therefore draw gradually nearer and finally meet in at the centre: rather in a world where every road, after a few miles, forks into two, and each of these into two again, and at each fork you must make a decision." (Lewis, p.viii) He goes on to point out that these decisions are "either-or," for we cannot keep some earthly or hellish quality and journey with it into Heaven. All evil either falls before grace, or (if embraced in even the smallest way) leads to detours of the worst sort (as the pilgrim Christian discovered) and perhaps headlong into the path of eternal danger.

Pascal said that "Between us and Heaven or Hell there is only life half-way, the most fragile thing in the world." (Kreeft, p. 142) In his commentary on this statement, Peter Kreeft draws a diagram placing earth at the crossroads between Heaven and Hell. The roads connect at the cross of Christ. "For the message of the cross is foolishness to those who are perishing, but to us who are being saved it is the power of God," Paul says in 1Cor. 1:18.

Notice the movement he indicates by the words "are perishing" and "are being saved." We are all going towards some eternal end. Everyone is here at the crossroads. Like the crossing at Times Square, New York we scurry through this intersection every which way, distracted by light and sound, looking for truth and searching for answers. "Life half-way" is a life of longing, yearning for something infinitely better, unfulfilled until our merciful God will "guide our feet into the path of peace." If we ignore God, however, we endlessly wander aimlessly, chasing after lies.

Our life on earth is life at the crossroads, quite literally. G.K. Chesterton wrote, "For the circle is perfect and infinite in its nature; but it is fixed forever in size; it can never be larger or smaller. But the cross, though it has at its heart a collision and a contradiction, can extend its four arms forever with out altering its shape...The cross opens its arms to the four winds; it is a signpost for free travelers." (Chesterton, p. 23,24) The cross stands as a challenge in the center of every person's life, and at the center of the cross itself the challenge confronts us – will we see merely suffering and death or gaze upon the wounds which give us salvation and life? We must make our choice and step upwards towards Heaven or downwards towards Hell.

Choice at the Crossroads

But what is the nature of this choice at the crossroads? Is it an instantaneously fixed choice, which determines our way forever, or do we make a series of choices that led us onward towards an everlasting goal? God created us as beings that are able to freely make choices, in fact, both spiritual angels and physical/spiritual man, were made in this way.

Choices have consequences; good choices lead to good results and bad ones lead to bad results. Adam and Eve made a bad choice in the garden when they freely willed to disobey God. The consequences of their choice had far reaching implications, affecting every person by causing our souls to die and separating us from God and condemning us to hell along with the evil angels.

In order to remedy the results of the disastrous fall into sin, God devised a plan of redemption in order to restore us to fellowship with himself. If we are ignorant of this plan, we wander about in confusion, unclear about our mission and destination. We often ask ourselves the questions – why am I here, and where am I going? The world is an enigma to us. We are faced with choices but we do not seem to be able to discern the consequences that might arise from making those choices.

The Catholic Catechism makes a very interesting observation about the questions we face: "The two questions, the first about the origin and the second about the end are inseparable. They are decisive for the meaning and orientation of our life and actions." (Catechism, p. 82) Each one of us wants to be connected to the Creator and to feel his providential love, and everyone wants to find rest in that love forever. Finding the answers to the questions drives our choices and actions for they become the steps we take upon the road of life.

The early church father, Irenaeus, wrote this about our freedom of choice: "For God does not use force, but his intention is at all times for man's good; and therefore his design for all is good. He equipped man with the power of choice, as he also equipped the angels...all have the same nature, with the power of accepting and achieving good, and the power likewise of spurning it and failing to achieve it." He also writes about the outcomes of the exercising this ability to choose: "God, with his perfect foreknowledge, has prepared for each class a fitting habitation; to those who seek the light of immortality and hasten towards it he graciously grants the light for which they long; for the others who spurn the light . . . he has prepared darkness." (*Early Church Fathers*, p.98,99)

Although we are sinful by nature, we still have, though the light of conscience, if not the ability to actually make the proper choice, we are able see that there are good and bad choices to be made. But other than having this knowledge, this feeling that something must change, we are essentially helpless to do anything about it. Something needs to happen to assist us in choosing well, so God provided for our redemption a way to change the orientation of our hearts so that we are redirected to God's way. As Paul explains in Rom. 5:10, "...we were reconciled to him through the death of his Son, how much more, having been reconciled, shall we be saved though his life!"

Isaiah 59:2 states that "your iniquities have separated you from your God," meaning that our sin nature has automatically caused us to be alienated from God. The prophet goes on in this chapter to discuss the desperate depths of our terrible plunge into sin, describing in detail our enslavement and hopeless condition.

But he also speaks of choice – "their feet rush into sin," (v. 7) and "they have turned them into crooked roads." (v. 8) Maybe these are inevitable choices, but they are choices nonetheless, for as James says, "Anyone, then, who knows the good he ought to do and doesn't do it, sins." (James 4:17)

Because of our innate knowledge of right and wrong, our longing for what is good, and the work of the Holy Spirit in the world to convict of sin, righteousness and judgment, we may wish to walk in God's ways but realize that we are powerless to do so. At this point, the only thing one can do is to make *a cry for help*. The pivotal fork in the road has been reached. One must now receive God's help or reject it; one must seek after God or turn away from him. Jesus said, "Come unto me," inviting everyone to walk on the road to heaven. He also said, "whoever comes to me I will never drive away." (Jn. 6:37) Jesus alone rescues repentant sinners and gives them the faith they need to be saved.

Now we begin the process of walking in the power and purpose of God on the heavenly road. In the epistle to the

Christ at the Center

Philippians, Paul discusses this dual process – God works powerfully in us and we work because of this power. "Continue to work out your salvation with fear and trembling," he writes, "for it is God who works in you to will and act according to his purpose." (Phil. 2:12,13)

The salvation of a soul is forever fixed with God, but it is a linear process for us. As we go through life, we experience change, decay and surprise; things which require us to make the right decisions and choose our steps carefully. Everyday, even on the dullest of days, we walk a thousand steps in a thousand ways on the road to Heaven. If our faith comes from God, we will not fail to reach God, but if our faith is false, it will desert us in the end.

Walking in Virtue

The life in Christ, the life on the narrow road, is a life lived in the strength of *virtue*. I've already talked about the virtues of the heart – faith, hope and love, without which no one can hope to begin in Christ. The three theological virtues form the basis for everything Christian – our salvation, our discipleship and our destiny. But along the way and in the body, we are called upon to practice the four cardinal (practical or human) virtues while we make our way through this world to heaven. These virtues are: Prudence (wisdom), Fortitude (courage), Temperance and Justice.

Teaching about the life of virtue has become a lost art in the evangelical church, chiefly because some confusion has arisen over whether or not the Catholic Church teaches that practicing the virtues is a means by which salvation is obtained. They have been perceived as a sort of doctrine of "salvation by works." But I do not believe this is truly the case. While the Catholic Catechism defines virtue as "an habitual and firm disposition to do good;" that is to say, they are learned traits which cause us to act in a manner that is good and godly, it also states that the virtues, while integral to godly living can only be lived out by the work of Christ in us. (Catechism, p. 495)

As Christians, we are still subject to sin in this life. Sin is constantly counteracting the work of grace within us as Romans

7:18 says, "I know that nothing good lives in me, that is in my sinful nature. For I have the desire to do what is good, but I cannot carry it out." Paul concludes that the resolution to his dilemma will only come through the power of Christ, who, indwelling him, causes him to do good. The life of virtue, states the Catechism, is made possible because: "Christ's gift of salvation offers us the grace necessary to persevere in the pursuit of the virtues." (Catechism, p. 498) Living a virtuous life is contingent upon receiving the gift of grace.

The cardinal virtues are further directed outwards toward others. While the theological virtues guide our hearts in our relationship with God, the cardinal ones guide our conduct in the arenas of human relationships. In Philippians 4:8, Paul urges believers to think and meditate on true, beautiful and worthwhile things, making them the reasoning behind virtuous actions.

In the next verse, he makes two practical observations about how to implement proper thoughts and actions. First, we must consider "Whatever you have learned or received or heard from me, or seen in me." Virtuous living comes from a process of education, beginning in our youth as our parents teach us godly things. Moses told the Israelites to teach the commandments diligently to their children. We often say that good behavior is "caught and not taught," but this is not necessarily true. If we could catch the alphabet or arithmetic, we would not need to be educated at school. But these things, along with virtue, require someone outside of us to reveal them to us. Jesus was a Rabbi, a teacher, and as such, he invites us to come and "learn of me."

Second, the teachings on the virtues must be translated into actions – "put into practice," Paul says. It is never enough to just think grand thoughts about God, or to listen to good sermons about God, for at some point we must begin to do great things by the power of God. "Faith without works is dead," James declared. The Christian life depends on an active faith. At every turn in the road, we are called upon to make a correct decision, to speak a proper word or to make a significant difference.

C.S. Lewis wrote, "...a man who perseveres in doing just actions gets in the end a certain quality of character. Now it is the quality rather than the particular actions which we mean when we talk of virtue." (Lewis, p. 80) We will, in other words, become what we do. A child who is taught to say "thank-you;" who repeats the phrase over and over and takes to heart in increasing degree the Scriptural admonitions on thankfulness, will grow up to be a person with a thankful heart. Virtue is indoctrinated, inspired and ingrained. In time, it becomes almost innocuous, like a river running to the sea, flowing through us as we walk on the Heavenly path.

Prudence (Wisdom)

Of the four cardinal virtues, prudence or wisdom is considered to be of primary importance. It has been called the chief of the virtues because it acts as a guide or a foundation for the other three. Making prudent decisions and implementing consistent Biblical analysis is the core of godly living. This virtue may be defined as determining the right thing to do along with the right way to do it. (Catechism, p. 496) It is the practical application of truth to everyday life.

I like the way the Biblical writer James is so down to earth in his discussion of wisdom: "If any of you lacks wisdom" (and we all do!), he admonishes, he should (simply) ask God [for it]." (James 1:5) He reassures us that this request will not be scorned or belittled, for God "gives generously to all without finding fault." He goes on in the epistle to list the character traits wisdom imparts – a peaceful attitude, a selfless disposition and a generous nature. (James 3:17)

Then he adds a warning: if wisdom is betrayed, we will find ourselves doing the very thing wisdom teaches us is the wrong thing to do, and willfully doing a wrong thing is sin. (James 4:17) Wisdom demands obedience to God, not self-righteousness.

The wisdom exercised by the Christian is heavenly wisdom that comes to us through Jesus Christ "who has become for us wisdom from God." (1Cor. 1:30) It is not like human wisdom that focuses on the knowledge of facts interpreted by current philosophies. It is not relative, based on feelings that change like the direction of the wind, but it is set firmly on the revelation of truth in Christ.

Paul says that godly wisdom is "a stumbling block to Jews and foolishness to Gentiles." (1Cor. 1:23) People lacking the influence of the Holy Spirit lack discernment and heavenly perspective, but Christ gives the believer the ability to see the world through God's eyes in order to make good decisions in light of the Word of God.

Fortitude

Fortitude is the virtue by which we practice courage and persistence in the practice of doing good or being good. It helps us to endure in tough circumstances and to exercise strength in difficult times. (Catechism, p. 496) As we work for God's glory and man's good, we must learn to triumph over obstacles in the power of Christ.

Fortitude is a two-fold characteristic: 1.) It helps us to resist temptation and 2.) It gives us strength in trials. Both of these conditions may cause us to be afraid, so fortitude gives us the ability to overcome fear. Once again, it is James who speaks to the double purpose of fortitude. "Blessed is the man who preservers under trial," he says, "Because when he has stood the test, he will receive the crown of life..." (James 1:12)

In the next few verses he explains how temptations are different from trials, for they arise from evil impulses and lead to sin. Yet, the same determination found in fortitude is needed to fight the battle on both fronts. He says both "Persevere" and "Do not be deceived." This is courage in action; holding up in a bad situation, over which there is little or no control, or consistently resisting and gaining control over a temptation coming from an ungodly source. The courage that comes from fortitude faces danger and endures pain. It is a solid rock in a shaky and uncertain world.

Temperance

The word 'temperance' is commonly thought of in relationship with abstinence from drinking alcoholic beverages, but when referring to the virtue itself it is much broader in scope and less specific in its application. Temperance was indeed a part of the "temperance movement" of the 19th and early 20th centuries, when citizens were asked to completely curb their appetites in one particular area – excessive drinking.

But while temperance is about moderation and balance in the exercise of all bodily pleasures, it also extends to keeping the same kind of evenness in the acquisition of material things and properly maintaining one's desires. A temperate person will look for balance in life and seek to find healthy ways of looking at the things God had given us for our good. (Catechism, p. 497) Temperance is the virtue of living a godly life in a practical way. It is, as Paul said, learning "to be content whatever the circumstances," so that as situations around him fluctuate he is still certain that he can "do everything through him who gives me strength." (Phil. 4:12, 13)

Temperance is practiced in humility; for example, Jesus warned us against practicing behaviors like the Pharisees who wished to be observed as they made their prayers. A temperate person never desires to have attention focused upon him. Also, the temperate person does not pass judgment on others, but instead seeks to make his life a living sacrifice to God, seeking first and foremost to please God.

Justice

Justice is the virtue which strives to give God his due as the great Judge of all mankind, and, at the same time, helps us to enable others to secure their rights as human beings made in God's image. (Catechism, p. 496) God alone is truly just, for he always makes fair judgments and, at the same time, he is the only one who can offer true mercy. God is consistently fair and true.

Christ has called us to be agents of his justice by being emissaries of the message of ultimate divine justice in Christ, who justifies all who believe. We are further called to bring just practices to oppressed people. The virtue of Justice compels us to act fairly and honestly with others and to defend those who have been unfairly and ill-treated. A just person will seek harmony in relationships and be true to his word.

Justice has become a popular concept lately in evangelical thought, especially among young people as they become aware that the injustices of this world abound and multiply at an alarming rate. But bringing God's justice into hopeless situations is very difficult and not for the faint-hearted. Bringing justice involves more than mere lip service, it involves getting down and dirty with the sin that brought about the evil in the first place. God is the ultimate source of justice for he defeated sin and passed judgment on all. In order to practice justice we need to possess the power of God who works in us to accomplish the good works that benefit the oppressed.

The life of virtue is the practical outcome of life on the narrow road as we draw closer to Heaven by the power of the Holy Spirit. As we live this life, the focus of living shifts off of ourselves and what we do and on to Christ and what he does within us. We become the workmanship of Christ who works in us so that our virtuous actions have good effects on others. They are not meant to boost our self-esteem or to turn us into impeccably good people. The life of virtue is a life of self-denial and Christ-exultation, as we grow in his likeness.

The Other Road
But there is another way in which life may be lived, a type of life that leads to an entirely different destination than that of the virtuous life. It is path to Hell or the Lake of Fire into which Satan, the evil angels and "all the nations that forget God" will be thrown at the end of time.

The road leading to this place is not always obviously corrupt. It seldom seems full of ruts, potholes and obstructions, and if these do occur, they are hastily labeled "road construction," signifying human attempts to fix various problems. "Broad is the way that leads to destruction," Jesus said. A bad road should *look like* a bad road, but it rarely does, and many travel it unawares.

The road to perdition is paved with immaculately presented lies. Satan is the father of lies and feeds the world a steady diet of them. From the deception in the Garden to the headlong crash into Hell, he lays down a glossy surface of lies, which appeal to millions traveling on the downward trail.

Christ at the Center

We all begin life on the broad road. Ever since Adam and Eve turned the corner onto it in Eden, everyone has started life on this treacherous path, due to the sin nature we are born with. For us to permanently get off of the broad way, God must intervene and move us over to the narrow way. When speaking to God the Father, Jesus said, "For you granted him [Jesus] authority over all people that he might give eternal life to all those you have given him." (John 17:2) God gives the gift of salvation permanently – he says his sheep will never perish and will not be able to fall out of his hand. (John 10:27,28)

However, salvation can be faked, and Jesus himself ruefully said, "Not everyone who says to me 'Lord, Lord,' will enter the kingdom of heaven, but only he who does the will of my Father who is in Heaven," (Mt. 7:21) Although it is certainly not up to us to judge who is saved and who is not, notice how the Bible gives us a standard to measure salvation by, that is, what a person **does**. Scripture indicates this in many places telling us that, like a tree, one is known by the quality of his "fruit," like a farmer, we will reap what we sow, and "out of the overflow of the heart the mouth speaks." (Mt. 12:34) What we do, the decisions we make and the thoughts we express all point to the true condition of our hearts and the force behind our actions, either the Holy Spirit or the fallen sinful nature.

Strange as it may seem, many people on the road to destruction are content to remain there. After all, walking downhill is a whole lot easier that walking uphill, as it were. And anything goes; there are no real rules on the broad road, only one's own rules that can change at a moment's notice. Once someone has traveled on this road for a while, it becomes hard to imagine walking any other way.

Jesus said, "Remember Lot's wife!" (Lk. 17:32) The story behind this admonition, found in Gen. 19, reveals much about the attitudes of unbelievers. Lot and his wife had been living a life of compromise in a very evil city, Sodom. When God punished this place, he was merciful to Lot's family by giving them an escape route; however, he warned them not to look back at the burning city. But Lot's wife, perhaps still drawn to her old sinful pleasures and godless leisure, turned and looked back. The raging residue from the sulfuric fires overcame her. By stopping to pine over her loss, she became a pillar of salt – the classic victim of the broad road to Hell.

The broad road has ever been littered with such victims, silent statues which others hurry past, who, on closer inspection (if anyone had the time to stop and look) bear the horrified expressions and desperate poses of similar victims found in the excavations of the volcanic ashes of Pompeii.

The people who walk on the broad road to destruction display differing ideas about their status. Some are truly fearful and long for escape. Christian, in *Pilgrim's Progress*, was one of these. "He was...greatly distressed in his mind and as he read, he burst out...crying, 'What shall I do to be saved?'" (p. 14) Pascal called these people "seekers," for they are looking for deliverance and long for stability. He says that they are "busy seeking him and have not found him," and consequently they are "unhappy and reasonable." (Kreeft, p. 211)

If they persist in their search, they stand a good chance of finding hope, for, as God said to Jeremiah, "You will seek me and find me when you seek me with all your heart. I will be found by you, declares the Lord." (Jer. 29:13,14) Others, who are self-centered, see nothing but "what's in it for me?" They attempt to travel alone, caring for nothing or no one except themselves. Heedless to all around them, they careen downwards at an ever-accelerating pace until they fall headlong into Hell, where they will forever be utterly alone.

Finally, there is the most desperate group of all, the ones who stubbornly stay on the evil path, knowing the dangers, yet denying them; living the sinful life, yet disgusted by it; fearing their tragic end while inviting it to come. They seem to be unredeemable people, choosing to stay in an eternal state of degradation.

Looking at these hopeless situations we ask the same question the disciples asked, "Who then can be saved?" (Mt. 19:25) With sorrowful tears, Paul described these people as the "enemies of the cross of Christ. Their destiny is destruction, their god is their stomach and their glory is in their shame." (Phil. 3:18,19) The truth is that one never gets off of the road to Hell unless Christ rescues him, but some, inexplicitly, do not wish to be rescued.

The broad road ultimately leads to destruction and ends in utter ruin. Every soul has an eternal destiny, and souls left to their own sinful devices will end in eternal tragedy. The parable of the rich man and Lazarus, told by Jesus himself in Luke 16, makes this abundantly clear. Lazarus, a poor beggar, who is however, rich in faith, dies and goes to a place called "Abraham's side." The rich man, who was poor in faith, also dies but he goes to a place known as Hades or hell. The two locations are spiritual places, but they are real, nonetheless. Abraham's side is a place of rest and peace where God's chosen ones abide after death, while Hades is a place of torment and distress.

The great question often raised about this story is: why does one go to Heaven while the other ends up in Hell? The rich man is the one who gives us the clue to discovering the criteria for who ends up where, for he tells Abraham that his brothers would **repent** if a messenger came to them from beyond the grave. Repentance from sin through faith in Christ is the key to obtaining heavenly life after death. Non-repentance, rejection of Christ, leads to everlasting torment and death that never ends.

The final destination of unbelievers has been and will remain the same throughout history. As the parable teaches, it is Hades, also known as Hell. Jesus confirms the reality of this place, when he says that those who willfully sin are "in danger of the fire of hell." (Matt. 5:22) After the final judgment, this place will be emptied into the Lake of Fire. Revelation 20 tells us that all of "death" and Hades will be absorbed into the Lake of Fire along with Satan, the evil angels and people whose names are not recorded in God's book of life, a record God keeps of the names and identities of his children. In this awful place, they will be forever alienated from God.

The final destination for believers, however, changed from "Abraham's side" for Old Testament believers to "with Christ" for believers who come to faith after Christ's resurrection. Paul said that he desired to "depart and be with Christ," (Phil. 1:23) and Peter tells us where that is – "Christ…has gone into heaven and is at God's right hand." (1Pet. 3:22) Peter also indicates that

Jesus, after his death, gathered the believers from Abraham's side and delivered them into heaven where, subsequently, all believers also go after death.

Suffering on Both Roads

The one thing common to travelers on both the narrow and the broad roads is something which neither group desires – suffering. No one wishes to experience pain, sorrow, disappointment and death, but we all do. Ever since Paradise was closed to us, trying to find the answer to the question of why we suffer has been a constant and universal search. It appears that we would rather know *why* we suffer than *how* to accept it.

Some people think that all suffering comes from sin. Before the fall of mankind, they believe, nothing decayed, felt pain or died, because no sin had touched the human race. Even though it was a far better world in Eden, things still underwent change. All earthly created things are physical and deteriorate by nature. Any physical living thing will eventually die, even though it may live for a very long time.

It is interesting to note that after the Fall and before the Flood, it is said that people lived for an incredibly long time – almost 1,000 years in some cases. Maybe the rate of decay in Eden and the antediluvian earth was imperceptibly slow, but it was happening nevertheless. Death was happening in the Garden because Adam and Eve knew what it was and what it meant. Also, God said that people should not eat the fruit from the Tree of Life in the center of the garden because it imparted everlasting life -- implying that ordinary created life was not meant to be eternal. If nothing else, plants were dying when they were picked and eaten for food.

Death happens because physical life changes. Decay and degeneration accounts for much of the discomfort we experience. There is nothing wrong with this per se, (it is just the way the physical universe works), but it is exacerbated by sin and the presence of evil. For example, if we approach a trial with fear and anger, its impact will be worse than if it is approached with godly confidence and joy.

Christ at the Center

In the account of the Curse recorded in Genesis 3, only three painful situations are specified: 1.) The "offspring" of the woman will crush the serpent's head, and the reactionary strike of the serpent will inflict pain, 2.) Women will suffer pain during childbirth, and 3.) Men will endure painful work and stressful toil.

The first reference is a veiled foretelling of the greatest example of suffering and death, the sacrifice of Christ on the cross, which, along with the resurrection would destroy the power of Satan. The other two instances of pain -- childbirth and work -- were disciplinary actions instituted by God. Along with spiritual death, they were the punitive results of the Fall.

All other pain, suffering, sickness and distress comes from the fact that we are spiritually dead people living as fallen people in a physical world. What we do, for good or ill, impacts that world, as the wounded world, in turn, distresses us.

The question is commonly asked, "How can a good God allow pain and suffering to take place?" Believers and non-believers alike raise this question, for everyone is attacked by evils at some time or another. The answer lies not so much in God allowing or permitting it, but rather that God dictated it; he said it would happen. Pain came from God's directive issued in the Garden.

God is just and gives righteous laws. Through the curse, the Law, and the death of Christ, he identified and punished sin. But because God practices perfect justice, he is also a God who redeems and sets things right. If God had turned his back on us and allowed sin and the pain and suffering it engenders to continue unabated, he would have been unjust. So, through Jesus who died for us, taking the pain and suffering of sin upon him, God made a way to make things right.

By his death and resurrection, Christ defeated Satan, the source and object of the first clause of the curse. The second clause, the pain of childbirth, is redeemed by forgetfulness (Jn. 16:21) and the third, toil and work, is redeemed by Sabbath rest. (Ex. 23:12)

God, having decreed suffering and having redeemed it, must work this redemption in us within the context of time, and this is where our frustration primarily lies. In time, everything is not yet redeemed. We suffer along the earthly road. We lose patience with God and ask, "Why am I afflicted?"

From God's perspective, however, everything has been rectified, exactly as it should be. But God, due to his great love for us, goes above and beyond positional redemption. He gives us strength and perspective in trials. He gives us joy in difficult circumstances. He gives us peace in pain and comfort in death. Suffering may be overwhelming, difficult and distressful, but God, who is good, is greater than any wrong situation. When the journey is hard and hurts us, he must help us.

In the end, two outcomes are destined for pain and suffering. They will stop, never again to be experienced by the Church, or they will continue on and become the unbeliever's all-consuming fate. Heaven has no suffering. John prophesied, "God will wipe away every tear from their eyes." (Rev. 7: 17) By contrast, hell is all suffering. John writes, "They will be tormented day and night for ever and ever." (Rev. 20:10)

The final judgment concerns what people *do*, that is to say, it is contingent upon either the actions of virtue arising from God's interaction with those who follow him, or upon the evil actions of those who are devoid of spiritual life and under the control of sin. Those who are in Christ will be set free from suffering and the memory of it, while those without Christ seal their fate to suffer endlessly.

A Glimpse of Heaven

Heaven is a place existing purely in the spiritual dimension; it is spiritual, but not ethereal, for it is very real. It was created in the beginning as a dwelling place for the angels of God, where God also "dwelt," not that he needs a place in which to live, but that he, although everywhere present, inhabits that glorious, spiritual place. There, the angels worship, praise and serve God in his presence; however, at the same time, God "lives in unapproachable light." (1Tim. 6:16)

Nehemiah said, "You alone are the Lord. You made the heavens, even the highest heavens and all their starry hosts, the earth and all that is in it, the seas and all that is in them. You gave life to everything and the multitudes of Heaven worship you. (Neh. 9:5-7) God is described as living in heaven, but in truth, he transends Heaven; God is his own dwelling place. Solomon said, "The heavens, even the highest heavens, cannot contain you." (2Chron. 6:18)

In John 14, Jesus tells the disciples that he is going to this place (he calls it "my Father's house,") where places to stay already exist, but he is going to create further places of residence for his followers. If we think temporally, this is where Christ is now, so believers' souls go here when they die. Jesus is working on additional heavenly dwelling places that will be given to us after he comes again.

I believe the Bible teaches that there will be three heavenly places constituting "Heaven,' and together they will be the dwelling places for believers in the eternal state, which begins after the final judgment. The first of these three is highest heaven, referred to above, which was created perfect and eternal by God and will not change or end. The throne of God is there as described in Rev. 4, surrounded by a glass-like sea and seven lamp stands.

John records that he sees there the 24 elders who worship God and lay their crowns down at the foot of the throne. He also observes fantastic angelic beings flying through the air and praising God. In the next chapter, John further describes his vision of Heaven, saying that he sees Jesus Christ as the Lamb of God enthroned in glory and the innumerable angels encircling the throne and singing to God. At the same time, he hears every creature in heaven and on earth singing praises to God.

The second heavenly place is the new heavens and earth described by Peter in 2Pet. 3:13: "We are looking forward to a new heaven and a new earth, the home of righteousness." This present physical universe (outer space, atmosphere and earth) will be annihilated by fire and the type of physicality we know today will end.

Remember, this universe was created "good," not perfect, but the new universe will be perfect. It will be constituted of a perfect-physical-spirituality that will make it very different and more real or solid than what we experience today, but I believe it will be very beautiful and earth-like. God will, I think, make a world that brings together all the best of creation, but without the constraints of death and decay.

The third heavenly place is the New Jerusalem, described in Revelation 21. This city descends from Heaven and hangs like a beautiful shining globe in the atmosphere of the new earth. We know that it is a real place, not a spiritualization of the glories of Heaven, because John is given a measuring stick and is told to take measurements of the city, its walls and the gates. Ezekiel, who sees a vision of a future temple of God, is also told to measure it.

I believe these two prophets saw incredible visions; so incredible that they were rubbing their eyes and questioning the reality of what they were seeing. So God said, in effect, "It's real, alright – go ahead and measure it." They would not have, nor could they have measured something purely spiritual. Revelation 21 also describes specific details of the city, such as the gems that make up the gates, the streets of gold and the river with the trees of life on each bank.

We often use these characteristics as indicative of what heaven is like, but they really only apply to the New Jerusalem, the place Jesus prepares for us. In fact, the church is so closely tied with the city that the angel who shows it to John calls it "the bride, the wife of the Lamb." (v. 9) We will be at one with our dwelling place, for we will be with Christ and in Christ, together forever, living eternal life together.

Wishing, perhaps, to play on the element of surprise, God has not told us very much about the heavenly places. But here are the few facts we do know. All three will be timeless. (Or, perhaps, time will be different; multi-dimensional, so to speak.) Time, as we now know it, is a restraint placed on the physical universe and when the present physical universe is destroyed, it will end. Everything we experience then will be in the *present*, for no time will exist to flow immediately and inexorably from the past to the future. But it will be the present *in motion*, for the love of God will be the force behind everything.

The new earth will combine the best of the physical world with the spiritual world, but the physical will no longer be merely good (as it was originally made) -- it will be perfect, because it will have been redeemed. As such, it will not be subject to the laws that govern it now; however, when we see it, it may seem familiar to us.

When describing the redemption of physical things, Paul says, "Meanwhile we groan, longing to be clothed with our heavenly dwelling...so that what is mortal may be swallowed up by life." (2Cor. 5:2,4) This longing is two-fold; we long for our new spiritual bodies ("the body that is sown is perishable, it is raised imperishable" -- 1Cor. 15:42), and we long for the place where we shall live and experience "an inheritance that can never perish, spoil or fade – kept in heaven for you." (1Pet. 1:4)

In fact, it seems that the new body, the new place and Christ himself will be somehow united – we *are* where we are and Christ is everything! Paul says that the Holy Spirit, who indwells us now through our faith, is "a deposit, guaranteeing what is to come." (2Cor. 5:5) As Christians, we have God the Holy Spirit in us today, showing us that in the future we will literally dwell in God.

The biggest hurdle we must overcome in our understanding of heaven is that it is not necessary to be able to picture what heaven is like. When the Apostle John tried to describe the New Jerusalem, he found that he had to resort to sweeping metaphor and earthly parallels, yet the measuring stick in his hand told him that what he was seeing was also very real. The apostles and prophets who saw glimpses of heaven had a hard time putting what they saw into words. It was almost as if the language hadn't been invented yet.

Something about Heaven defies explanation. Paul quotes Isaiah when he writes in 1Cor. 2:9, "No eye has seen, no ear has heard, no mind has conceived what God has prepared for those who love him." He is saying that in our present physical state, we cannot understand or picture a spiritual place. It is going to take a different kind of perception to see heaven. We will receive this ability when we are given our new bodies at the time of the resurrection.

But after Paul says that our physical senses cannot comprehend spiritual things, he adds an interesting comment –

an afterthought, as it were. He says, "But God has revealed it to us by his Spirit." (v. 10) This statement is the key to a true understanding of Heaven. He does not mean that some descriptive passages of Heaven will be written later in the New Testament such as those found in the book of Revelation. He means that, as Heaven is spiritual, we should not be looking for physically-based descriptions, but instead for descriptions of real spiritual things. Spiritual things (truths) are made real to us now by faith and grace, and they will become even more real in the eternal state.

These realities are, of course, all the things that God *is*. He is good. He is life. He is love. He is our peace. He redeems us, frees us, satisfies us and delights in us. God is for us, he is with us, and he surrounds us and never leaves us. All of these things, and far more which lie beyond our comprehension, are who God *is*.

When speaking of our future redemption, John says, "We shall be like him, for we shall see him as he is." (1John 3:2) Jesus said, "Blessed are the pure in heart, for they will see God." (Mt. 5:8) This simple idea, taught by these passages of Scripture -- that we may become so intimate with God that we shall see him at every turn, turns what we only see by faith here into what we shall constantly, in totality observe in Heaven. St. Augustine writes, "We shall see God and we shall see him with the utmost clarity as being everywhere present and as regulating the whole universe, including material things...in Heaven, wherever we turn the eyes of our spiritual bodies we shall see the immaterial God." (St. Augustine, p. 539)

Imagine what it will be like to "see" things like faith, hope and love where seeing becomes an actual experience of fellowship with God! When Paul said that the Holy Spirit reveals these things to us in our daily, earthly existence, he is saying that the insights we gain into spiritual truth here are but a small representation of the great and glorious vision to come – the face of God.

Another description of Heaven comes from the fact that we will be *with* God. In Revelation 21:3, this proclamation is given, "Now the dwelling of God is with men and he shall live with them." Remember, Jesus said that he was going to create a place for the redeemed to live in; a place that has within it many dwelling spaces. This idea of dwelling, abiding, being forever at home, is a picture of what Heaven is. It is living in God.

Today, as Christians, God lives in us -- "Christ in you, the hope of glory" – but in Heaven, it will become us-in-Christ. We will finally be completely able to "participate in the divine nature," a process which begins here and will be endlessly real there. Not only will we behold the face of God; that is, to merely see the glory of it, we will live in Glory, the very life of God.

Here's where it gets a little tricky for most of us. Spiritual qualities and truths made real, alive and eternal seem – well – so inactive, so ethereal, so *same*. What can be done with a truth? How is joy lived? What will be done without time to do it? Once again, we face dilemmas of this sort because we cannot comprehend physically what will come to pass spiritually. Therefore, we must walk by faith and not by sight.

After thoroughly contemplating this question, St. Augustine concluded that our one activity in Heaven will be praise: "Every fiber and organ of our imperishable body will play its part in the praising of God. On earth these varied organs have each a special function, but in heaven, function will be swallowed up in felicity, in perfect certainty of an untroubled everlastingness of joy." (St. Augustine, p. 540) From our earthy perspective, singing praise all day long may seem a bit dull, but this praise that goes beyond simple singing and shouting – it is the praise of action.

What we do in heaven is an eternal sacrifice of praise as we fulfill timeless dreams and aspirations in eternal tribute to our Savior. Every offering of praise will be laid at the feet of Christ as a beautiful endeavor given to magnify his glory. We will be truly fulfilled and filled with joy in finally being able to bring lasting honor to God in actions of love. But even though we can be assured that this is what we will do, we really have no idea of how we will do it, because our world simply doesn't work that way.

Even though we cannot see Heaven here on earth – except with the eyes of faith, which must grow in their perceptivity –

Christ at the Center

sometimes we are granted a glimpse of Heaven. Jesus permitted James, John and Peter to see his heavenly glory on the Mount of Transfiguration. From Peter's blundering comment ("Hey dudes, let's build three shelters!") we see how utterly out of their element they were. The only thing they could do was stand around in shock and speak ridiculous nonsense.

But to see Heaven – to see Christ exalted in splendor, even if only by faith – defies the logic of experience and set us on an earth-altering course. John and Peter note this change of direction in their writings. John speaks to this quality of Heaven through which we shall see God. He writes, "The word became flesh and made his dwelling among us. We have seen his glory, the glory of the one and only, who came from the Father, full of grace and truth." (John 1:14) He is expressing the beatitude of heaven in which Christ is seen and our eyes are forever turned on him. It is the glory of finally meeting Christ, who left Heaven in order to give his life to bring the redeemed into his intimate friendship.

Peter wrote a similar observation: "He was chosen before the creation of the world, but was revealed in these last times for your sake. Through him you believe in God, who raised him from the dead and glorified him, and so your faith and hope are in God." (1Pet. 1:20,21) The glory of Heaven is the glory of salvation eternally lived as a life of spiritual truth made real, constantly lived in God. He also says that we are like "living stones," which are even now being built into a spiritual house of which Christ is the cornerstone. (1Pet. 2: 5) Maybe Peter was thinking of his crazy comment about the temporary shelters when he wrote this. He finally realized that the true meaning of living in God's presence is living out our eternal salvation, now and in the life to come.

Personally, I do not always know what to make of the accounts of those who claim to have died and gone to Heaven and returned to tell the tale. I cannot say if they saw a heavenly place or not. But such a story has had a profound impact on my life. My mother, a loving Christian woman, died when I was two and a half years old. I remember when she died and seeing her in the casket, and I even have memories of her when she was alive. I know that it seems improbable that such a young child could retain memories of this sort, but I have always believed that God gave them to me as a gift of love, for he wanted me to always remember my mother's love.

Sometime after my mother died and my father remarried, and I was still quite young, a friend of our family told us a story about my mother's death. She related how, when she was visiting my mother in the hospital, my mother told her that even though she wanted to stay with her husband and two daughters, *she had seen Jesus* and knew that she must go to be with him. Her heart could not turn back. My father tended to downplay this story, thinking perhaps of the sheer improbability of looking into glory – but I took it much to heart.

Imagine, I wonder, how amazing Heaven must be, how full of comfort and joy beyond telling, that my mother would gladly go there leaving her family in the gracious hands of God. This story, my tiny incredible glimpse of heaven, has called me for over 50 years like a requiem of grace upon my soul, telling me that to be at home with Christ is everything!

Luke 12:48 says, "From everyone who has been given much, much will be demanded." Anyone given a glimpse into the infinite glory of Heaven is changed forever. Paul, who may have had a vision of heaven, said, "Although I am less than the least of all God's people, this grace was given me: to preach to the Gentiles the unsearchable riches of Christ..." (Eph. 3:8) If we wonder why we do not now see or know very much about Heaven, it is because what little we do know is meant to be powerful enough to propel us into action for Christ.

In John Bunyan's great book, *The Pilgrim's Progress*, Christian and Hopeful meet the Shepherds in the Delectable Mountains. The Shepherds show them two incredible sights – a glimpse of Hell and a glimpse of Heaven. They give the pilgrims a telescope through which they may look upon Heaven, but their hands are shaking because they had recently viewed the nightmare of Hell. "They could not look steadily through the Glass; yet they thought they saw something like a Gate, and also some Glory of the place." (Bunyan, p. 140, 141)

Christ at the Center

This is they way we, too, see the future, for God has not left us ignorant of the end of the journey. We fear for those who rush to Hell upon the broad road and, at the same time, we long to enter the Gates of Heaven. The journey to Heaven is not just our story, it is God's story, written on our hearts by faith and proclaimed through our words and deeds to the world. Even though our vision of heaven is cloudy or shaky, it is still real, and it is our motivation behind all that we do. It is holding on to an amazing story or a dream that seems very, very real and making it the goal of our life's work.

When at last we arrive at our heavenly home, all the work and labor of this life will be poured as a cup of water into a stream of praise to God. Yet, for now we walk the narrow road by faith, dimly seeing the light of hope beyond, and filled with love for our Savior, who we long to always see and desire forever to know.

Bibliography – Heaven or Hell

Bunyan, John. *The Pilgrim's Progress*. New York:: Barnes and Noble Books, 2005. Print.

Lewis, C. S. *The Great Divorce: A Dream*. New York: HarperCollinsPublishers, 2000. Print.

Kreeft, Peter. *Christianity for Modern Pagans: Pascal's Pensees Edited, Outlined and Explained*. San Francisco: Ignatius Press, 1993. Print.

Chesterton, G. K. *Orthodoxy*. New York: Doubleday, 1990. Print.

Catechism of the Catholic Church. New York: Doubleday, 1995. Print.

The Early Church Fathers. New York: Oxford University Press, 1956. Print.

Augustine, Saint. *City of God*. abridged ed. New York: Doubleday, 1958. Print.

About the Author

Janet Rea was born and raised in Peoria, Illinois. She attended Baptist Bible College of PA, where she earned a B.A. in Christian Education. After spending a year working in a campus ministry at Northern Iowa University, she enrolled at the University of Illinois where she earned an M.S. in Information and Library Science. For over fifteen years, she worked in public libraries, public schools and Christian schools. She now devotes her time to writing, teaching classes at her church, and needle arts of all kinds.

It was while attending Bible College that Janet developed her desire to make God's word more accessible to others. Whether teaching young children, teenagers or adults, she endeavors to make the Bible and the Christian faith understandable for laypeople. Her experience as a librarian has made her an adept researcher, and her love of literature has allowed her to develop a solid foundation of literary apologetics. Today, Janet and her husband Michael jointly teach courses in Christian Apologetics, Christian World View and Christian Literature for adults and teens.

Janet and her husband, Michael, are currently living in Temecula, CA where she is currently working on her next book.

www.ingramcontent.com/pod-product-compliance
Lightning Source LLC
Chambersburg PA
CBHW070548050426
42450CB00011B/2764